Teaching Art and Design in the Primary School

Gloria Callaway and Mary Kear

Illustrated by Abigail Leach

David Fulton Publishers

London

David Fulton Publishers Ltd
Ormond House, 26–27 Boswell Street, London WC1N 3JZ
www.fultonpublishers.co.uk

First published in Great Britain by David Fulton Publishers 1997
Reprinted 2000

Note: The right of the authors to be identified as the authors of this work has been asserted by them in accordance with the Copyright, Designs and Patents Act 1988.

Copyright © Gloria Callaway and Mary Kear. Illustrations © Abigail Leach

British Library Cataloguing in Publication Data
A catalogue record for this book is available from the British Library

ISBN 1–85346–598–4

Typeset by Kate Williams, Abergavenny
Printed in Great Britain by The Cromwell Press Ltd, Trowbridge, Wilts.

Contents

Preface   v

Acknowledgments   vi

1   Introducing Art and Design Education   1

2   Drawing   18

3   Painting   36

4   Printmaking   55

5   Computer Art and Design   74

6   Photography   83

7   Bookmaking   96

8   Collage   106

9   Sculpture and Box Modelling   115

10 Modelling   131

11 Puppets and Masks   144

12 Clay   153

13 Fabrics and Thread   174

14 Developing a Context for Learning   196

    Appendix: Artists and their Work   209

    Bibliography   213

    Index   215

Preface

We wrote this book for our students and colleagues, who enjoyed the notes we made to support workshop sessions and courses in both the Faculty of Education and local schools. We have tried to communicate, through the text and the illustrations, our belief in the value, centrality and power of the visual arts in education, particularly in the primary years.

Some time ago, we took inspiration from the excellent cookery manuals of Delia Smith and Madhur Jaffrey, whose clear instructions and interesting background information we have both found inspirational in our own culinary efforts. We have tried to root the practical in the theoretical, to explain carefully the principles which underpin our practice, as well as offering a day-to-day reference book for classroom use. We have therefore included ideas and examples of cross-curricular work which retain the integrity of visual arts teaching within the structures and strictures of today's primary schools. How far we have achieved this aim we leave readers to judge, but we trust that both specialist and non-specialist colleagues will find the book helpful.

Gloria Callaway and Mary Kear
University of the West of England
Bristol, March 1999

Acknowledgments

Particular and very special thanks are due to the children, especially Camilla, Robbie, Carla and Johnny, whose work is included in the book. Our students have also given us inspiration and some fine pieces of work to illustrate various techniques.

The following schools and teachers deserve individual mention: Fiona Childs at Cheddar Grove Primary, Christchurch Clifton Primary, Hannah Buchan (student) and Brian Walton at Four Acres Primary, Stanshawes Court Primary, St. Michael's Primary, Sefton Park Juniors, and Penny Richards who taught us how to make a Japanese sketchbook.

We thank our colleagues, Tim Knowles and Andy Pinner, for assistance with the photography and Siamak Alimi and Ed Crewe who gave essential ICT support.

We are also grateful to all the artists (listed in the Appendix) who took both time and trouble to provide us with examples to show how artists' work can inform and inspire teachers and children alike. We chose to use local, practising artists, whose work is both dynamic and accessible, and who prove that not all visual artists are 'dead white males'.

Most importantly, we owe a considerable debt of gratitude to Abigail Leach, a fine ceramicist, whose illustrations not only inform but delight.

CHAPTER 1

Introducing Art and Design Education

Figure 1.1 *Looking at the Sunflowers*. Crayon and paint by an eight year old. Size: 60 × 45 cm

Teaching art is one of the perks of being a primary school teacher. It brings delight to the children and adults alike, enabling them to celebrate ingenuity, inventiveness, and creativity through the making and viewing of works of art. We write at a time of uncertainty about the role of art and arts education in the primary sector, so it is with some ambivalence that we open this chapter by quoting at length one of the most powerful statements we have read in support of the arts in schools, from a recent OFSTED publication.

> . . . the most persuasive argument for an education in the arts concerns the benefits of attainment in the arts for its own sake.
>
> • The arts . . . are intrinsic components of human culture, heritage and creativity. They mirror the whole repertoire of human experience, and are worthy of study in their own right.

It is difficult to imagine a world without arts, with no drawing, music or painting for example. Few, if any, cultures are without these elements.

• The arts are a response to our thirst for knowledge, insight and revelation. They give people opportunities to explore their feelings, come into contact with the spiritual, increase their knowledge, develop their skills, and articulate and realise their aspirations. They provide ways of knowing, representing, presenting, interpreting and symbolising, and a context for appreciating and valuing.

• Contact with the arts requires the abilities to question, explore, collaborate, and extend and develop one's ideas, and the ideas of others. The creation of art requires a sense of structure, discipline, rigour, and a positive response to challenge.   (OFSTED 1998)

Making art actively supports intellectual, social and emotional development, while offering opportunities to develop essential skills, knowledge and understanding that apply across the curriculum. Some aspects of cognitive development and understanding cannot be taught except through the arts, and of these, some are only accessible within the visual arts. As primary teachers, we need to be reminded that art education is concerned with essential elements of thinking and learning:

• first-hand, practical, sensory experiences;
• developing, processing and representing ideas;
• responding to problems;
• developing critical, visual awareness;
• refining practical skills in the use and control of materials and equipment;
• investigation, exploration and discovery;
• study of the ideas, processes and products of other artists;
• developing personal and individual modes of expression;
• observing and scrutinising in detail.

A major contribution to thinking about art education was, and remains, what is commonly referred to as *The Gulbenkian Report*, from which this statement comes:

We see the arts making vital contributions to children's education in six main areas:
• in developing the full variety of human intelligence;
• in developing the ability for creative thought and action;
• in the education of feeling and sensibility;
• in the exploration of values;
• in understanding cultural change and difference;
• in developing physical and perceptual skills.   (Calouste-Gulbenkian Foundation 1982)

Children usually enjoy art activities; they learn more productively when motivated, enthused and suitably challenged by an area of the curriculum that they respond to positively, and teachers should encourage them to:

• express ideas, observations and feelings with confidence;
• make choices about the media and tools to suit the task and match their preferred mode of working;
• understand the processes and techniques of particular media;
• develop an appreciation of art and the work of artists.

While art can, on occasion, prove relaxing, the real satisfaction comes from actively responding to challenge. In the best taught art sessions, there is sometimes little talk, and almost no off-task talk. Children are focused and absorbed, if the teacher has framed the task in such a way that they are confident, but never under-stimulated.

The National Curriculum describes Art and Design with its own values, aims and outcomes, achieved through the Attainment Target: Knowledge, Skills and Understanding.

The visual and tactile elements of art and design are referred to as requirements to be taught at each Key Stage. For ease of reference, these have been summarised and defined at the end of this chapter, and are referred to in each medium-specific chapter. While streamlining and cross-curricular planning is an established aim in effectively managing the demands of the primary school curriculum, art teaching should be considered in its own right as well as in conjunction with other curricular areas.

> However, this is not to say that art exists in a vacuum (for its own sake) as though it didn't by its very nature feed off life and, just as important, nourish it. Indeed, art can have a part to play in the Viking topic, or any other element of the curriculum which we might choose to use as an example, but it must be used positively, integrally, and not merely as an after-thought. (Sedgwick and Sedgwick 1993)

PLANNING FOR ART

Art needs to be planned as a discrete subject, although it may also complement learning in other disciplines, as this list of the characteristics of good art teaching demonstrates:

- a sequence of lessons is thoroughly planned;
- classroom assistants share the planning of lessons and understand the learning objectives;
- resources are well organised, and materials and equipment are accessible when needed;
- lessons are targeted on teaching specific skills;
- the purpose of the lesson is fully explained to the pupils;
- the introduction is supported by well-chosen visual resources;
- the teacher demonstrates a practical technique confidently;
- pupils receive focused support from the teacher and classroom assistants;
- individual, group and class discussion of the work helps in its assessment;
- the teacher evaluates and monitors both the process and outcomes of the lesson so that planning for progression can be systematic;
- the quality of display does justice to the high standards of pupils' work, and provides both a learning resource and an assessment tool. (OFSTED 1998)

Art needs distinctive documentation to support planning and classroom work, such as the school's policy documents and curriculum statements. The *specialist curriculum* leader has a duty to share personal interests, knowledge and skills with colleagues, to select appropriate materials and consumable resources, to keep up to date with relevant research, identify ways of enhancing and promoting art within the school, and keep in touch with local and national arts organisations and galleries. *The class teacher* should:

a) have a clear grasp of the educational role of the arts, an understanding of how children learn through the arts, and a knowledge of the different stages of the child's aesthetic development;

b) be personally interested in and familiar with at least one or two art forms;

c) be confident in encouraging creative work across the whole range of the arts;

d) be able to recognise and evaluate the artistic quality in children's work.

(NCC Arts in Schools Project Team 1989)

Class teachers need to examine the context in which the teaching takes place, with particular reference to:

- the requirements of the National Curriculum;
- the school's art policy documents;
- the school's overall planning policy;
- available resources, materials and equipment, and storage;
- organisation and arrangement of available space in and outside the classroom;
- the size of the class or group and its dynamics;
- the age, abilities, interests and enthusiasms of the children;
- the teacher's own skills, interests and enthusiasms;
- the teacher's preferred style of classroom management.

The interrelationship of practical work and 'critical studies' (as defined in the Attainment Targets prior to Curriculum 2000), has proved problematic for some teachers whose knowledge and understanding of art and artists is, they feel, limited and insubstantial. Separate planning helps. For example, children working on painting, within a topic on the sea, might look at artists such as Hokusai, Turner, and portraits of sea-farers, videos and photographs of the sea in different moods, observe water at first hand through play and draw on personal experiences through family photographs, postcards and movies. Such research also informs history, geography and English, speaking and listening, reading and writing, as well as art. But within *art* sessions, work focuses on teaching art. The notion of 'input and output' may be helpful. *Input* consists of:

- the work of artists in the medium or media the children have as their current focus through displays, books, videos and CD Roms;
- the subject matter, related to the current topic, including books, video, photographs, and artists' work in different media on the relevant theme;
- the skills and techniques children will learn about, through demonstration, experimentation and investigation.

Figures 1.2 and 1.3 are examples of artists' work which might inspire children. (See Appendix, page 209–212 for more information about the artists).

Output takes place through children's own responses to the subject via the medium.

TALKING ABOUT CHILDREN'S WORK

A major skill of primary teachers is that they understand when and when not to talk to children as they work. If the teacher is clear about aims, that is, what the children are to learn, discussions are better focused, and the teacher is able to teach through discussion and questioning, rather than by offering solutions. Tasks should enable children to begin with confidence, using appropriate resources, with a clear idea of what to do, and why. If the aim is to teach about colour and texture using collage, this can be explained carefully at the outset.

Figure 1.2 *Untitled*. A lithograph by Andy Pinner. Size: 8 × 10.5 cm

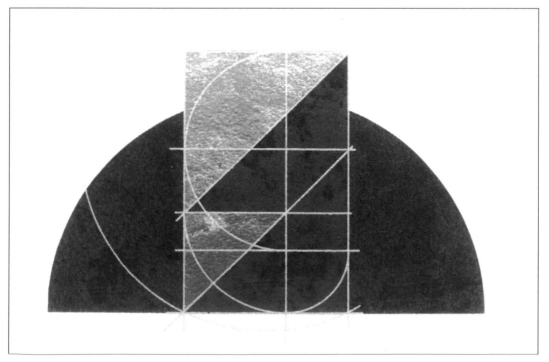

Figure 1.3 *Golden Section, Los Angeles*. A screenprint with gold foil by Stephen Hoskins. Size: 22 × 12.5 cm

Teacher/child talk depends to a large extent on the role the teacher adopts; flexibility is essential to differentiation. This analysis of teachers' roles within the creative arts is summarised from NCC Arts in School Project Team (1989):

- facilitator: enabling pupils to participate practically in the arts and providing stimulus materials, artifacts and ideas;
- mediator: helping pupils to link their own experiences with the world of the arts, and to communicate as artists;
- assessor: conveying, through informed discussion, how fundamental self-assessment is to the process of art-making;
- partner: taking an open-ended, negotiated and supportive approach in an area where solutions are not predetermined;
- questioner: generating and encouraging alternative points of view and critical awareness to the pupils' and others' work;
- instructor: directly teaching techniques and skills, or providing information to encourage self-directed learning;
- artist: sharing personal skills with pupils to inspire them and, occasionally, as an exemplar for their own work.

ART AND DESIGN ACROSS THE CURRICULUM

Every National Curriculum subject at primary level needs to be exploited in terms of its cross-curricular potential. Many skills, concepts and areas of knowledge within the art curriculum are relevant to other subjects, but we should bear in mind that:

> Illuminating one subject through another is quite different from pushing subjects together and hoping they might have something in common. The cross-curricular links must be genuine and not forced . . . The very nature of each subject elicits a different response and understanding and skills are developed in different ways. (Barnes 1989)

Art, like language, pervades all aspects of learning. Observation and recording, discussing and planning, predicting and imagining, experimenting, exploring and problem-solving, are all essential in the art making process. This list highlights how art education might feature across the curriculum; further suggestions are made in each chapter.

English

- Understanding relationships between text and illustration.
- Responding verbally to the quality of illustrations in story and information books.
- Appreciating the concept of genre in art and in English: e.g. descriptive, narrative; forms and styles in art.
- Looking at text in artwork, e.g. Hockney, and links with poster art; use of typefaces, decorative texts, computer generated text etc.
- Considering the arrangement of sounds and letters in written and spoken language.
- Discussing relationships between creative works and where and when they are made, e.g. myths and legends, like works of art, are products of their time, place and cultural setting.

Mathematics

- Using scale, e.g. enlarging sketches for a finished frieze.
- Exploring number patterns, symmetry and tessellation.
- Looking for pattern in natural phenomena.
- Looking for similarities and differences in textured surfaces.
- Studying the construction and design of patterns.
- Measuring and estimating for frames and mounts, and in 3D construction.
- Sorting equipment, such as paintbrushes, pencils.

Science

- Working on light, colour and pigments, studying the spectrum.
- Closely observing animals and plants through art.
- Understanding changes in materials, e.g. mixing dry pigment with water or oil to make paint, consistencies of clay.
- Studying the nature of pigments, e.g. geological (ochre, lapiz lazuli) and botanical (indigo).
- Discovering absorbency of different fabrics and papers.
- Using and depicting minerals and other natural phenomena in art, e.g. copper, brass, gold (leaf), silver, bronze, iron, wood, stone, glass.
- Recognising natural patterns in the environment that indicate cause and effect.

Information and Communications Technology

- Using CD Rom programs to access information about art and artists.
- Using graphics programs to create original work.
- Making multi-media work combining traditional tools and computer technology.

Design and Technology

- Comparing different types of materials, e.g. pliable, rigid.
- Designing artifacts and technological implications.
- Recycling of materials and ideas.
- Applying appropriate technology.
- Analysing package, poster and other 'everyday' design.
- Developing the use of typefaces in printing.
- Seeing how pattern results from technological processes, such as weaving.
- Addressing the health and safety implications of using tools and equipment.

Geography

- Discussing art and artifacts of particular places and cultures.
- Using art to record the environment through sketches, photographs etc.
- Using appropriate local technology.
- Comparing landscape as depicted in photographs and artwork.
- Exploring sources of pigments and other materials used in art such as inks.

History

- Using art as historical evidence.
- Studying developments of techniques and materials through international trading, e.g. papyrus, paper, indigo.
- Recognising symbolic representation in art and architecture.
- Studying how art is used to depict or glorify religious or secular leaders and its role in media propaganda.
- Seeing architecture as a product of its time, culture and place.
- Considering the place of women in art, as artists and as subjects.
- Looking at art of a particular period, e.g. Victorian.
- Studying the history of traditional patterns, e.g. Paisley or plaid.
- Tracing the development of 'everyday' design, e.g. furniture, tableware.

Music

- Making musical instruments, e.g. clay drums.
- Linking art with genres in music: narrative, descriptive etc.
- Using instruments and players as subjects for artwork.
- Constructing patterns of sound to make music.
- Combining music projects with art: movement, dance and drama.
- Studying how music and music-making has been depicted in art.
- Recognising relationships between visual and aural/oral elements.

Physical Education

(See Figure 1.4; p. 211.)
- Studying how movement is depicted in works of art (see Figure 1.4).
- Making patterns in dance.
- Using symbolism in dance and movement.
- Using body movement to describe line, shape, repetitive pattern.
- Using video to study movement.
- Making links with movement in puppetry.
- Recognising how choreography and spatial awareness are related to composition.
- Sketching classmates, if children have to sit out for a physical activity.

Religious Education

- Studying the use of art for devotional purposes: shrines, Eastern gods and goddesses, and the architecture of places of worship.
- Looking at religious narratives in art, e.g. Old and New Testaments, Rama and Sita.
- Recognising pattern in Islamic art.
- Developing a sense of wonder, e.g. through the sea and sky depicted in art.
- Looking at how relationships are described in art, e.g. mother and child.
- Looking at how emotions are depicted in art, e.g. Munch, Picasso.
- Learning about celebration and ceremony through art and artifacts.

Figure 1.4 *Billy's Balloons (1995)*. Oil painting by Elza Scoble. Size: 60 × 90 cm

Painting, sculpture, crafts, music, drama, dance and poetry can all be seen as ways of exploring, investigating and communicating. To learn to do any of them effectively it is necessary, as in any activity, to learn how to interpret experience. Gaining experience, interpreting it and communicating what emerges involves a bringing-together of knowledge, understanding, skill, imagination and reason.

(Wenham in Moyles 1995)

In our experience, making art particularly complements children's learning in mathematics and literacy. Increased fluency, more developed visual discrimination, increased concentration span when working through a process, describing that process and evaluating the end product, all enhance development in reading, writing and speaking. Judging quantities, working with space and form in three dimensions, using symmetry and asymmetry, looking at the origin and structure of pattern, all make use of and consolidate numeracy skills. An art-based theme, such as pattern, can be extended across many areas of the curriculum, as is evident from the cross-curricular examples above.

PLANNING FOR PROGRESSION

Beware the 'timed test' approach to art, when everyone has to make a picture or item of a given subject, following a prescribed formula, using identical materials, by a given time, which will be judged according to its close resemblance to the model from which it was copied. This strategy belies the principles of good art teaching in every respect.

There are times when specific input through a demonstrated technique is helpful to teach children skills and techniques on an apprentice model, as long as they then have the opportunity to use, develop and take ownership of their own work.

The National Curricula set out teaching aims in a content-free way. Experiment with visual elements, such as space, shape and form, might be achieved through 3D work in any of several media (see Figure 1.5), and in connection with almost any subject matter. The outcome, or product, may be a cardboard castle, a papier mâché sculpture, puppets, or 'abstract' constructions in clay or wood. Planning principles are similar, and the teacher needs to include each of the following in planning for practical work:

- examples of art and/or artifacts in the given medium;
- research about the subject matter;
- time to experiment, play and revise skills in the medium;
- opportunities to extend knowledge of the medium, through learning new processes, techniques and uses of tools;
- time to consider, reconsider, modify and adapt original ideas through practical work and ongoing research;
- time to stand back and review progress at intervals in the designing and making process.

This cannot be achieved in a single taught session. Time needs to be carefully apportioned, with children working for some time on a single idea, from inspiration, research, drafting, reviewing, editing, redrafting, modifying, to finished product. Children need to tackle preliminary ideas, have a break, and then come back refreshed to consider what to do next.

DIFFERENTIATION AND MATCH IN ART EDUCATION

When making art, as with most practical activities, all pupils should engage at their own level in processes such as mixing and using paint, constructing with clay or closely observing and drawing the texture of an object. If they can use personal experience, and focus on personal responses to given starting points, rather than conforming to prescribed products, they have more 'ownership' of their work. In this way, the teacher can better differentiate to meet their needs, and provide an effective match between child and activity, equipment and media. Differentiating 'by task' does not always mean asking children to do different things, but ensuring that:

- there is a degree of success in all activities, so children gain skills and confidence in themselves as artists and designers;
- expectations of process and outcome are commensurate with the child's level of development and ability;
- equipment and materials provided match motor control and manual dexterity;
- children are very clear about the minimum requirements and potential developments of the task;
- children better understand what you aim to teach them to do;

Figure 1.5 *Heads*. Drawings with wire by students. Size: 20 cm diameter

- plans include time for demonstration and instruction as well as ongoing supervision;
- you plan for regular feedback to the whole group;
- you allow time to warm up before creative work, and time to clear up at the end.

SPECIAL EDUCATIONAL NEEDS

It is essential . . . that children with special needs are given many opportunities for creative expression and the use of hand-eye coordination. However we need to encourage such children carefully, appreciating what they are capable of doing while recognising that their work has a special value of its own; a value which may be different from that of other children's work. We must also be careful not to use standard adult expectations to judge unsophisticated forms.   (Lancaster 1990)

We tend to use 'special educational needs' as a general term, although it covers many aspects of need, from physical or emotional problems affecting the smooth running of practical or discussion work, to pupils whose special knowledge of art and art processes is beyond that of their peers and teachers. Other books deal with special needs in the detailed and specific ways in which they deserve to be considered. The work we suggest is adaptable to all types of need, depending on the teacher and the resources available. However, we heartily endorse these statements with regard to special educational needs in the arts:

The value of the arts in the education of pupils with special educational needs is not to compensate for abilities that children and young people don't have, but to identify and develop the abilities they *do* have:

- a range of opportunities commensurate with the needs and abilities should be on offer to all pupils, rather than disabilities become the basis for limitation of experience;
- all pupils are individuals and, as such, can be seen as having special needs, gifts and talents which have to be met in order that they realise their full potential;
- disability as such should not be the basis for denial of access to the Arts and their varied forms.   (NCC Arts in Schools Project Team 1989)

WORKING IN GROUPS

The National Curriculum requires that children should be given opportunities to work individually, in groups, and as a whole class. When children work together, ideas, opinions, attitudes and feelings can be expressed, shared and modified. Group work can:

- encourage confidence to tackle tasks that seem daunting to the individual;
- spark off an outpouring and sharing of ideas;
- encourage consideration for others, and awareness of others' individual approaches to art;
- enable sustained or prolonged work, where concentration and motivation is supported by the interest of the group;
- help develop a range of cross-curricular skills;

- promote negotiating, problem-solving and decision-making skills;
- stimulate effective evaluation of process and product.

Group work can take place through:

- children planning and making individual contributions to an item, e.g. a decorated tile to place with others in a panel, or a single building to add to a model village;
- working collaboratively to design and make a large painting or sculpture;
- a group discussing, planning and organising work on a piece of art, agreeing different roles to adopt in producing a book or frieze, a display of art work, stories, poems, information or artifacts that represent learning through a topic.

ASSESSMENT AND EVALUATION IN ART EDUCATION

Assessment and evaluation in the appreciating or appraising role is necessary to teacher and pupil. The teacher needs to know what and how a child has perceived and learned, and, as far as possible, felt, in order to extend the repertoire. The child needs to know how to incorporate what is learned and felt to the next stage/level of production/appreciation.

(Treacher 1989)

The National Curriculum requires that assessment is made of pupils' knowledge, skills and understanding in art and design. To address this, assessment of art and design should:

- be an integral part of the school's policy;
- be part of the curriculum planning process, closely linked with the teaching aims of the unit of work;
- use methods that are appropriate to the task and sensitive to different ways of working;
- not inhibit art processes or delivery of the curriculum;
- be flexible to account for developments that occur during the process of making art;
- give feedback and encouragement to pupils;
- be formative to facilitate monitoring of process and product;
- provide diagnostic information about pupils' abilities and levels of attainments;
- help teachers in future planning and practice;
- use summative strategies to assess pupil achievement;
- inform curriculum continuity and progression;
- give a framework for reporting to parents.

The sketchbook is invaluable, for children of all ages, to help them and the teacher with assessment. Other strategies for carrying out assessment in art are:

- portfolios of examples of 2D work, and photographs of 3D work to demonstrate development and progress;
- adding descriptive accounts or photographs of artwork to pupils' profiles;
- using self-assessment sheets for pupils;
- keeping notes of discussions with pupils as work progresses and is completed;
- setting a specific task as a focus for assessment, negotiating the criteria for assessment with pupils at the outset.

Displays offer a useful vehicle for children to assess their own finished work, which often looks more accomplished and satisfying when it is appropriately mounted. This is a very different type of assessment from ongoing decision making. Displays of artwork should be discussed in some depth with the children who made the work. A lesson plan helps to ensure that this discussion is appropriately focused on the original aims of the work, as well as allowing for more general and free-flowing talk. Displays also offer teachers evidence about children's achievements, their use of particular processes and their ability to work independently on completing a set task. (See Chapter 14.)

> Teachers involved with art, craft and design education sometimes feel that the evaluation and assessment of children's work inhibits creativity, personal responses and individual development. If evaluation is based upon arbitrary external criteria this will sometimes be the case, but if it is seen as an essential part of the process of education it will already be an integral part of the learning strategy. Teachers are continuously involved with evaluation in both formal and informal contexts. (Barrett 1990)

The following sections list 'elements of learning' which help in evaluating children's work adapted from NCC Arts in Schools Project Team (1989).

- *Concepts:* Contextual concepts are developed through familiarity with and experience of a wide variety of media, materials and approaches. Children should see that their own work is growing within cultural contexts which are likely to exercise an influence on its form and style. Aesthetic concepts relate to the form and organisation of the work, e.g. rhythm, symmetry, contrast, balance, harmony, tone.
- *Skills:* Children's art development does not just happen because they get older: creative work needs practice, learning, teaching. *Perceptual* skills include observation, discrimination, interpretation. *Productive* skills include knowledge and practical application of materials, tools, techniques. *Discursive* skills include developing vocabulary and understanding to enable appropriate responses to be articulated effectively.
- *Values:* Feelings are evaluations of events. The arts offer ways of raising questions of value and perceptions. Children need to develop the confidence to express and question their own values and attitudes, a willingness to consider others, and a sense of self-worth from positive achievement.
- *Information:* Children need to know about the subject matter of their work, and about the medium in use. Relevant information enhances their understanding about the medium, and increases understanding of context and convention in their own and others' work.

Evaluating and assessing each child's every piece of artwork is a daunting prospect. Unless it is helpful to child and teacher, it is not worth the time. A simple cumulative checklist can help to summarise and record data, to inform ongoing planning, and to acquaint the next teacher with relevant information. Filed with the lesson plan, a copy can be completed for each group as the children work through the task (see Table 1.1).

TALKING ABOUT ART AND ARTISTS AND DESIGN AND DESIGNERS

There is an onus on the teacher to be familiar with the particular processes and media being taught, and about how artists have used them. If the art work is linked to a topic like

Table 1.1 Summary of group achievement/needs

Class:	Term:		Group:
Medium:			2D/3D *e.g. drawing, painting, sculpture, etc.*
Aims:			*(write out or refer to lesson plan)*
NC ref. AT1:			
AT2:			
Task:			*(write out or refer to lesson plan)*
Names	Response to artists' work (date)	Notes on process (date)	Notes on product (date)

weather, children can explore how artists depict the weather of the region in which they worked. Within an 'ourselves' project, self-portraits, portraits, sculptures etc., representing people, inspire children to work in a more considered way.

One of the pleasures of being a primary teacher is the opportunity it offers to browse through art books as part of planning. Story-time can include the biography of an artist whose work is on display in the classroom, such as Frink, if her work is used as part of a project on animals. On occasion, during quiet reading time, children can browse through books about art and artists, and later share impressions.

While it is impractical to insist that every primary teacher should be an art historian, it is nonetheless important that teachers are informed and able to talk at some level about the work and lives of artists, craftspersons and designers, as appropriate to children's ages and levels of understanding. If they are painting, provide paintings to look at; if printmaking, use prints. For 3D work, use the work of sculptors, architects and designers. Discussion may focus on the subject-matter, how and why children think it was made, and how children respond. Allow them time to think aloud and compare and contrast pictures, rather than guessing what you want them to answer. Subsequent discussion might be based on any of the following.

- *Content or subject:* think of what it is about, or in response to; what the artist was interested in when making it; when and where it might have been made.
- *Medium, tools and equipment:* consider what materials were used; how were they applied or worked; the scale of the original; surface marks, textures and the medium itself (print, drawing, bronze sculpture etc.), all give clues.
- *Exploring colour:* identify the range of colours used; those which dominate the eye may be different for one person compared with another; experiments with colour may be illustrated in the work, e.g. Impressionist and Renaissance artists, and designers such as William Morris from the Arts and Crafts Movement.
- *Ideas behind works of art and design:* finding out about the philosophies of artists and designers (e.g. Surrealism, Art Deco) can be a challenge.

- *Why it was made:* it may have been a commission, or an investigation into the way light can be represented, as with some of Rembrandt's work, and fire or landscape, e.g. in Australian Aboriginal painting.
- *Children's responses:* include, and go beyond, whether or not they like it; compare colours, content or composition with other work they know, which may promote language and vocabulary around the mood or emotion it conveys.
- *Developing personal preferences:* looking critically at a wide range of art of different historical periods and cultures helps develop art appreciation, particularly looking at examples of work by artists at different times of their careers, or alongside others of the same school or group.

WORKING WITH ARTISTS, DESIGNERS AND CRAFTSPERSONS IN SCHOOLS

Many artists who work in schools say that they learn as much as the children. They may be employed to run *Artist workshops*, where the artist teaches the children specialist skills and processes through working alongside them, usually on a one-off basis. *Artists in residence*, on the other hand, spend a more prolonged period of time in the school, using it as a studio base, so children can observe the process, or they work alongside children to achieve a particular, possibly ambitious, project.

Artists, designers and craftspersons will require payment commensurate with their professional status. The school may have to raise funds for this, so it is vital to make a form of written contract which states the fee, what is included, materials or tools, how long the artist will work, including preparatory visits, travelling costs, number of children involved, etc. Teachers must check the artist's credentials, experience and suitability. Ensure that all staff and parents are aware of the event, the timing and location. Art coordinators probably have a file of contacts, including circulars sent to schools by artists seeking employment in this field. For further information, look up the internet, or contact:

- local and regional arts organisations through yellow pages;
- local art galleries and museums;
- other schools in your area;
- local press reports of such events;
- craftspersons or artists through their own guilds, organisations or associations.

THE BASIC ELEMENTS OF ART

Within traditional media, such as paint, sculpture and printmaking, there are discernible elements, conventionally described in the terms defined below. These conventions have, to a great extent, been questioned and challenged by some modern artists, such as installation artists and by work in video and computer art, but the visual and tactile elements of art still serve as useful terms to explore with children and to describe aspects of most of the artwork they will produce and examine in their primary years. Each chapter in turn describes how some or all of these elements apply within particular media.

Line

Line is the basic element of drawing, a device for describing, e.g. shape, by the use of outlines (which do not exist in nature). Three-dimensional form can be represented on a two-dimensional surface. Line can be used to tell a story, to express ideas, to report on what is seen (see Figure 1.6), or to make patterns, maps, writing, etc. A line is essentially a continuous mark, which can be thick, thin, straight, curved or a combination of qualities. In two-dimensional work, lines are made on paper or other flat surfaces with tools such as pencils, biros, brushes or fingers in paint, sand etc. Line can be descriptive (as in a cartoon) or decorative (as in embellishment of a page). Handwriting is essentially a series of lines and dots, made

Figure 1.6 *Bicycle.* A pencil drawing by a five year old. Size: 10 × 10 cm

within recognised conventions of the language community, e.g. Roman, Greek. In three-dimensional work, line is usually superimposed on the form by incising in clay or print blocks, painting on papier mâché or models, and with resist processes on fabrics.

Colour

Primary colours cannot be mixed from other colours:

- red
- yellow
- blue

Secondary colours can be made by mixing any two primary colours:

- red + yellow   ➜   orange
- red + blue   ➜   purple
- blue + yellow ➜   green

Complementary colours contrast, and are opposite each other on the colour wheel; a primary colour contrasts with the secondary colour made from the other two primaries.

complementary	*contrasting*
blue and orange	(yellow/red)
yellow and purple	(red/blue)
red and green	(blue/yellow)

- *Hue:* The actual colour itself, e.g. red, yellow, purple etc.
- *Tint:* This is a colour to which white has been added.
- *Shade:* This is a colour to which black has been added.

   ⬅ lighter ⬅ tint ⬅ HUE ➜ shade ➜ darker ➜

- *Tone:* indicates a degree of lightness or darkness, the depth of colour or the density achieved with different drawing media, e.g. crayon or pencil. Children need to understand the difference between colour contrast (i.e. of hue) and tonal contrast (i.e. of light/shade). 'Monochrome' means gradations of one colour, as in black and white drawings or photographs, or sepia (brown) photographs.

Shape

Shape is an area with clear boundaries. It can refer to both geometric shapes and non-geometric shapes. In art, it usually refers to something flat and two-dimensional.

Form

This could be considered to be the three dimensional equivalent of shape. Form is the term used to describe things in the round, such as sculpture or modelling. A painter may also describe the illusion of form in a painting.

Texture

Texture can mean the actual surface qualities of things around us, which can be seen or felt. Texture can also be created by making marks to produce the illusion of a textured surface in drawing, painting, etc. Paint, for instance, can be laid smoothly on the paper but still describe texture. It can also be applied thickly so it has its own texture.

Pattern

Pattern refers to the repetition of shapes, formal and random. Throughout history, pattern has been used universally to decorate and embellish: Paisley, Scottish plaid, checks and stripes. Regular patterns are found in natural objects such as flowers, honeycombs and some spider webs, and in the built environment in railings and windows. Repeat patterns are used in designs for fabrics and knitwear, in bricks and roof tiles; irregular patterns are found in some animal markings, trees and buildings. Pattern is used in Australian Aboriginal painting, Indian miniatures and Islamic designs.

Composition

Putting together some or all of the elements above will create a relationship between components (colours, hues, textures, shapes) to create a picture, design or form (see Figure 1.7).

Figure 1.7 *Clown.* Drawing in felt-tip by an eight year old. Size 15 × 30 cm

CHAPTER 2

Drawing

Children draw, almost every day, in almost every classroom. Their drawings fulfil many functions, and are often taken for granted. Nonetheless, drawing is a major, overarching activity, central to every facet of the visual arts. It requires and develops skills in:

- looking, responding, analysing and coordination of mind, hand and eye (see Figure 2.1);
- gathering of essential data and information and the processes of researching, working out and thinking through ideas (see Figure 2.2);
- solving problems in response to design briefs in relation to meeting a whole range of human needs;
- communicating ideas to others through use of sketches, plans, designs, diagrams, scribbles, doodles and so on (see Figure 2.3).

Figure 2.1 *Pinks.* Fibretip drawing by a seven year old. Size: 17 × 27 cm

Drawing is mark-making, with every tool and material known to the human race: graphic tools, brushes, fingers, hands, imprinting, using modelling and cutting tools, threads, fibres, wires and whatever else is or ever has been available. Drawing is an attitude of mind, a form of enquiry; not an end in itself so much as a way of understanding, of seeing potential, or of using. Drawing deepens understanding through involvement, by utilising an intensity of looking, selecting, organising . . .   (Sedgwick and Sedgwick 1993)

Figure 2.2 *Bicycle.* Fibretip drawing by a seven year old. Size: 20 × 20 cm

Figure 2.3 *The Farm.* Biro and wax crayon drawing by a five year old. Size: 25 × 21 cm

Drawing is pleasurable for children. From the marks they make, in the early years of childhood onwards, they build a graphic vocabulary, a personal language which they use to communicate a range of ideas and feelings. In school drawing occurs across the curriculum, to illustrate stories, poems and topic work, represent plans and designs, record, explore and analyse observations and responses. 'With a drawing, the whole idea is visible all at once and you can work at it with addition, alteration, modification, change, etc.' (de Bono 1972).

To exploit the potential of drawing as a vehicle for expression, children need access to a range of tools and media, instruction and support in their use, and adequate time to experiment and explore. Thus they develop understanding about the relationship between the drawing implement and the type and quality of the mark it produces, and move towards being able to match tools and media to tasks. In this way, they develop confidence, skill and fluency, and begin to acknowledge their own graphic style and preferences that inform the way they work.

> There is a natural progression for the learner from the examination of a single object. Drawing an object in a secure and comfortable environment helps to focus research while confidence and skills are gained . . . These activities involving seeing as well as recording skills help to develop the learner's ability to order their responses to direct experience. This can lead to learners encountering the need to extend their understanding and further refine the personal qualities of their response to a learning situation.   (Newlands and Rubens 1983)

THE CROSS-CURRICULAR POTENTIAL OF DRAWING

Drawing is a part of every subject in the National Curriculum, and the following types of drawing indicate how it enhances and develops work in all subject areas.

Illustration/narrative drawing

Making pictures to go with stories, poems or other work, children consider relationships between information and ideas best portrayed in words, how drawings may complement words. Studying the work of book illustrators in fiction and information books may help them to make decisions about the balance and layout of books, articles or poems they write for themselves.

Sketching

Making preliminary drawings towards an art product in any of a number of media, e.g. paint, printmaking, modelling or a more finished drawing, enables children to draft work, preferably in sketchbooks. Gathering ideas towards finished work helps children to organise thoughts and make decisions.

Designing

Design can take account of previous research and exploratory work, reference to ideas noted in sketchbooks, developing them through trying out 3D designs in 2D (see Figure 2.4). The computer is a particularly useful drawing tool for design.

Communicating

When the viewer understands what the drawer intended, there has been communication. Transmitting information, instructions, ideas or emotions through drawing does not indicate a lack of facility with either spoken or written words, but another, complementary and equally important skill (see Figure 2.5).

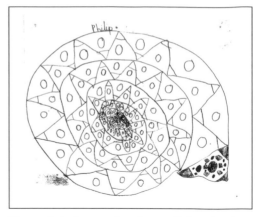

Figure 2.4 *Ammonite*. A pencil drawing by a ten year old. Size: 20 × 18 cm

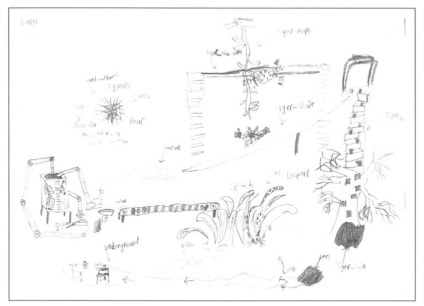

Figure 2.5 *Tiger Environment*. A pencil drawing by an eight year old. Size 40 × 30 cm

Investigating

Drawing and recording information, while looking at an object or a person, enables the drawer to investigate how the individual features of the subject fit together to make the whole. Equally the subject can, with imagination, be transferred to another setting within the drawing; parts or whole of the subject may be drawn; focus may be on pattern, line, tone or surface texture of the subject. These are ways of investigating the subject, and getting to know it, through the drawing.

Analysing

Drawing a subject from observation or memory enables the drawer to analyse the structure of an object, artifact or person: to see what is intrinsic to the form and function of the item, and what is surface design, pattern or feature.

Making studies

Studying a subject in detail, with a viewfinder or a magnifying glass, enables the drawer to focus attention on those parts which attract or create particular responses, such as the lines of veins in leaves, the pattern on a single petal, or the arrangement of leaves and flowers on a stem. Making several studies of a subject helps the drawer to become familiar with aspects of an object, the better to understand its structure and form.

Figure 2.6 *Big Cat and Babies.* Fibretip drawing by a six year old. Size: 27 × 33 cm

Note-making

Quick recording of essential detail is a skill akin to taking brief notes when reading or listening to language. This aide-memoire will later remind the drawer about how windows are placed in a building's facade, the relative proportions of the door, patterns made by brickwork, roof tiles, etc.

Researching

These processes are part of a research approach to making art; the study of the subject through visual observation and note-making adds to the drawer's knowledge, understanding and appreciation of the subject, which might be landscape, portraits or crystals.

Expressing

To draw in response to an event, experience or emotional trigger is a valid way of recording what the particular stimulus meant to the drawer personally (see Figure 2.6). It is up to the person making the marks to decide on the most appropriate focus, on the form, and emphases within, the drawing. Without a wide repertoire of mark-making skills and tools, the drawer is limited, and the response therefore tends to be more shallow or formulaic.

Figure 2.7 *Indian Artifact.* Pencil drawing by an eight year old. Size: 30 × 14 cm

Embellishing

From doodles in margins to the expert and beautiful calligraphic borders of manuscripts, drawing skills are essential in being able to embellish and decorate work of all kinds. Familiarity with the potential range of marks to be made with particular tools and media, such as ink with pens or brushes, helps the drawer to work more skilfully and gain greater satisfaction. Figure 2.7 shows embellishment of design based on observational drawing.

THE BASIC ELEMENTS OF ART IN DRAWING

Line

Line is integral to drawing. 'The (narrow) continuous mark, as one made by a pencil, pen or brush, across a surface' (Collins Concise Dictionary, 1988) is used in all forms of drawing. Line in children's earliest drawings depicts a range of characters and situations. Their use of the drawn line expands, as manipulative control and fluency develops, until an abundant vocabulary of marks is used to describe content, shape, space, texture, surface, depth and detail. Children also use linear marks to draw into print blocks, and to manipulate the mouse to draw on a computer screen.

Colour

Drawing occurs in most art activities that use a colour medium. Children apply paint to surfaces with applicators using strokes, marks, and lines. The shape of coloured crayons and pastels define the marks that can be made with them. Coloured pens produce the continuous line so characteristic of drawing.

Pattern and shape

The organisation and manipulation of drawn lines is evident in both drawn composition and pattern-making (see Figure 2.8). When children create patterns on different surfaces, they use drawing techniques to represent form, shape and texture, to devise decorative features and indicate the division of space.

Texture

Surface texture can be both represented and created in drawing. Texture on a dragon can be drawn from imagination, or a fossil surface recorded from close observation. A decorative, textural pattern can be incised on a clay tile, or drawn on fabric. Shapes cut from collage materials, where the scissors become the drawing tool, can be combined to form textural surfaces.

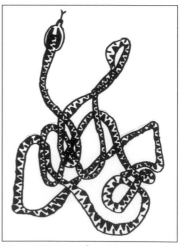

Figure 2.8 *Snake*. Fibretip by a nine year old. Size: 21 × 30 cm

THE DEVELOPMENT OF CHILDREN'S IMAGERY

To teach art well, the teacher needs to understand how children's mark-making develops, evidenced in the outpouring of drawings and paintings of early childhood and the lively intensity that the work displays. While many theories exist about the significance and possible interpretation of these marks, there is a consensus about general developmental trends.

Each child is a changing, developing individual, whose physical, emotional and intellectual growth usually follows a pattern in common with other children, but at a different rate in each case. Similarly, children's art work is seen to follow a predictable pattern, evolving from first scribbles towards consistent symbols which, over time, become the conscious representation of ideas and objects.

At every stage, children's art reflects their ability to reason and problem-solve. Progression is age-related, although not age-determined, and is observed in whatever media the child uses. It is continuous, but for convenience has been split up into a number of stages. The following paragraphs briefly summarise these stages as described in several books about children's art development.

- *Scribbling:* happens from early infancy, when children explore through broad physical whole-arm movements, making accidental marks and images, experimenting through play.
- *Symbolism:* at pre-school, infant and early junior age, less apparently random mark-making leads to more considered placing of marks, increasing introduction of representational elements in the selection of shapes, forms and colour. More variation and detail indicate increasing awareness of the environment and developing motor control.
- *Schematic images:* these appear during early and middle junior years, with increasing emphasis on realism or representational work, evident through more logically

Figure 2.9 *My Friend.* Drawings in pencil by ten year olds. Size 30 × 40 cm

conceived and analysed shapes, the use of plan and elevation, x-ray drawings, and an interest in technology when building objects and models. Figure 2.9 is an interesting example of the convergence of representational images as the two pictures were drawn by unrelated children from different schools but show striking similarity.

- *Attempts at realism:* at the latter stages of junior school, children aim for realism, and are more self-conscious in relation to their drawings, particularly of the human figure, with greater awareness of detail and the inter-relationship or overlapping of objects. The sky meets the horizon. There is less exaggeration, distortion and omission of body parts.

The stages are not always chronological, and scribbling may be very appropriate for older children, even adults, getting to know a new medium, like charcoal or pen and ink drawing. When trying something new, children often seem to go back a stage or two. Once familiar with it, they can use skills they already have in developing their proficiency and ideas with the new materials.

A key point is that children will draw better, more confidently and with greater skill, if they know the medium and the subject they are working with, if they have been set a task which allows them freedom within defined parameters, and if their work is taken seriously. When a child is dissatisfied with a piece of work, the teacher needs to find out in what way it is disappointing, to identify areas which are satisfactory, and to make suggestions as to how to improve the whole. Thus, children learn about drawing, rather than how to draw according to a set formula.

ARTISTS WHO DRAW

Not everyone who draws is an artist, and it is really quite surprising to note how many occupations make use of drawing skills in one way or another. Some may be called artists, others would eschew the term, but nonetheless use similar skills to work on and communicate ideas, to make visual notes, or to calculate measurements and quantities: interior designers, engineers, draughtspersons, mathematicians, architects, ceramicists, graphic designers, weavers, couturiers, botanists, quilt-makers, cartoonists; the list is almost endless. In almost every society, there is a function for drawing in terms of passing on information, instructions and explanations. Drawings shown in Figures 2.10 and 2.11 show sketches towards 3D artifacts. Figure 2.12 is a drawing for its own sake, not a sketch towards another piece of work.

Artists in Western cultures almost all draw in one way or another. Their sketchbooks reveal just how much time and effort is put into working out ideas and thoughts, organising and reorganising compositions, trying out different effects in the easily accessible, cheap and portable medium of drawing. Goya, da Vinci, Dürer, Hockney, Van Gogh, Moore, Picasso and Miro are among those whose sketchbooks (published, and available from libraries) are testimony to the way they worked.

For children, to look at the sketchbooks of artists whose work they have encountered is illuminating. They get an idea of how the art-making process works for some people, and begin to appreciate how working on initial ideas through sketches is similar to collecting ideas for a poem or a story.

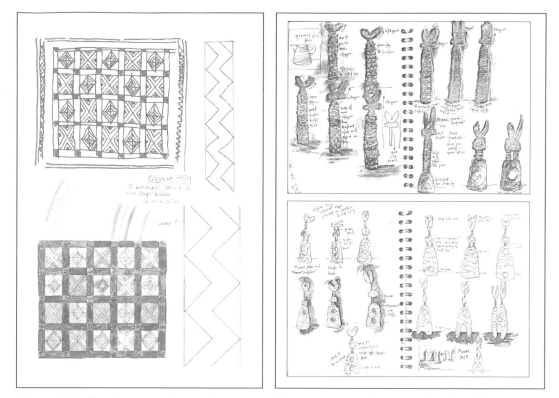

Figure 2.10 Sketches towards a quilt by Mary Kear. Size: Imperial sketchbook (see Chapter 13)

Figure 2.11 Sketches towards a bottle by Abigail Leach. Size: A5 (see Chapter 12)

Figure 2.12 *Windows*. A mixed media drawing, by Alfred Huckett. Size: 43 × 65 cm

Visual resources, such as book illustrations, can be copied (always check copyright). Posters of drawings mounted for display, make drawing a feature in its own right. Children can then see similarities between their own mark-making and the lines, shades and tonal effects achieved by artists. You may be able to borrow sketchbooks from artists or art students to show them the real thing.

SUITABLE TOOLS AND MEDIA FOR DRAWING

Dry drawing media: monochrome

Pencils

Everyone uses the humble HB, Hard-Black, pencil for everyday writing and drawing. Despite this, it has a very wide range of mark-making potential for the skilled user, depending on how it is sharpened, how it is held, the amount of pressure used, and the surface to which it is applied. Children can investigate its potential by making as many different lines and textural effects as possible on different papers. There are a lot! Harder leads are designated H, 2H, 3H etc. H pencils are used by draughtspersons, as they give a very hard, thin line, rather faint if the pencil is lightly held. Softer, blacker leads are designated B, 2B, 4B and so on, up to a very soft 9B, used for flowing, soft lines and a range of tones. Some pencils have charcoal centres, or flat casings, like carpenters' pencils, designed to run smoothly along a straight edge.

Charcoal

Charcoal breaks: this burned wood is brittle and best snapped into small lengths before use. It comes in a range of sizes, from quite fine to massive chunks used by scene-painters for initial drawings. It is best used boldly and with due respect for the lovely quality of texture and tone which can be achieved, especially used on its side with sweeping, relaxed movements, on fairly rough paper. Charcoal sticks are available in a range of blacks, greys and even white, although we do not understand how burnt wood becomes white charcoal. Its kinship with chalk, especially blackboard chalk, is clear.

Dry drawing media: colour

Pencil crayons

Ordinary coloured pencils offer great scope for detailed work, with a subtlety and range of colour and tone which can be achieved according to the type of pencil and the way it is used. Watercolour pencils are best used on a dampened surface, giving very interesting effects. Coloured pencils are best used in sets, or sorted into colours in containers with leads uppermost. Make sure they are sharp, clean and that children have the opportunity to choose from a range of reds, greens, yellows, etc.

Wax crayons

Over-used, but often under-rated, ordinary wax crayons give a range of exciting effects, e.g. layering different colours, or using in combination with other drawing media, such as water-colour, ink or dye in a wax-resist technique. Extend the range with fluorescent and metallic crayons, or extended colour boxes. Stubby, block crayons come in a good range of colours, and handle well. Always present these sorted, in clean containers, to avoid those gungy waxy crayon boxes, so off-putting to serious work.

Chalks and pastels

Soft and brittle, chalks and pastels have a limited life-span but are essential tools for primary children. Oil pastels are less fragile than chalk pastels: the oil binding gives a more opaque quality and greater intensity of colour. Pastels work best on a rough surface like sugar paper, so chalky characteristics are heightened. Colour range and texture can be extended by building up layers on the paper. Pastel drawings can easily be smudged or wiped off. If no fixative is available, separate with sheets of protective tissue paper. New boxes of pristine and inviting colours are quite delicious, and inspire most children to very good work.

Felt and fibre tipped pens

These can give a sharp, regular flowing line. They are often rigid and stiff when new, but wear down and soften with use. With practice, it is possible to achieve a wide variety of marks and textures. Use only water-based pens. Offer a variety and present them attractively.

Liquid drawing media

Ink

Waterproof ink drawings can be washed over or added to without the ink being removed or smudged. It is also waterproof on clothes, and will not wash out. Water-based inks can be diluted for paler drawn lines or colour washes.

Paint

All types of paint can be used for drawing, with various applicators. Thin water-based paints offer the greatest fluency.

Tools to use with liquid drawing media

A comprehensive list is impossible, but to start with, try:

- drawing and fountain pens with different sized nibs, dip pens;
- brushes and ink or water colour;
- computer drawing packages;
- long sticks attached to brushes that lengthen the arm-span;
- all types of paintbrushes, and Chinese calligraphy brushes;
- ordinary sticks, sharpened at the end (or not).

Children can also make their own tools, such as:

- sticks broken or sharpened to a point;
- feathers;
- sponges on sticks;
- fabric screwed to a point;
- charcoal from wood they have watched burn.

Other media to draw with

Mark-making skills are also used when drawing:

- in clay, for instance on a tile or dish;
- on commercially produced scraperboard, or over layers of wax on paper;
- in print, especially monoprint, and in string etc. on blocks for printmaking;
- in sand;
- in thin florists' wire, in 3D: a challenge to which children respond with enthusiasm and interesting results.

Papers and grounds

Provide a range of good quality paper for drawing, and avoid flimsy, shiny paper which does not provide a firm surface for the mark-making tool. Label paper trays accurately with the type and weight of paper, to help children to choose with discrimination, e.g.:

- cartridge;
- black sugar paper;
- light coloured sugar paper (off-white, beige, pale colours);
- green, brown and blue sugar paper;
- kitchen paper;
- tracing paper;
- textured wallpaper.

Note that no bright colours are recommended, because they tend to overpower the often subtle marks of children. The use of general purpose rough paper devalues the drawing activity and encourages rough work. 'Draft' paper is a much more useful label.

PLANS FOR TEACHING DRAWING TO ALL AGE AND ABILITY GROUPS

First experiments: scribble!

Each child stands by a large, open newspaper on the floor, with a large wax crayon. Ask them to scribble over the paper in various ways, to help them appreciate the range of muscles they use, and how their movements are reflected in the marks on the paper. This can be useful as a warm-up, prior to more controlled, detailed work. Large and fine motor movements are familiar from movement sessions, and links can be made with scale in drawing. If children try making marks on other people's scribbles, a talking point is provided to discuss how different marks can be identified within a scribble, and about the nature of 'composite' images. A possible sequence of instructions follows.

- Bend from the waist, and scribble to a count of five. Look at the marks, and think about how hard you pressed, and how the shapes differ.
- Moving your arm from the shoulder, make circular and zig-zag marks.
- Hold the crayon on its side or in a clenched fist, and try again.
- Kneel down, and make marks by moving your arm from the elbow.
- Close your eyes and scribble; see if the marks look as you expected.
- Close your eyes, scribble with a crayon in each hand; see what happens.
- Crouch , make marks from the wrist, compare with 'elbow' and 'shoulder' marks.

Investigating mark-making

Provide a range of drawing materials, all black:

- brushes/pens of various shapes/sizes to use with ink;
- charcoal and charcoal pencils;
- black crayons, different sizes;
- a range of pencils: soft, 4B, 3B, 2B, HB, etc.;
- pastels, oil crayons and oil pastels;
- several types of white paper in several sizes;
- newspaper, large and smaller pieces.

Experiment with a selection of mark-makers to see what you can do with them. As you work, notice how marks change according to how you hold the drawing implement, how hard you press, whether you use the tip or the side of the mark-maker. Work on different types of paper to produce an interesting range of textures.

Decide how to arrange the marks on the page, to make an interesting composition, but try not to make it look like anything. Focus on the quality of the texture, and getting to know the media. Explore the potential of each medium. Discover the different types of line and marks and the range of tones that can be made with each, for instance:

- the various marks you can make with a brush and ink;
- the lightest/darkest tones possible with an HB pencil;
- contrasts made by grouping lines closely together or placing them farther apart.

Investigating specific media

Pencils
- Introduce the full range of pencils; choose two different types, make the lightest and the darkest possible mark with each and compare them.
- Make a row of similarly spaced, straight or curved lines.
- Vary the length or space between the lines and group them on the page.
- Press hard, press soft.
- Use a continuous curved line with no angles or corners.
- Use a continuous straight line with corners and angular turns, no curves, to draw all over the page; make up your own rules before you start, e.g. don't cross over lines, always go in the same direction, only turn through ninety degrees etc.
- Start from the centre and work outwards.
- Start from several points around the edge and work inwards.
- Work without lifting the pencil, varying the tone as you go, until the paper is covered with a continuous line.

Crayons
- Draw with quick movements, then slowly, smoothly, erratically.
- Work on a very small scale carefully.
- Work on a large scale boldly.
- Try using a crayon in each hand at the same time.
- Try using your 'other' hand.

Charcoal

- Explore the possible range of marks from different surfaces of the charcoal on rough paper.

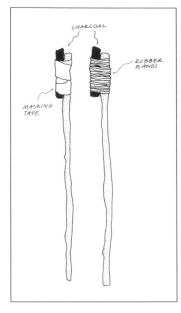

- Work with the whole arm in sweeping movements.
- Shade in a large area with different types of marks made with the charcoal.
- Tie charcoal to a stick, bend over from the waist and see how large an arc you can draw on newspaper.
- Smudge your drawing to see what happens.

Figure 2.13 Charcoal on a stick. Attach with masking tape or rubber bands. In both cases ensure 'drawing end' is protruding slightly over end of stick to prevent breakage of charcoal

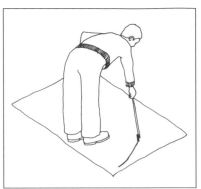

Figure 2.14 Drawing an arc with charcoal on stick

Ink and small brushes

- Use the same ideas as above for pencil: how do the media differ?
- Try to create a texture (like the surface of water or tree bark) using wavy lines and varying the thickness.

Biro or thin felt pen

- Using a ruler to help you, work over the page drawing straight lines; group them close together or further apart.

Mixed media: collaborative work

- Work in pairs on a large sheet of paper, using different media and a range of marks, to create an interesting surface that is content-free but varies in line, tone and intensity, making full use of space and the relationships between areas of marks.
- Make marks sequentially, changing, developing, making each a little different from the one before.
- Work cooperatively by taking turns to draw and then passing on to others.
- Work from the middle in dense marks creating an area of dark tone, then work out towards the edge, gradually lightening the tone.
- Work from one corner, making your marks relate to one another, contrasting or blending.

Drawing from observation: texture and line

Display

- originals, or reproductions, of artists' drawings in different styles;
- shells, bones, dried seed heads, fossils, etc., with interesting surface texture;
- magnifying glasses;
- viewfinders (Figure 2.15).

Drawing media

- a range of pencils, sorted by grade: HB, 2B etc.;
- a range of charcoal sticks;
- a range of coloured pencils in black, browns and ochres;
- small wax crayons in similar colours;
- fine felt and fibre-tipped pens in similar colours;
- white chalks, oil and wax crayons.

Papers

- a range of white papers, e.g. cartridge and sugar paper, in different sizes;
- a range of light, neutral colours, e.g. beige and pale grey;
- black sugar paper of different sizes.

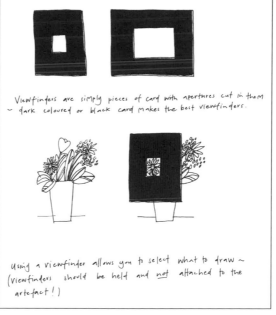

Viewfinders are simply pieces of card with apertures cut in them ~ dark coloured or black card makes the best viewfinders.

Using a viewfinder allows you to select what to draw ~ (viewfinders should be held and *not* attached to the artefact!)

Figure 2.15 Using a viewfinder allows you to select what to draw (viewfinders should be held and *not* attached to the artifact!)

Introduction

Look at artists' work on display, and discuss whether the artist was most concerned with line, or tone, or the effects of light and shade etc. Focus on how the artist works, as well as on the subject of the drawing. Children realise how much they already know about drawing and mark-making from their own work. Compare and contrast the drawings:

- Did any two – or more – artists use the same medium? How can you tell?
- Which drawings do you think were big in the original, and which were very small?
- Were any of the drawings made in preparation for a painting or sculpture?

Task

Select from the display an object that excites interest, something that you find pleasant to look at or to touch. Use a magnifying glass and a viewfinder and focus on a small area of the surface.

Select the mark-making tools you most enjoyed using in previous sessions. Use the range of marks and graphic vocabulary developed during previous experimentation, e.g. to represent textural qualities to explore the surface of this area. Do not attempt to draw the whole object, but try to represent the small area that you have isolated. Remember the artists' work you have looked at, and see if your marks are similar.

Afterwards, discuss the range of marks, favourites, surprises, the effects on different qualities and tones of paper, different types of black, and of the space between marks. Choose some of your experiments and arrange them on a mounting sheet. Move them around until they give a pleasing and balanced impression with equal borders, then stick them down. The drawings made may be the basis for later printmaking or sewing work, particularly if focused on the use of line and texture, rather than on depicting objects.

'Still life' observational drawing

Drawing directly from an arrangement of objects such as a 'still life', children need to explore different aspects of the task before attempting a final composition.

Line

Observational drawing in the Western tradition implies getting the shapes of the objects on paper in some sort of proportion. Encourage children to look at the shapes, to allow their eyes to travel around the edges of the objects and to appreciate how the individual shapes relate to each other. Use a pointed finger in the air to trace the outlines, and the spaces in between. If appropriate for the children's ages and skills, get them to draw these shapes, on newspaper, while looking at the objects, and not looking down. This is very hard, but fun. Using newspaper means the drawing is not precious, so they work in a less inhibited, freer way, allowing their eyes to tell their hand what to do. Parallels with riding a bike, in that the hands steer according to information sent from the eyes to the brain, may be obvious to some.

Patterns, textures, colour

Work in sketchbooks, perhaps on newspaper, responding in turn to the patterns, the textures and recording the colours they see, helps familiarise children with the object or objects and the setting from various viewpoints.

Introducing tone

One way of encouraging children to look at tone and tonal values, as well as colour appreciation, is to provide resources which help them to compare, contrast and describe the nuances and subtleties within a limited range of coloured artifacts. In this case, the resource might be 'the black and white bag'.

Into a large, preferably black, shopping bag, put some black and white items (at least one for each child), wrapped in black and white paper, or newspaper. Objects might include:

- white china articles, such as teapots, cups, plates;
- shiny and dull black ceramics, such as bowls, ornaments, vases;
- pieces of black and white fabrics, such as silk or wool scarves, cotton shirts, sheets, tablecloths, net curtain material;
- leather items, such as shoes, handbags, camera cases;
- plastic ware, such as computer discs.

Create a 'set' to display the objects on as they are unwrapped, for instance a few boxes to provide different levels, covered with plain black and white cloths. A strong light is useful.

Take the objects one by one from the bag, and ask children to unwrap them. Help them to see the differences between the blacks and whites, to compare the shiny black of metal or ceramic with dull fabrics or plastics, and how surface texture is informed by colour. They discover that black is not just black, and white is not always white. Children can then take some of the items to draw, using black and white media. This type of approach works well with other colour ranges too.

Shading

It is best to teach children to look at the range of tones and shades in real settings, rather than to introduce so-called rules about how light works on a surface. In fact, the 'theory' almost never applies in practice, because in the real world light sources are rarely definite and uncomplicated. In cartoons, shading one side of each item or person in a picture can be effective, but in observational work it is best to point out the shapes of shadows, the darker tones of colours in different parts of an object, or how reflections work on non-matt surfaces. Older children can use a viewfinder, to isolate a small area of the subject of an observational drawing, because dealing with light and shade on a large scale can be daunting. They might try putting a viewfinder over a small piece of plain fabric scrunched up on the table, and recording the shapes of shadows in the fabric, made by the way the light falls on it.

Artists such as Rembrandt made use of 'artificial' light sources on their work, and individual children who are ready and interested in representing light and shade in their work might usefully examine paintings such as *The Nightwatch* to see how this artifice is employed, and decide for themselves if it is realistic or not.

Perspective

Teaching perspective is worth a special mention. Our advice is, on the whole, don't. Teach children to look, look and look again, to see how much of one object another obscures, and to decide whether to represent this in their drawing. Even showing children classic 'disappearing lines', on a railway line or down an avenue of trees, will not necessarily be helpful at primary age. Children can represent shapes, relative proportions and spatial relationships between objects in many ways, so we feel that the 'vanishing point' is best left until they are older and can cope with the ideas better. Asking them to use 'accurate' perspective complicates the observational aspects of drawing for them, and often for the teacher.

Figure 2.16 *Making music*. Drawing from life in pencil, by an eight year old. Size: 40 × 30 cm

Drawing a person

The principles of drawing a person from observation (Figure 2.16) are the same as those for drawing anything else. Use the same introductory ideas as described above. Encourage children to look closely at different parts of the body through a viewfinder, and to record what they see in detail before trying to put together the whole figure.

SKETCHBOOKS AND SKETCHING

Sketchbooks are usually books with blank pages. Children often keep scrapbooks and collections that reflect personal and individual interests and preferences. A sketchbook can be viewed in this way too. It is really a storage system for a collection of observations, ideas, evidence and information, for children to retrieve and use subsequently in their art, craft or design work, gathered with a particular piece of work in mind, or as an ad hoc collection, such as work from other art, craft and design activities, e.g. notes and drawings of textures on shells taken during a school trip, or experiments with a new medium or technique. Other resources might include photographs with a theme of particular appeal, or reproductions of artists' work that excite. Work can be drawn or painted directly in the sketchbook or pasted in. 'Artists and designers keep sketchbooks for very good reasons, filling them with collections of drawings and annotations because it helps them to think, to find out, and build up relevant source materials for their work' (Morgan 1993).

There is no standard size for sketchbooks; they can range from small pocket-size up to A1. General topic work books, already available in school, may not be suitable, because sketchbook paper needs to be of sufficient quality to support work carried out using a range of drawing and painting materials. Stapling a book together is satisfactory if there are limited pages. A sewn book is one of the best methods to make books for use in school. Both types are described in the chapter on bookmaking.

If you take the children outside the classroom to sketch, in the playground or further afield, plan carefully to promote active learning. Clarify your aims, i.e. what you want the children to learn, and to experience. Decide what is best discussed, best read and best simply observed. Explain why you have set certain tasks, so they understand clearly the point of the exercise. Think about the curriculum focus, concepts you aim to reinforce and consolidate, and information you aim to convey. Do you want them, for instance, to:

- be able to use a simple map?
- notice architectural details, and to understand how the outside of a building reflects its original purpose and function, or its present-day use if this has changed;
- record mathematical relationships, in shapes or proportions?

Include tasks such as: 'tell your friend what you can see', as well as asking for written responses. Tasks should help children in their explorations, to look carefully, to take in the ambience and the setting, to make a record, an aide-memoire of a feature of particular significance.

Take clip-boards which will support the work, cartridge or other good quality paper with a fairly rough surface, and several sharp pencils, fine fibretip pens, a biro and a viewfinder for each child. Children need to be comfortably positioned, to rest clipboards on laps. Some may want to tuck into a corner so their work is not exposed to passers-by.

Encourage them to select a subject that is not too daunting, e.g. a stair-rail, gargoyle, part of a boat or a section of a roof. They need to look, with time to try out several drawings of the subject, and not worry about getting it right first time. Avoid even taking erasers. No attempts should be discarded, but kept in a sketchbook for later reference.

Encourage children to make notes on their sketches, such as the colours, the size or anything else that strikes them, which is not represented in the drawing. They may like to look at the shapes between, e.g. the relationships of sizes of windows to panes of glass, or panels in a door.

Children may decide to work very large or in miniature, but be sure they know to use appropriate tools to make analytical drawings which record the basic outline of the subject, the shapes within it, and its structure.

Remind them to look at their subject while they are drawing, to let the eye tell the hand what to do, to think about what is structural and what is decorative, to add frills last. Most of all, it is important that they relax, and enjoy engaging with the subject they are working on. Encourage them to 'make friends with the subject' by getting to know it well.

Bear in mind how the work will be used, e.g. for a class zig-zag book, a display or exhibition, to provide a focal point for subsequent discussion and reminiscence. The photocopier can be used to blow up children's illustrations for the display.

Tasks on location

Make notes, in whatever graphic form you like, of the sounds you hear over a five minute span. If several children work at the same time, they can compare results later. How do the sounds reflect the place? Children can record sounds in different places and later compare, for instance, street sounds with garden sounds. Re-create the sounds in the classroom from the notes, using voices, hands and basic percussion.

Take five minutes each to draw what is above your eye-line, below you and ahead of you from the same spot. Children may focus on roofs, skylines and details of landscape or cityscape. They may find interesting detail in a church roof or a pattern in tiles or slates. Looking ahead can be more difficult than it seems, especially if there is a lot to see, so encourage children to be selective. Looking down may reveal a detail in the pavement, some small flowers in grass or pebbles on a path. A viewfinder often helps.

Use a hoop or string circle to mark out a small area, not necessarily on the ground. Record what you see in the frame, which may be a section of a wall, a window or, inside, an detail on an item of furniture or a commemorative plaque or icon. The frame or viewfinder, large or small, will help you and the children to focus on a smaller, more manageable area by eliminating extraneous detail.

CHAPTER 3

Painting

Figure 3.1 *Owl*. A painting from imagination by a seven years old. Size: 38 × 20 cm

Painting is a traditional mainstay in primary schools, to decorate classroom and school, almost always linked to current topic work. In the process of making paintings, children learn about technical skills and how paint works. They also learn about the visual and tactile elements of art, integral to the Western tradition of painting and part of the National Curriculum requirements. Through helping children to develop knowledge, skills and understanding of the processes involved in painting, teachers can empower them to use paint as a medium for learning, to illustrate, for personal expression or for decorative purposes as appropriate. Paintings also inform and promote thinking, in particular when comparing how artists worked at different times to depict similar subject-matter: myths and legends, aspects of nature, ideas and emotions.

> Only through the direct, sensory experience of exploring paint and making their own discoveries can children develop an intelligence about paint. Only through having the opportunity to use a variety of brushes can children develop sensitive handling of the medium.
>
> (Gentle 1993)

Painting immediately implies colour. Colour names and associations are usually well established before children set foot in any school. The acquisition of a highly developed sense of colour, through appreciating nuances and relationships, and the ability to manipulate pigments to control the colours in making a painting, are central to primary school teaching and learning. Work on colour as a theme can help children focus on how it affects our senses and emotions and enable them fully to explore a range of colour media. A colour display might include, along with the work of artists, natural and manu-factured items of different materials, textures, forms, shapes and sizes, thus motivating children to develop their vocabulary through searching for descriptive terms to contrast, compare and describe what they see.

THE CROSS-CURRICULAR POTENTIAL OF COLOUR IN PAINT AND PAINTINGS

English

- Developing colour-specific vocabulary, e.g. tone, shade.
- Reading descriptions of colour and colours in poetry and prose.
- Learning similes and cliches associated with colour, e.g. green as grass.

Mathematics

- Sorting fabrics, papers, brushes etc. by size, shape and other qualities.
- Colour coding, in graphs or charts.
- Using colour as data, e.g. for graphs.

Science

- Studying light, e.g. splitting light through a prism or water to produce a spectrum.
- Investigating sources of natural colour in minerals and plants.
- Observing colour in nature, as a device to warn, attract or repel.
- Experimenting with a range of pigments and coloured materials to establish opacity, translucency, transparency and density.

Information and Communications Technology

- Using the computer screen as a painting medium, with graphics programs.
- Using CD Rom to access information about colour, paint and artists.

Design and Technology

- Using colour in communication: road signs, traffic lights etc.
- Using colour in design using construction kits.
- Exploring colours in modelling materials: play-dough, plasticine, clay.
- Investigating colour in packaging.

Humanities

- Discussing colour stereotypes in relation to gender.
- Learning about colours associated with traditional festivals and celebrations, e.g. weddings.

- Exploring natural pigments and their origins.
- Observing colours in landscape, and as depicted in paintings.
- Observing colour as related to climate and the weather.

Music

- Making links between musical and art terminology, e.g. texture.
- Combining musical and visual compositions: stage shows, set designs, celebrations.

THE BASIC ELEMENTS OF ART IN PAINTING

Colour

Understanding colour concepts comes through practical work with colour media, discussion and basic analysis of colours in the environment, as used by artists and by the children. Dry media, like pencils and crayons, help to enhance understanding, but it is traditionally through liquid media, usually paint, that children learn about colour, how to manipulate, use and control it.

Pattern

Very much an aspect of composition, pattern refers to the repetition of shapes, formal or random. Along with texture, patterning features in the depictions of fabrics and natural forms in realistic paintings. Matisse and Cézanne used patterning as a major element of composition in some work, using the surface pattern of the objects in the paintings to show their outline and form. Pattern itself, mathematical patterns, patterns in nature and in architecture, are often the subject of abstract, decorative and expressive paintings. Australian Aboriginal paintings use symbolic patterning, Islamic work features complex geometric pattern and traditional Indian miniature paintings place strong emphasis on calligraphic and other patterns in their compositions.

Composition

The process of putting together colours, textures and pattern is an act of composing: the artist decides how to place the pigment on the paper or canvas to give a satisfactory overall effect. Some compositions may be purely textural or colour-based, in abstract work by artists like Riley or Matisse. Some may be representational compositions, like portraits or landscapes. Children learn how composition affects the impact of a painting by comparing how different artists have depicted similar subject matter, such as Canaletto and Turner in Venice, or by trying out various ideas themselves.

ARTISTS WHO PAINT

Children need to build up knowledge about artists, their work and methods, for reference, research and inspiration. Artists use different, individual starting points, and most continue to explore and experiment with their chosen media as they work on finished pieces. Artists' sketchbooks give fascinating insight into the processes involved, as do published letters, like those of Van Gogh. Three paintings in different media are reproduced in Figures 3.2, 3.3 and 3.4.

Figure 3.2 *The Dance of the Cockerel (1991)*. Oil crayons by Lalit Kumar. Size: 90 × 60 cm

Figure 3.3 *Portrait of Carla*. Oil painting on canvas by Elza Scoble. Size: 90 × 60 cm

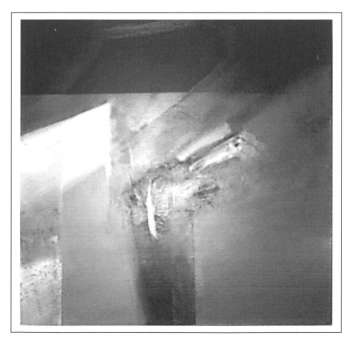

Figure 3.4 *Mir – Version 2 (1995)*. Synthetic resins on panel by Julian Scott. Size: 61 × 61 cm

There is a strong tradition in Western art of painting from direct observation for representational, and some abstract work. In traditional Australian Aboriginal art, inspiration comes from familiar landscapes, historical and current concerns. We must respect and honour the spiritual significance of these paintings, as well as enjoying the work.

Creative pursuits almost invariably draw on personal experiences in one way or another. Children need inspiration, based on first-hand experiences and engagement with the work of others, to which they can respond personally. If working on flowers, they need real ones to look at, touch and smell, as did Monet and O'Keeffe. No one else can possibly have the artist's own inspirations and ideas, let alone skills and knowledge, so the practice of copying their work (rather than understanding their processes) needs very careful thought.

Cutting up reproductions to copy in sections destroys the notion of composition, balance, wholeness and 'finish' of the original. Encouraging children to copy gives the message that their own responses to stimuli are not valid. Similarly, painting 'in the style of' has its limitations for children of primary school age. Instead, show a range of artists' work on a similar theme, discuss the similarities and differences in their approaches, and allow the children to take inspiration from them, using ideas and techniques discussed to their own advantage. The apprenticeship model has much to recommend it, but few teachers can make it work, particularly with younger children, whose efforts can be no more than mere parody.

EQUIPMENT, TOOLS AND MATERIALS

Liquid colour media

Powder Paint

Commonly available in primary schools, powder paint has the potential for wondrous effects, and offers more potential for subtlety of colour and range of texture than any other paint appropriate for the primary age-range. It is very cheap, and, properly used, can work well on most paper, although thin, non-absorbent surfaces, like photocopy paper, are unsuitable. From the beginning, teach children to mix their own paint from a limited range of dry pigments, usually primary colours and white; younger children will anyway experiment on the paper. On occasion, a wider range of pigments may be appropriate, such as sets of greens and blues, or yellows and oranges. Black pigment is often best kept separate, so children try other ways to make a colour darker; black often dulls other colours, and, once added, is almost impossible to compensate for.

Mix powder pigment like concrete, custard powder and packet soups: add the water little by little to the powder. Once mixed to a creamy consistency, it can be thinned. Too much water too soon results in murky liquid with bits floating uneasily on the top. Some pigments dissolve more easily; certain reds and most blacks require more work, due to the minerals from which they are made. This paint dries lighter than when it is wet; children learn to judge this as they work. Silver and gold metallic powder pigments are particularly useful, and mixing them is in itself fascinating!

Each colour pigment should be stored in a separate container, and decanted with a brush or a spoon, never poured on to the palette. The same goes for the water. For larger quantities, use a spoon to decant water and paint into a wide-topped container. Different colours can be shaken together before adding water. It can be made thick, having some of the qualities of oil paint, or thin, as a watercolour.

When dry, it can effectively be covered over with a thicker layer to obscure the first, so work can be changed and developed over several sessions. Other media can be overlaid, like charcoal, felt-tips etc., to provide special finishes. There are many ways of changing the consistency of powder paint with additives, used in addition to or instead of water to mix the pigment, or added to pre-mixed paint, such as glues and pastes, pva medium mixed with water, or washing-up liquid.

Different substances can be added to vary the textures. Present these in small quantities, in separate containers, each with a small spoon. They can be mixed directly into the wet paint, or sprinkled on to the paper. Apply a thin cover of glue, leave to dry and then paint. Rice, lentils etc. need quite strong glue, and cannot easily be coloured with water-based paint, but try these:

- sand, of different sizes of grain;
- fine sawdust, or woodshavings (from the pencil sharpener);
- crumpled dead leaves;
- small shredded paper, or dots from hole punches;
- crushed pasta, pulses or rice.

Ready mixed paint

This comes in a wide range of colours, opaque, like poster paint or translucent, but it lacks the versatility of powder paint. Water, palettes and a range of applicators should be available, so children can experiment with different consistencies and textures. Individual containers, like those for powder paint, are useful for decanting small amounts, to keep colours separate and to minimise waste. Use a funnel to pour back surplus paint. It is expensive and tends to dry out if containers are not fully airtight; clingfilm may help. When not in use it tends to separate out like curds and whey, requiring much time and patience to reconstitute. It can be used for printmaking, for covering a large area with a flat colour, and for painting models, depending on their surfaces. Use additives to make finger paint.

Paint boxes

Paint boxes can be organised with a minimum of fuss to illustrate and decorate work in all curriculum areas, as an everyday medium. Once very popular, they are now sometimes considered expensive and unsuitable. In fact, with appropriate tuition, even young children manage well, if brushes are of appropriate size and quality, and water is clean. Children familiar with mixing powder pigment should easily grasp the principles of the water-colour paint-box solid pigments and should eventually be able to produce fine detailed painting such as Figure 3.5. Experimentation is essential, e.g. dampening the paper before painting and

Figure 3.5 *Berries*. Observational watercolour by a six year old. Size: 35 × 20 cm

mixing paint to different consistencies. Separate palettes are easier to handle than box lids. Ensure boxes are carefully wiped with a damp sponge before being put away, so they are always available. The type of paint block varies according to the manufacturer, so shop around to get the ones you want. Paint boxes are normally used for small-scale work, so provide good quality small, light coloured paper. Sugar paper is probably too absorbent, so cartridge paper is the best ground.

'Brusho'

This powder ink is mixed with cold water. It contains quite a strong pigment, but can usually be washed off. It should be mixed by an adult, and kept in a screw-top jars, then decanted into small containers for immediate use. It has a vibrant, translucent quality of finish on particular surfaces, especially fabrics, useful when a strong colour is needed in a very thin consistency. It also works well on heavy, fairly absorbent paper such as cartridge, but it tends to stretch flimsy papers. It works well over dry colour media: wax crayons, water-soluble coloured pencils, oil pastels etc. Clean brushes thoroughly after use.

Finger paint

This is commercially available, including additives for pre-mixed paint, and fluorescent and glitter paint are a treat to use! Below are recipes to make your own.

- *Cornflour paste*: Use 3 parts water, 1 part cornflour and food colouring. Bring the water to the boil in a thick saucepan. Dissolve cornflour in a little cold water and add to the pan, stirring constantly, until clear and thick. Add colouring. A tablespoon of glycerine makes it glossy, or half a cup of soapflakes makes it lumpy.
- *Flour paste*: Use 1 part water, 1 part plain flour and powder paint or food colouring. Add flour to water in a bowl, stirring constantly. Add colour. Salt or sand will vary the texture.
- *Soapflake paste*: Use 1 part soapflakes, 1 part cold water, colouring. Put soapflakes in a bowl and add water little by little, stirring to a thick paste. Add colouring. It turns out like scrambled egg.
- *Whipped soapflake paste*: Use 2 parts warm water, 1 part soapflakes, colouring. Put water in a bowl, and add soapflakes. Beat with electric beaters until stiff. Add colouring. Do not dispose of this down the sink: it blocks drains. Bin it instead.

Brushes and applicators

Artists' brushes

The number on the handle indicates the size of the brush, i.e. the amount of hairs or bristles in the metal holder, regardless of the type of 'head' or handle, so small and large-handled brushes can have the same number. Overall size and shape determine what marks are made: wedge shapes are easier with flat-fiche brushes.

Handles are shaped in a particular way, to lie easily in the hand. The brush will normally balance just below the grip, the fat bit, where it should be held. Only short stubby stencil brushes are designed to be used end-on; all other types should be used to stroke the paper.

Sort and store different sizes and types separately, so children can choose according to scale, effect required, type of paint etc. Paint brushes should never, even temporarily, be left in paint, ink or water. 'Keep the hair in the air!' After use, rinse immediately and replace, handles down, in the right container, to prevent damage to bristles, and to reduce the domestic chores later.

Other applicators

Try these ideas for large-scale work (see also Figure 3.7):

- 1", 3", 4", 8" house paint brushes;
- wallpaper pasting brushes;
- crumpled up balls of newspaper, bubble wrap, sponge, foam pieces;
- tooth and nailbrushes, scrubbing brushes, hand brushes, hairbrushes, bottle brushes;
- spoons to dribble, e.g. tea-straining spoons.

Home-made applicators

- foam, fabric or newspaper, attached to a stick with elastic bands;
- 'dabbers': fabric wrapped around a ball of crumpled paper or fabric, secured like puddings with elastic bands, sometimes with handles;
- pieces of card of various weights and sizes, cut in wedge shapes or with serrated edges, to use as spatulas or spreaders.

Palettes

Children need to mix paint and try it out before applying it to work in progress. Teach the routine: *water, paint, palette, paper* from the start. The palette often takes over from the

Figure 3.6 Keep the hair in the air!

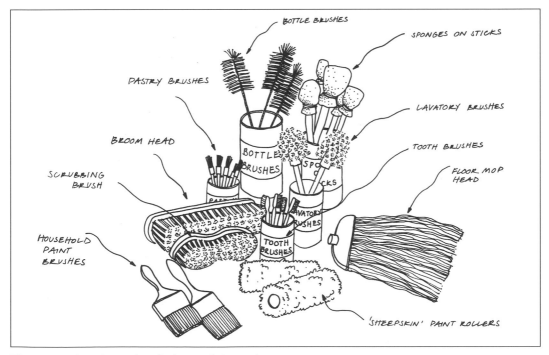

Figure 3.7 A variety of tools for applying paint

painting as the main focus of attention, because it is here that colours mix, merge, change and develop. Commercially produced palettes come in two basic types: flat and bun-tin. Heavy-weight dinner plates, lids of large plastic tubs or ceramic tiles serve just as well. White is best. Store paint in separate containers, and keep palettes for mixing only, because putting little heaps of paint on to them is wasteful and distracting.

At the end of the session, once work is left to dry, make quick prints with the remaining paint using sponges on old kitchen paper, to get interesting effects and minimise washing up! Hold the palette briefly under the running tap and clean with a house-painting brush. Stack clean palettes in piles, with a sheet of newspaper between each to absorb the wetness and prevent them sticking together, and place immediately back into storage.

Water pots

Get stable, wide topped pots. Lay them out empty and half fill them from a jug. Use two pots per pair of children, one to mix with paint, one to rinse brushes.

Paint pots

These often contain ready-mixed paint, with brushes permanently stuck through holes in the top: children cannot see what quantity, colour or consistency of paint is inside, and cannot decide what applicator to use. Brushes get ruined! Small tins or stable plastic pots are useful for small quantities of mixed paint.

Easels

Often used in early years classrooms, these are best for drawing with dry media: any but the thickest paint dribbles unsatisfactorily.

Drying racks/clothes lines

Flat-bed drying racks are expensive but useful. For non-dribbly work, a clothesline with pegs is adequate. Work can dry on newspaper under working surfaces.

Aprons/overalls

Use old adult tee-shirts and shirts. Proper aprons should be properly fastened.

ORGANISING PAINT IN THE CLASSROOM

Painting tools and materials should always be readily available, carefully stored, labelled and displayed. Teaching good 'studio practice' from the outset encourages independence, so children help with, and are responsible for, as much of the setting up as possible. A diagram of 'how to lay the table' is useful (Figure 3.8).

Laying the table for painting

Lay plenty of newspaper to overlap and cover the entire surface. The top layer can be removed if it gets grubby. On this place old kitchen paper mats, to define working areas. Leave room for consulting visual reference, sketchbooks or objects being painted. Ensure materials are in easy reach and children have space to move. Standing up takes less space

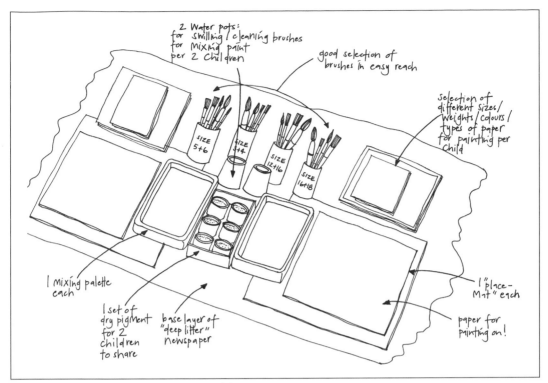

Figure 3.8 How to 'lay the painting table'

than sitting down. It is usually best to work on a tabletop. A central area for paint mixing, with spoons and brushes, another to set out different applicators, and a third for painting helps traffic flow when several children are applying paint to a larger piece.

Put out brushes and applicators, sorted into sizes and types. Each pair of children needs a set of dry pigment, two waterpots, a piece of foam to wipe brushes, two palettes and a range of papers to choose from. Dirty water can be tipped into a bucket, and pots refilled from a jug of clean water.

Allocate drying space as part of the planning, so children know beforehand what to do with completed work. At clearing up time, designate a space near the sink to sort and stack washing up. Allocate jobs:

- emptying water pots and replacing to store;
- cleaning, stacking and storing palettes;
- putting away dry paint, topping it up if necessary first;
- checking brushes are properly placed in the right containers;
- discarding the top layer of newspaper and folding the remainder for re-use.

HEALTH AND SAFETY

Avoid using glass jars with younger children. Use only water-based products as a rule; check before using non-water-based products if there are any children with allergies. Never leave brushes in waterpots; they may topple.

TEACHING COLOUR MIXING

Understanding how colours work is best learned through first-hand experience with pigments, light sources etc. It may not be appropriate to introduce the terms 'primary' and 'secondary' colours, but it is vital that children's visual perception of the relative qualities of each colour is developed.

If children want to know how to make green, a good strategy is to compare some green objects with the primary coloured pigments: yellow, blue, red. Ask which is closest to green, and the chances are that they will choose blue. Ask which other one is close, and probably, they will say yellow. Children can then mix them, to see what happens. If the 'wrong' colour is chosen, e.g. red, the mixing will prove unsatisfactory. Try again. Show a limey green, which is closer to yellow, and a turquoise green, which is closer to blue, as well as the original examples. Using a colour wheel for reference is definitely not recommended. Encourage the children to 'see' colours in other colours, rather than rely on a formula.

Children use sight and practical engagement to enhance their understanding of green. They may add more blue, yellow or white, to make a range of colours which satisfy the description 'green', and link each to a known object, e.g. apples, limes, spinach. Thus they take control of colour mixing for themselves. Look at artists' work to see how many colours have been used in a 'green' area of a painting. If a child cannot see that green contains elements of blue and yellow, it may indicate limited colour vision ('colour blindness'). But such problems rarely arise if children are able to really look at, discuss and experiment with colour.

An initial colour-mixing session

This plan is adaptable for any age range, to introduce or recap on paint mixing. Make separate plans for discussion and practical work.

Aims

- to look at colour in artists' work;
- to teach the process of paint-mixing;
- to give experience of how colours affect each other when mixed;
- to encourage good practice in caring for art materials.

Display

Colour stimulus material, reproductions of artists' work, representational and abstract, colour photographs, good quality magazine images, etc.

Preliminary discussion

Draw children's attention to the range of colours available, and assess how they see colour and colours, their use of descriptive vocabulary and associations. They might sort a range of objects and images into different colour groups, and compare and contrast the work of several artists.

Practical work

Resources:

- newspaper to cover tables;
- a range of brushes, sorted in pots;
- a range of small papers: light, dark and black sugar, kitchen paper, cartridge;
- one set of powder paint and two water pots per two children;
- one mixing palette per child;
- small pieces of sponge;
- place mats.

Session plan

Explain aims and expectations of session.

Children each choose a small brush, and compare the size, shape, number, and point of balance with a friend's. Put the brush into the water. Hold it up. No drips! Place the brush carefully in the centre of one paint container, avoiding the sides. Mix water and pigment on the palette. Take more water, more paint, and add to the palette. Continue until a reasonable amount of paint has been mixed. Try the colour on one or two of the papers.

Wash and rinse brush; remove excess water on the sponge. Try another colour in the same way, on another part of the palette. Take some of each colour and mix together. Repeat, and record the colours made on different papers.

As children work, monitor progress, and set new challenges:

- Does a different brush change the marks on the paper?
- How do the colours look on a different type or colour of paper?
- Add more powder – how does the paint change?
- Add more water with your brush – how does the paint change?
- Add white to the colours: what happens?

Older or more experienced children may try to match skin or clothing colours, or a range of fruits, leaves or flowers displayed on the table so they can easily refer to the colours. Emphasise the need to look at the *colour*, rather than the *form* of the object.

Evaluation

Compare and contrast the range of colours made on different palettes and papers. How well do the children think they managed to mix a range of colours, match particular colours and make paint of different consistencies: thick, thin, runny etc.? Can they explain how they achieved particular effects? Do they notice how colours respond to each other, i.e. the paint colours themselves, and the effect of different papers? Decide whether to display their work, or put it in sketchbooks.

Look again at artists' work:

- Are there colours similar to those the children have mixed?
- Is the artist's paint thick or thin?
- What sort of brushes do they think the artists might have used?
- Why do they think the artists chose those particular colours?

Large scale work

Discussion of artists' work to precede this session may include reference to abstract artists like Mondrian, Riley or Heron, as well as representational work. For practical work, designate, if possible, separate areas for paint mixing, display of applicators, for working on the large group piece.

Aims:
- to extend understanding of colour mixing, paint consistency and texture;
- to encourage use of a range of paint applicators;
- to focus on colour composition;
- to work collaboratively in groups.

Resources:
- a range of large paint applicators;
- a small number of larger-sized artists' brushes, for mixing only;
- dry pigment in medium sized containers, each with a spoon;
- water pots and spoons for decanting;
- small papers, for testing;
- large papers, for composition;
- palettes.

Session plan

Explain the aims of session. Demonstrate paint mixing process using spoons, i.e. decant a spoonful of paint and a spoonful of water into the palette and mix with a brush. Children mix, record on small papers, and compare results.

In small groups, use one or two colours to cover the entire surface of the paper with different textured marks. Use smaller brushes to mix the paint, but only large applicators for applying to the paper. The group decides the colour range, paper type and composition collaboratively. Spare paint can be applied to another paper, or mopped up with sponges etc., and printed, to make a different textural composition with similar colours.

Evaluation

Once dry, paintings can be temporarily displayed. Each group explains the techniques used, and recounts the way in which decisions were made during the process. It is often helpful if they can rehearse feed-back first. The teacher can assess how well children have grasped the processes, how confidently they made decisions, what reference was made to other artists' work, and how strong their colour sense is when working with a restricted range. Later, work can be displayed alongside artists' work, together with quotations from the children's presentations, as artists write statements for gallery exhibitions. Descriptions of the process may be set out separately from evaluative and descriptive comments about the work.

Extensions: texture focus

Discussion

Use a display, with magnifying glasses and viewfinders, to promote tactile engagement with, and discussion of, responses to different textured surfaces. 'Feelybags' work well with all ages. Objects can be sorted, compared and contrasted. The display may include:

- natural objects and artifacts with natural textured surfaces, e.g. coconuts, oranges, bark, fleece, shells;
- manufactured items, e.g. baskets, sandpaper, fabrics, carpets;
- artists' work with examples of texture in the paint: Van Gogh, O'Keeffe, Turner, Australian Aboriginal artists;
- artists' work depicting textural qualities in a particular way: Rembrandt, Constable;
- photographs which emphasise textural qualities of objects and living things.

Practical work: tasks

- With a viewfinder, select a section of large-scale work and enlarge it, using different applicators to achieve the same textural and colour qualities on a larger scale. This requires close examination of texture, and careful recall of how colours were achieved. Deciding which segment to use is the key to the composition of this piece.
- Attempt to re-create the textures using newspaper soaked in paste, to give a papier mâché quality. Scrunch it up on a fairly heavy base, and paint when it is dry. The original starting point may get lost, but this is not always important, since the new piece is a development in its own right.
- Work on the above tasks, using conventional brushes to investigate the potential for a range of marks within a piece. Colour might be limited to one or two primaries, to extend understanding of the potential of colour range within a given set of hues.
- Use pattern as a basis for composition. Consult artists who use pattern, e.g. Riley, American Indian, Islamic and Alari designs. Develop work from the original pattern, using different colours and textural surfaces.
- Take items from the display, and make rubbings with crayons on thin paper, to use as a starting point for painting, re-creating the texture through paint on the paper. Focus on texture and colour, rather than form or shape.
- Choose an item from the display. Mix every colour you see on its surface. Record these on your paper systematically as you mix, or create an abstract design. Do not paint a picture of the item itself. Try to match the variation in colours and tones, according to shadows cast on the objects.

Evaluation

Children discuss how well they feel they met the criteria outlined, and give reasons for decisions made. The quality of this discussion, together with observations of them at work, in particular the nature and amount of support required, guides the teacher's assessment and evaluation. Children can be specifically asked to refer to the display and artists' work in the feedback.

OBSERVATIONAL PAINTING

For a classic 'still life', flowers, fruit, bowls, vases etc. are arranged on a background, often a fabric, which may provide a neutral 'setting' or be a vibrant part of the colour and pattern of the composition (see Figure 3.9). Artists' work in different styles and media, such as the Impressionists, Dutch School and Renaissance, can promote discussion about how these artists solved problems of depicting 3D objects in 2D painting.

Figure 3.9 *Still life with fish*. Powder paint by a nine year old. Size: 30 × 40 cm

Some artists focus on colour composition or depicting surface textures, and some use still life within a narrative painting. Many will have worked from direct observation of items carefully arranged to suit their needs. Similarly, children might select and arrange items for themselves, or like a painting they know.

The very process of making a painting is a learning experience, but there is nevertheless a need to outline clear expectations of the product. Artists often make preliminary sketches of form, composition (arrangement) and colour before working on the final piece. Paintings need time for inspiration, stimulus, planning, drafting, evaluation, modification. It is said that Cézanne's onions sprouted before he finished one piece, so leave the arrangement in position for some time, for children to consider:

- colour: identifying, mixing and matching the colour range they see;
- form: identifying and capturing shapes of and between objects;
- pattern and texture: deciding the amount of detail to be included;
- composition: deciding how much of the display will be included and how to place the items on the paper.

Preliminary work helps children to get to know the subject of their painting. They work at different paces, and a few may take a 'preliminary' idea through to a final piece. They may try some or all of these suggestions in sketchbooks:

- use viewfinders to try different compositions within the arrangement;
- sketch with thinly mixed paint and fine brushes, using a paintbox, focusing on line, shape, matching colour and texture in turn;

- try these on different papers;
- draw the spaces between the objects on display;
- paint a small sample of the background cloth, or a pattern on an object.

The children's task is to record, in paint, their personal responses to the display, rather than to produce a pre-determined composition to a fixed set of criteria. Before working on the final piece, children need to decide what sort of paint to use, what scale they will work to and what paper to use, and may consider what artists have to decide before they start work. You may ask if they will:

- emphasise colour, or composition or pattern;
- emphasise tones, light and shade, or shape and form;
- look for detail, or for overall effects of colour.

Once they have started work, if a part of the painting is causing anxiety, another part can be worked on for the moment. If a colour is not right, leave it to dry, and work on mixing a more satisfactory shade using trial paper, or concentrate on another part of the painting for now.

Most children benefit from a break, when they put paintings to one side, clean brushes and renew water, then take a few minutes to evaluate the work so far. Coming back to look at it from a different angle helps the decision-making process. Persistent problems can be resolved, by cropping a part of the painting altogether, sticking paper over the offending area, or even starting again, and keeping this one for the sketchbook.

PAINTING FROM IMAGINATION AND MEMORY

Many imaginative artists, including book illustrators, use observational work as the basis for their compositions and paintings, such as the Surrealists and Rousseau. To work creatively from imagination and memory, children need memorable first-hand experiences to stimulate them. Children rarely lack imagination, but do need stimulus and information on which to base their creative work. This may be immediate, such as collecting references towards a particular work, or from previous work in sketchbooks.

Direct copying is to be discouraged, but gathering and using visual reference is appropriate at all ages. Children painting three little pigs or tropical rain forests might collect photographs, painting reproductions and drawings of animals and plants. Videos help them see how different animals move, before trying out these movements for themselves. They can investigate what pigs' tails and snouts really look like, what colours different species of monkey are, and how many greens and browns there are in a local garden, let alone a tropical forest. Children's research-based paintings tend to be more individual and personal; the bird in Figure 3.12 was painted from memory after a visit to a bird sanctuary.

Start with exercises similar to those suggested for still life, where they play with ideas and compositions and colours, gathering and juxtaposing images to suit the purpose, and gradually preparing for work on the final piece. If children have had good experiences of working from observation, they gain a repertoire of ideas and skills which can be put to good use in imaginative work. As an adult, think how you might approach an instruction to paint a picture of something or somebody, what reference and inspiration you might

Figure 3.10 *Sun God.* 'Brusho', oil pastel, fluorescent wax crayons and felt pens by an eight year old. Size: 27 × 27 cm

need. Ask the children what they need before they start, and help them to research, by consulting and assembling resources. Figure 3.10 shows what an eight year old can produce as an end result of this process. See also ideas in the chapter on collage.

ILLUSTRATING STORIES OR POEMS

Sources of inspiration for imaginative work might include poems, extracts from stories, as with Figure 3.11, factual descriptions of a landscape or building, passages from history

Figure 3.11 *Ned Kelly.* Pen, ink and wash, by a nine year old. Size: 27 × 21 cm

texts or even close examination of a map where features can be incorporated into the painting. Children are accustomed, from an early age, to well illustrated books with well composed text. The complementary nature of the illustrations and story are usually discussed during joint reading of texts. Just as artists' paintings inspire and inform children's visual art, these books provide models for the creation of story books, poetry anthologies etc. Collaborative work, where children either write or illustrate in partnership, can be very rewarding for all concerned, as exemplified in so many author-artist teams. At planning stage, children can research and draft both stories and illustration, and consider layout. The word processor is most helpful for paste-up, as is a story board, described in the photography chapter.

A PROJECT BASED ON WATER

Work on a theme such as water must include first-hand experience. This might be at the seaside, a local stream, pond or lake, as well as viewing video recordings of the calm, stormy, rough or smooth sea, from which children can make notes in sketchbooks. Practical work suggested can be tackled over several sessions, or the class can work in groups, moving from one activity and task to the next. A whole-class project requires sufficient adult support and time to meet the teaching aims and health and safety requirements. The following are useful for display:

- reproductions of paintings of water by artists working in different periods and styles;
- photographs, postcards and books about water, especially those with water and sky in colours other than blue;
- magnifying glasses and viewfinders to isolate and examine small areas of images.

Necessary materials and equipment may include:

- water to play with, in large and smaller containers;
- small objects, e.g. pebbles, to place in the water;
- overhead projector with shallow transparent plastic container to place water in, arranged with health and safety implications in mind;
- bottles and plastic containers to pour into;
- water-based coloured liquids, e.g. premixed 'Brusho';
- droppers to place coloured liquids into clear water;
- substances to change the water's viscosity, e.g. pre-mixed paste, salt, oil, sugar;
- a selection of drawing and painting media in colour, black and white;
- brushes of different sizes and shapes;
- papers of different colours and weights, e.g. tissue, foil, cellophane;
- adhesives, spreaders, pots.

Session plan

Play! Experiment with the water to see how it moves, how small drops of colour spread in the water; how different colours merge in the water. Put water carefully in the container on the overhead projector and watch the effects on the screen, wall or ceiling. Note in sketchbooks how the colours behave in the water.

Look! Closely observe reproductions, photographs, postcards and other images of water on display. Note how artists in different times and different places have depicted water, and how colours reflect the climate and season and location. Consider how many types of water there are, and how the artists have recorded their responses to it. Use viewfinders and magnifying glasses to examine images. Record your responses in sketchbooks or on papers provided.

Another starting point is to tear from magazines small irregular sections of photographs of water. These are pasted on to paper and hidden, through using paint, inks, pastels or paper collage to develop colours, textures and patterns over the surface of the paper.

Figure 3.12 *Big Bird*. Painting with brush and ink by a seven year old. Size: 60 × 70 cm

CHAPTER 4

Printmaking

Figure 4.1 *Crocodile*. Polystyrene block print by a six year old. Size: 14 × 14 cm

The tension between the calculated and the unpredictable is one of the delights of printmaking at all levels, from initial tactile experiments with hands and fingers to professional use of a highly versatile, challenging and creative medium. The textural surface of a block, the quality of the colour medium and the surface and absorbency of the paper all affect the quality of the print. Many artists choose printmaking both for the qualities of surface which can be achieved, and for the facility of generating multiple, individually produced, copies of an image. Design is an essential part of printmaking, with planning and predicting outcome and an understanding of the stages of the print process being central to good practice. Each print is a discovery; even professionals experience the excitement of uncertainty each time they pull a print.

Accidental fingerprints are children's first printmaking experience, so almost every child comes to school with some prior knowledge of the process. Children need to discover and appreciate the nature of texture, pattern and surface relief. They gradually learn to predict results, taking ownership of techniques at their disposal. Learning printmaking is cumulative: each step reinforces and develops previous understandings.

Regularly revisiting known processes helps to effect continuity through building on past expertise; an annual autumnal leafprint exercise can develop knowledge, understanding, control and decision-making if planning and teaching incorporate both continuity and progression. Keeping a series of hand and footprints can record growth in size and printmaking skills throughout the primary years.

Block printmaking and monoprinting involve the transfer of an image from one surface, the block, to another, the paper. The print block may be an inked or painted surface onto which the paper is directly applied, as in monoprinting, or a relief block which is inked so the top surface of the relief design prints. Multiple images can be produced from a single block, which may be a hand, a cotton reel or a card block, re-inked as necessary. The potential range of blocks is endless, from crumpled paper, sponges and rollers to carefully crafted or carved relief blocks, which can be reused almost ad infinitum. Intaglio printmaking involves making indentations in a block, where the ink is held until it is squeezed on to paper using a press. Screen printing is a different process, akin to stencilling.

Printmaking lends itself to a very wide range of applications. Commercial printing is all around, in magazines and journals, on fabrics and household articles such as food packaging. Distinguishing between these applications and the fine art printmaking process provides a good starting point for investigating the nature of print itself. Almost all the techniques and processes described in this chapter can be used on fabrics, walls or other suitably primed surfaces, as well as paper.

Textural and pattern qualities of rubbings and prints have much in common. Rubbing with wax crayons on thin paper over a textured surface is a complementary and parallel exercise for relief block printmaking; it aids understanding of the process and function of relief surfaces, and can be a useful starting point for block design. Rubbing the raised, or relief, surface of an artifact or natural object with a crayon makes the pattern on the paper: the crayon only comes into contact through the paper with the topmost layer of the textured surface. Most children have experimented with this technique, and so have some awareness of how basic relief-block printmaking works: only the raised surface of the inked block comes into contact with the paper, thus making the required mark.

Matching the task and the tools to the ability and stage of development of the child is essential. Manipulation skills, evidence of fine motor movement and dexterity of the pupils will help determine which processes are most suitable for which age group. First stages in school will probably include:

- using and making simple stencils;
- basic monoprinting: taking a print directly from an inked surface;
- block printing from hands, feet and fingers with ready-mixed paint;
- using found and natural objects as blocks, e.g. leaves, screws of paper, foam.

Children may go on to make their own blocks from clay, plasticine, cut vegetables etc., to print from pads of paint or ink. More sophisticated incised blocks, such as polystyrene, and built-up blocks, or collographs, introduce use of rollers and ink. Being more durable, these blocks allow almost unlimited numbers of repeats. Older children may also try screen printing. Preliminary experimentation and play are important at all stages prior to work on a finished set of prints. Basic technical expertise permits children to:

- select techniques and inks according to the end product and print surface;
- use print as one element of mixed-media work with paint, drawing tools, fabrics and thread or collage;
- build up decorative surfaces or patterns using repeats, overlapping etc.

PRINTMAKING AND RELATED TECHNIQUES

Original, or artists', prints are made by four main methods: relief or surface print processes, intaglio, lithographic and stencil or silkscreen. There follows a brief outline of the most common printmaking techniques used in schools, with suggestions for teaching them later in the chapter.

Monoprinting

This process, examples of which are shown in Figures 4.2 and 4.3, involves applying ink to a non-porous block, such as slate or formica, using rollers, palette knives or fingers. Paper is placed directly on to the inked surface, gently smoothed and pulled. Subsequent prints vary considerably as the ink transfers to the paper, each one individual, a monoprint. It is possible to draw into the ink directly before placing the paper, or onto the back of the paper once it has been laid down, to develop the technique.

Figure 4.2 *Miner* (1). Monoprint by a nine year old. Size: 35 × 25 cm

Figure 4.3 *Miner* (2). Monoprint by a nine year old. Size: 35 × 25 cm

Marbling: 'liquid monoprinting'

This technique is much favoured for preparing paper for book-making. Oil-based ink, dropped onto the surface of water in a shallow tray, forms a layer on top. The colour can be manipulated with brushes or bits of card. It is then possible carefully to lower a piece of kitchen or other absorbent paper on to the surface to make the print. The paper will retain an impression or print of the layer of paint when lifted off. Use oil paint or other paint media, mixed or thinned with turpentine or cooking oil. Supervision of both materials and process is essential. Kits are available.

Block printmaking

A block is a surface from which a print is taken. The simplest blocks for children are readily available: hands and feet. There follow descriptions of other types of block.

Found and natural objects

Leaf printing is a much underestimated technique; it is possible to make high quality prints suitable for fabric design. Traditional potato print blocks can produce quite sophisticated results. Use the smooth flat surface as it is, or cut in a surface design. Objects can be mounted on wood or card to make them more durable and easier to handle. Other ideas to try are: cotton reels, foam rubber, sticks, string, Balsa wood, small wheels, matchboxes, shoes, film canisters, candles, leaves, bark, stems, seeds, flat pebbles, seaweed, shells, cones, vegetables and fruit (see below).

Incised blocks

Vegetables

Many root vegetables can be carved: swedes, turnips, parsnips, sweet potato, carrots. The idea is deceptively simple, and quite subtle effects are possible with skill and application.

Clay, plasticine blocks

Firm, soft lumps of clay or plasticine are cut to have a smooth flat surface. This can have objects impressed into it, or be scratched or cut into to make a design. Being soft, this type of block is easy for young children to handle; it can be re-used and worked on during the development of the print. It is not durable, but good for trying out ideas.

Polystyrene pressprint blocks

Commercially available 30 cm square pressprint polystyrene blocks are scored or scratched with a biro or other sharp tool to incise the design. They can be cut to smaller or irregular shapes with sharp scissors. Manufactured blocks only should be used; harmful fibres are released from ceiling tiles or food packaging.

Figure 4.4 *Some People*. Pressprint block and print with watercolour ink by a five year old. Size 10 × 10 cm

Plaster blocks

A cardboard box filled with plaster of Paris is left until dry. Once removed from the box as a block, the plaster can be dampened and carved with a sharp implement to use as a print block. There will be dust, so masks should be worn. For carving, the block should be big enough to grip firmly by the child, or placed on a bench-hook to avoid accidents with sharp tools. This medium is best for older, more experienced children.

Lino and wood blocks

Balsa wood is soft enough for children to carve. Traditional lino and hardwood make durable, versatile blocks, capable of carrying very fine detail. They require very sharp specialised cutting tools, which need great care and expertise. Such caution, care and dexterity can rarely reasonably be expected in the primary school.

Built, relief card blocks: collographs

These have heavy card, like strawboard, as a base, on to which a textured surface is collaged, which holds the ink and makes the print. Pieces of card of a uniform depth can be cut to shape and stuck on, together with fabric, sawdust, string etc. The block is left to dry and covered with a thin film of watered down adhesive as a bond, since printing will put a strain on the join.

Intaglio (etching) plates

For this technique, a surface such as smooth metal, plastic or perspex is scraped with a very sharp instrument, or etched with an acid and wax process. Ink is carefully rubbed into the incised grooves. The top surface is wiped, so the plate is clean except for the ink in the incisions. Slightly damp paper draws the ink from the grooves when the plate and the paper are passed together through a heavy press. This quite advanced process needs more skill, strength and persistence than the average primary school child can muster, and is therefore rarely developed to any extent with young children. A printing press for this type of work is shown in Figure 4.5.

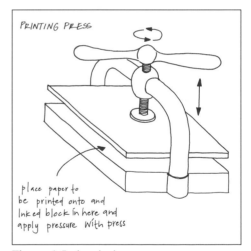

Figure 4.5 A printing press

Lithography

Primarily a commercial process, a greasy mark is drawn on a plate or stone, the surface of which is then damped with water. When rolled with ink, the grease attracts ink and the water rejects it. Prints can then be taken from the surface of the plate. Again, this process is rarely appropriate for primary children.

Stencilling

Stencilling involves cutting out an image from a firm, non-porous paper or thin card, traditionally waxed parchment, which is placed on the surface of the paper to mask a given area. When paint is applied, usually with a stipple brush, only the cut-out sections are coloured. It comes out the same way around, not like the reverse image of a block print. Stencilling is useful for decorative repeat patterns.

Screen printing

A printmaking screen is made from a strong frame, over which has been stretched gauze, nylon or other very fine fabric (see Figure 4.6). A stencil is placed on the paper, and the frame, gauze side down, placed on top. Special screen printing ink is placed inside the frame at one end, which has been 'masked' to form a reservoir. A squeegee is used to pull the ink evenly across the frame from one side to the other. The gauze makes the ink lie on the paper in an even layer, so quite a large area can be covered with one stencil. Some screen printing inks have a particular translucent quality, which offers potential for over-printing images. A more complex process will enable the stencil to be fixed directly to the screen gauze. so the frame can be moved from one print to the next with ease.

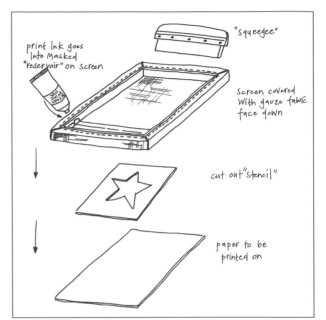

Figure 4.6 Screen printing

THE CROSS-CURRICULAR POTENTIAL OF PRINTMAKING

English

- Planning a picture book, designing the illustrations and preparing the text.
- Creating print blocks of alphabets such as Arabic, Hebrew, Greek, to use.
- Making instruction booklets of processes for other children.

Mathematics

- Printing directly from geometrically shaped blocks.
- Using different number symbols, e.g. Arabic numerals, as a basis for block design.
- Estimating the number of prints needed to cover a surface; measure, confirm.
- Using rotational symmetry to plan design over a large surface.
- Planning a large repeat print, deciding what size block is required.
- Printing a patchwork fabric, measuring squares and designing blocks.
- Using the roller itself as a block: the cylinder is essentially a curved rectangle.

Science

- Printing different blocks on different surfaces and comparing.
- Experimenting with and making printing inks, testing, comparing results.
- Investigating different printed surfaces; charting the different functions.
- Considering how friction affects printmaking.
- Using botanical studies for block designs.

Information and Communications Technology

- Using the computer to work out repeat patterns, colour combinations etc.
- Examining examples of patterns and designs in the memory of the computer graphics program for inspiration.
- Researching into printmakers and designs through CD Rom programs.

Design Technology

- Designing and making tools, e.g. squeegees, rollers or presses; evaluating.
- Designing a printed surface to fill an identified need; carry out process; evaluate.
- Discussing differences between commercial processes and 'printmaking' as an art form.

Geography

- Comparing forms of print used in different geographical or cultural contexts.
- Considering how local materials are used in printmaking, e.g. wood, metal.
- Using different language scripts for print blocks, e.g. Greek, Hindi, Chinese.

History

- Looking at processes and equipment from different historical periods.
- Comparing reproductions of prints from artists of different periods.
- Using historical symbols to design blocks, such as hieroglyphics.

Physical Education

- Making quick sketches during PE as ideas for monoprint.
- Linking hand and footprints with load bearing on balls of feet, heels, fingers.

THE BASIC ELEMENTS OF ART IN PRINTMAKING

Texture

The concept of texture, achieved through relief surfaces or impressions made in flat surfaces, is vital for the understanding of block printmaking. Uniform, smooth surfaces will not produce an image when inked and printed, unless the artist has manipulated the ink, or made an impression on the smooth surface by carving or building up layers.

Line

Incised line, using a pencil, biro or sharp tool, makes an image on the polystyrene, clay or plaster block (see Figure 4.7). Thread, string etc. affixed to a card block also makes a linear print. The quality of line can vary within a print, and can be used to complement other non-linear textured surfaces.

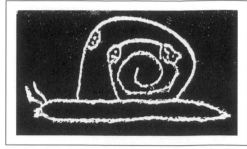

Figure 4.7 *Snail*, polystyrene print with oil-based ink, by a nine year old. Size: 26 × 9 cm

Colour

The range of tones and shades within colours is well demonstrated through printmaking, through effects achieved using the same block on different colour backgrounds (papers), using different colours and combinations of inks or paint. Decisions about colour are important but not irreversible. Blocks can first be printed with one colour, then adding small amounts of another, white or black, helps children learn how to achieve a range of tones within a set of prints. Overprinting demonstrates how colours mix and merge, often unpredictably producing a new set of secondary or tertiary colours when the print is pulled.

Pattern

Pattern is achieved both in the block design itself and in the arrangement of multiple prints on paper or fabric. Exploiting the design applications of printmaking processes encourages application and use of concepts such as tessellation and symmetry.

Composition

Inking a monoprint block requires compositional decisions: what colour goes where, how to balance the overall effect of texture etc. Making a block for block-printing requires decisions about placing the lines or textured marks or materials for collograph.

ARTISTS WHO PRINT

Most professional printmaker artists use sophisticated techniques (see Figure 4.8), but many also use more basic processes such as monoprint and collograph. Etching, lithograph and wood block are out of range for primary children, but they can learn about the principles and processes, to help them appreciate aspects of the artist's print.

Looking at prints like these, children may consider artist printmakers' use of composition, colour combinations, subject matter etc., and speculate about why an artist chose a particular medium for a particular work (see Figure 4.9). This may help them also to appreciate both the work of printmaker artists like Matisse and Dürer, who used the print as a vehicle for their work, and craft printmakers like Morris, who used print for design and manufacture of fabrics and papers.

There is a difference between the editioned print, produced to a specific number, perhaps 10, 50 or even 500, and the unlimited reproductions of prints produced by

Figure 4.8 *Harpyia*. Etching by Anita Ford. Size: 25 × 20 cm

Figure 4.9 *Golden Shell*. Collograph by Barbara Munns. Size: 9 × 11.5 cm

commercial publishers. In the case of artists' prints, each is original, because the artist has personally produced, signed and numbered it, in pencil so the numbering is clearly original. (Ink is easily technically reproduced, so can be faked.) The accessibility afforded by modern technological printmaking processes has tempted many painters to work in printmaking media, which offer the potential of making more than one sale from a single image. While this may be seen as a rather commercial approach to art, it is nonetheless important for artists to make commercial decisions.

An interesting new direction in the field of printmaking is the development of new, water-based screen printing inks, which have a particular translucent quality, and which have recently become commercially viable for artists and art students. Such technological developments often influence the work of practising artists, as does the rediscovery of old techniques. David Hockney learned how to use a particular sugar-based type of printmaking, and his work was for some time based around the potential of this once-forgotten technique. Biographies of artists often give interesting insights into how technological developments have inspired new directions, an aspect of the artistic process children frequently find fascinating. Computer printmaking is a developing technique, increasingly used by traditional printmakers in conjunction with other methods, described in the chapter on computer art.

EQUIPMENT AND TOOLS

Inks and paints

Always read labels on containers to ensure the ink or paint is designed to cope with the job in hand. For hand or small block printing, ready mixed opaque paint, the consistency of thin cream, can be poured on to foam pads on palettes. With more sophisticated blocks, the effects will be more satisfactory with inks.

Block printing inks are fairly cheap, and last quite well. Water-based paints and inks are best: oil-based inks take a long time to dry, and are difficult to remove. Younger children will work better with half full tubes; with new ones, a small squeeze releases a term's supply. Screen printing needs special ink, commercially available, or it can be made by adding an agent to some ready-mixed commercial paints.

Papers

Printmaking generally requires fairly porous paper, so the ink or paint is absorbed and does not smudge. Use good quality sugar paper, or cartridge for special prints. Non-porous photocopy paper is not suitable. Any shiny surface will probably only work well with professional inks. Tissue paper can be effective, but it is flimsy and needs careful handling. Large sheets of brown wrapping paper work well; use the matt side. Children might research types of paper and ink as part of the artistic process.

Trays for paint or ink

For hand printing, found object or vegetable printing, use flat palettes, plates or large plastic lids, with slightly smaller inserts of foam to give an even distribution of ink or paint across the block (see Figure 4.10).

Inking plates

Any non-porous, flat surface like melamine, plastic or formica, is suitable for rolling out inks to make a monoprint and for transferring ink evenly onto the roller before inking a block.

Rollers

These are used for rolling out ink on to a monoprint plate, rolling and transferring ink on to the surface of a printing block, androlling the back of the paper to ensure even distribution of ink. Designate wet (ink) and dry (paper) rollers to avoid getting unwanted ink on the paper. Most rollers have a stand to keep the inked roller clear of the work surface (see Figure 4.11).

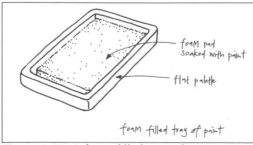

Figure 4.10 A foam filled tray of paint

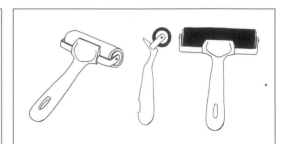

Figure 4.11 Rollers for printing

Dabbers

These are soft alternatives to the roller, made by affixing a ball of foam or fabric to a small handle, covering with fabric and tying with string or elastic bands. Figure 4.12 shows the shape of a foam dabber.

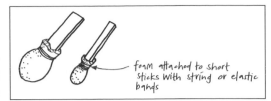

foam attached to short sticks with string or elastic bands

Figure 4.12 Foam 'dabbers'

Newspaper pads

Small pads of newspaper are put under the print block when it is being inked. If the roller goes over the edge, the ink goes on to the top layer of paper, which is removed and thrown away, so the ink does not get on to the print.

Drying lines

Printmaking sessions produce large amounts of work, which must be catered for in the organisation. Drying lines can be improvised with string and clothes pegs, across the room or along shelves, or put newspaper under tables. Commercially available drying racks are quite expensive, but useful. Ensure work does not stick to the next print.

Screens

A sturdy frame is covered with gauze and stapled firmly around the edges so the fabric is tightly stretched across. Around the inside, layers of brown sticky tape are placed as an inner frame, to mask the edges and provide a reservoir for the inks (see Figure 4.6).

Squeegees

These tools are used to squeeze the ink along the length of the screen, so it goes evenly through the gauze and onto the paper.

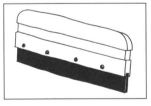

Figure 4.13 Squeegee

ORGANISING PRINTMAKING IN THE CLASSROOM

Printmaking can be a gloriously messy operation, but care and attention to basic organisation can minimise this (see Fig. 4.14), and make the experience more satisfactory for children and teacher alike. The following ideas may help:

- Layers of newspaper give a soft surface to work on and enable the top messy layer to be removed without having to completely re-cover the table.
- Isolating block making from the printmaking helps to effect an organised work space.
- Placing mats of used kitchen paper help define each working space, and, in the centre of the table, show where to replace tools and materials.
- Plastic bags taped to the ends of tables for rubbish such as soiled newspaper or bits of vegetable, during the session, to be disposed of at the end.

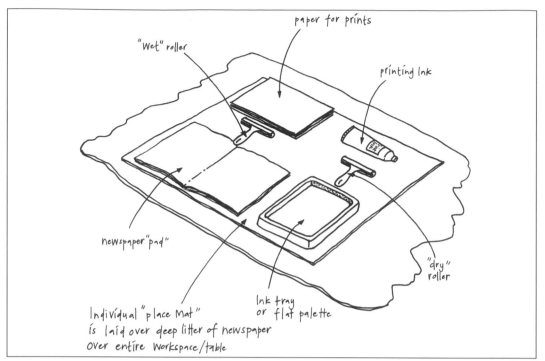

Figure 4.14 Placing of equipment

- Sign, date and number each print like an artist; children may like to devise an easily recognisable symbol (like Albrecht Dürer) rather than writing laboriously each time.
- Teach children to clear the work space each time they leave it.

PLANS FOR TEACHING PRINTMAKING

Handprinting

Using the hand as a print block is fun for very young children, and older children can achieve very exciting and imaginative compositions with this basic technique.

Aims

To introduce/develop the concept of block printmaking, including:

- the reverse image of the block on paper;
- the technique of carefully inking the block (hand);
- overprinting, using a range of colours;
- developing concepts of composition, colour and texture.

Organisation

Ensure sleeves are rolled up, and aprons are properly tied. Cover the worktop with several layers of newspaper, and set out:

- trays of ready-mixed paint on sponges in a range of colours;

- papers of different colours: sugar papers, kitchen paper;
- a washing line or rack to hold wet prints;
- pencils for signing prints before putting to dry.

Session plan

Explain aims to children. Ask them to examine the palms of their hands, feeling the contours with their fingers and tracing the lines with fingertip. Which bits are smooth? Are any bits rough? Do the lines on the palm go in or out? Children stretch their hands flat, to make a print block, and place palms lightly onto a sponge pad, to pick up the ink.

Examine the hands again. Where is there most ink? Can they see lines on their palms, or does the ink go into them? What will happen when they put their hands down onto the paper?

Press the hand carefully down on the paper; hold it still for a moment, then lift. What happened? Can you see the lines of your hand on the print? What happened to the paint on your palms? Why did some bits not print? Which way round is the print? Is it the same way round as the hand block? Why?

Try again, without washing hands, in the same colour. Put different colours on each hand, rub palms together, and print. Compare the prints. Is there anything different? Why? Sign the prints, and hang them up to dry.

Evaluation

Discussion at each stage helps children exchange ideas, formulate aims for the next piece of work, and put them immediately into practice. Discuss the quality of the print: techniques; ways of improving or developing the idea; the texture of the paint; the colours used and how they interact; similarities and differences between prints, and between the prints and the hand surface which formed the printing block. What have the children learned?

Printmaking with found or natural objects: session plan

Using simple, readily available blocks and basic techniques, children can make a fairly uniform set of prints and learn about repeat patterning, tessellation and estimating. At early stages it is best to focus on pattern, colour and textural qualities in a printmaking context, rather than making pictures. Previous or linked experiences might include:

- hand and foot printing;
- arranging in patterns a sets of shapes, perhaps using squared paper;
- examining fabrics and papers for repeat patterns;
- examining bricks in a wall, roof tiles, etc., for the patterns made;
- studying natural geometry, e.g. honeycombs, spirals;
- discussing books and reproductions of artists' work.

Aims

- to develop concepts, skills and knowledge of block printing techniques;
- to encourage experimentation with colour, shapes, overprinting;
- to develop concept of composition;
- to develop concept of pattern through arrangement of multiple prints.

Organisation

Cover the worktop with several layers of newspaper, and set out:

- trays of ready-mixed paint on foam pads;
- clean water for cleaning blocks;
- 'place mats' for each child;
- objects for print blocks, sorted;
- a range of small papers for trial prints;
- large papers for more ambitious or collaborative work;
- a washing line or other method for drying prints.

Session plan

Explain aims to children. Briefly recap previous sessions and principles of workshop practice. Demonstrate and remind them of techniques for block printing:

- gently press the block surface on to foam pad;
- check the block surface has enough paint on it;
- place carefully on paper and hold it there for a moment;
- lift gently so it does not smudge.

Children select a print block and examine printing surface. Which bits will touch the paper? How will the print look? What shape will it be?

Children select paper to print on and choose a colour, then make multiple prints with the same block on the paper. Assess how well each child can manage the process. Children may develop ideas using different colours and blocks:

- make a row of prints along the edge of the paper;
- try several prints without re-inking the block;
- make the prints look like rows of bricks;
- try rotating the block through a quarter turn each time you print;
- try printing with a different colour on top;
- try making two columns of prints, side by side;
- try making a spiral.

Evaluation

What have children learned about print techniques, colour and colour combinations, shapes and patterns, overprinting? How well did they manage to experiment and try ideas? Were any too teacher-dependent? Could they see connections between their own patterns and others they have examined?

Prints may be mounted in sets to demonstrate the range of colours, patterns and textural effects achieved. Some could go into sketchbooks, or into plastic wallet books for reference and further discussion.

Possible extensions

Children draw out their own guidelines for repeat patterns, and try to achieve symmetrical, asymmetrical and rotationally symmetrical designs.

Clay and plasticine printmaking

These soft materials allow for easy cutting or carving, so children can be responsible both for the design of the block and the patterns on the paper. Clay and plasticine blocks can be printed successfully from foam-filled paint trays.

Aims

- to effect continuity and to encourage experimentation and risk-taking in design;
- to develop concepts and technical skills of block printmaking;
- to reinforce workshop practice, health and safety routines.

Organisation

Set out printing area as for found object session (above), without blocks. Cover the block-making area with several layers of newspaper, and set out:

- table mats and cutting boards or edge blocks in each place;
- cutting tools: knives, small knitting needles, tapestry needles in corks;
- objects to press into surface: pastry cutters, plastic shapes;
- a prepared piece of clay or plasticine for each child.

Session plan

Explain aims of the session, and remind children about workshop practice. Recap previous printmaking work, emphasising composition, colour, texture, etc. Explain significance of 'block making' and 'printmaking' areas. Examine the clay/plasticine blocks. Which side would be best to print from? Experiment with different effects of mark-makers on print blocks. Move to print table; make experimental prints on various papers.

Some children need further support, others will quickly establish a routine: make marks on the block; replace cutters; go to the print area to experiment. Encourage them to persevere and print from one block in different ways before they go back to change the surface. Stop regularly to discuss how they achieved particular effects, and to predict what happens if . . .? Which cutters made the clearest impressions? Which bits of the surface printed? Which were left?

Evaluation

How well could children handle the materials and tools available? Were they prepared to experiment and take risks? How well did they establish the routine of using both areas appropriately? How well did they apply and develop previous printmaking skills? What connections were made with previous discussions of artists' work?

Potato printing: notes on process

The potato can be used just cut in half. To carve it requires more skill than plasticine or clay. Other root vegetables may be used to print in the same way and celery is fun too. With a large sharp knife, cut the potato firmly across the middle, so the surface is even and flat. Children may cut unevenly, and it is dangerous for them to use such sharp knives. Cut off the top, so the potato sits firmly on the cutting board when being carved. Leave time to allow juices dry out, which may later effect the quality of the print. Each child needs two or three blocks.

Organising the block-making area

Ensure plenty of room since children will be using sharp instruments. Every child should be seated. Each should have a cutting block, preferably an edge block. Place cutters (as sharp as you can safely entrust to the children) in the centre of the table within reach. Tape plastic bags to the table for rubbish.

Teaching potato block making

Demonstrate how to cut down into the potato and then across, to ensure a good depth of relief. If flesh is scooped out, the resultant print with be fuzzy. Place the potato firmly on the cutting block, and experiment with cutting. Teach children always to cut away from themselves, to avoid accidents. Make some preliminary experimental prints.

Making the design

Recap on previous printmaking. Remind them how effective a simple design can be, and that the nature of the potato makes it best for basic shapes. Some may wish to carve their initials, although they often print backwards, even if you remind them beforehand! (You can first draw with a fine water-based pen onto the potato.)

Printing the potato

The natural juices water down the quality of ink, so blot the potato block before use. The printing procedure is the same as above. The potato can be rinsed, blotted and reused. It will keep for a few days in an airtight box for reuse.

Evaluation

As above; emphasise the design, colour combinations and patterns achieved.

Polystyrene 'pressprint' blocks: notes on process

Best results are obtained using waterbased printing ink (see Figure 4.15).

Organisation

Block making area: cover table with newspaper and set out:

- small pieces of pressprint;
- incising tools: sharp pencils, fine biros, large blunt needles set in corks;
- cutting boards / edge blocks.

Printing area: cover table with plenty of layers of newspaper and set out:

- place mats, allowing for plenty of elbow room;
- a wet roller, a dry roller, an ink block, a small pad of newspaper per child;
- small papers and printing inks within reach.

Figure 4.15 *Face*. Polystyrene pressprint block print by a ten year old. Size: 14 × 14 cm

Teaching the process

For first experiments, use small sample blocks, about 10 cm square. Incising tools give a range of textural qualities which can be test printed and discussed. Rubbing the block with wax crayons before printing will give a good indication of how well the image or design will print. When children come to make a more considered block, they can work directly or make an initial design on paper before cutting it. The drawing can be traced lightly, using carbon paper or a rubbing.

Printing the block

Place printing block onto newspaper, face up. Select printing ink, squeeze about 5 cm from the tube on to the ink block. Roll out the ink with the wet roller to ensure an even cover on the roller itself. Roll the ink on to the block, to the edges; the newspaper mops up any surplus. Put the roller back on the ink block. Discard the top layer of newspaper, so the inked block rests on a clean layer.

Carefully place the paper over the inked block. Pat down gently, then use a dry roller to ensure the ink is evenly transferred to the paper. Lift up one corner to check the print. If satisfactory, gently remove the paper, admire the print and sign it. Hang it up to dry. Bear in mind that first prints are rarely entirely satisfactory, as blocks work better after a few attempts. It may need to be re-cut in some areas before it is ready. If so, rinse off under a tap, pat dry on some newspaper and return to the blockmaking area to work on it. Figure 4.17 illustrates some letter images.

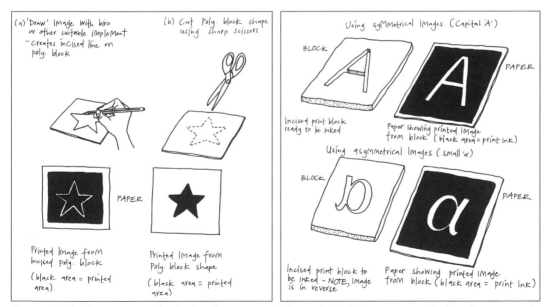

Figure 4.16 The process of printing from a polystyrene block

Figure 4.17 Using symmetrical and asymmetrical letter images

Extension

The print block can be cut to shape to make interesting non-standard sized prints. Small sections can be cut out and used to overprint (see Figure 4.16).

Collage/collograph block printmaking: notes on process

The printing process is the same as above; progression is achieved in the making of the blocks. For clay, plasticine, potato or polystyrene blocks, the image or design is incised into the basic material; collograph blocks are built up from the base, like other collage techniques they have used.

Organisation

Blockmaking area: cover with newspaper and set out:

- base blocks of heavy card or strawboard, about 15 cm square;
- a range of materials for building up the blocks, e.g. thin card, textured papers, string, threads, pieces of fabric etc.;
- cutting tools as appropriate, e.g. scissors, craft knives;
- pva glue and glue mats;
- cutting boards.

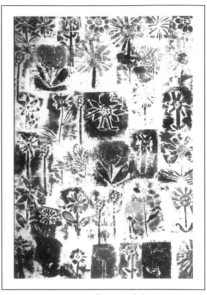

Figure 4.18 *Sunflower fabric print*. Collaborative work using collograph print blocks and water based inks by seven year olds. Size: 200 × 400 cm

Printmaking area: as above, for polystyrene blocks.

Making the block

Plan this session at least an hour or so before printing, so that the blocks can dry. Remind children of printing process, and how to use impact adhesives. Encourage them to think of themselves as researchers, testing out the properties of different materials. Focus on shape and texture rather than representational images. Make rubbings of the blocks before printing. Once the block is dry, the process is as for polystyrene blocks.

When printing multiple copies as a repeat, or over-print, the block is placed face down on the paper. Some considerable dexterity is required to ensure it is not smudged and that each print comes out the right way up, so test runs are again vital.

Monoprinting: notes on process

This technique encourages an experimental and risk-taking approach; principles and aims vary according to the children's age, experience, dexterity and confidence. Paper is laid directly onto the plate so the size and shape of both paper and inking plate influence the size of print. Inks are best, but paint is satisfactory with absorbent paper (see Figure 4.19).

Organisation

Cover the printing area with layers of newspaper and set out:

- printing plates: a large plate for collaborative work, small ones for individuals;
- a range of inks: primary colours to encourage initial colour-mixing, or more for more

experienced children; one or two colours only can encourage experiments with textural qualities;

- spreaders: different sized rollers, palette knives, spoons, spatulas;
- dry rollers and/or dabbers;
- papers: sugar paper and tissue paper work well.

Inking the block

Squeeze about 5 cm ink from a tube onto the inking block. Use applicators or fingers to spread it. Add more colours as required and mix. Keep the overall layer of ink fairly thin and even to start with. Do not add water at first but a little squirt from a plant spray may create an interesting effect.

Making the print

Select the paper and place carefully on top of the plate. Gently pat it in place. A 'dry' roller to roll over the back of the paper, a dabber for a softer effect, or fingertips, help to transfer the ink from the plate to the paper. Remove paper carefully.

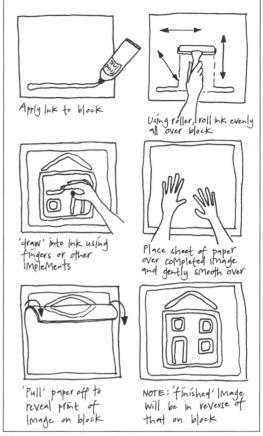

Figure 4.19 Monoprinting

Extensions

To draw on the monoprint, roll the plate with a thin coat of one colour. Place paper on top. Do not roll or dab. Draw firmly and boldly with biro or pencil on the back of the paper; be careful not to tear it. Lift the paper; the pressure of the drawing tool makes an image on the paper darker than the surrounding layer of ink. The outline is seen in negative on the block. Place another piece of paper on the ink block. Roll with a dry roller. Lift the negative print which shows where the first drawing lifted the ink from the block. This technique encourages quick, fluid work, partly because it is not possible to make corrections. Only bold lines really work, since the ink will dry fairly quickly but the print may have unforeseen textural interest in the background (see Figures 4.2 and 4.3).

CHAPTER 5

Computer Art and Design

Figure 5.1   *Untitled*, computer drawing by a nine year old. Size: 17 × 10 cm

The computer is an everyday tool in the primary classroom. While many teachers are familiar, competent, even expert in its use, children see the applications and potential even more clearly, and are, it seems, less fazed by technical hitches, malfunctions and limitations (see Figure 5.1). No book on primary art and design could be complete without a section on computer art, although we do not attempt to use technical language, or to discuss particular machines (hardware) or programs (software). We do aim to set out how well-established principles of primary education apply to the age of technology, and how using this comparatively new way of working can inform other areas of the art and design curriculum, as well as being a medium worthy of consideration in its own right.

> Use of IT should provide positive support for the development of pupils' learning in art and design. This may seem obvious; however, in practice, this fundamental consideration is often masked by the hypnotic quality of special effects, and often quite superficial visual trickery . . . Use of IT in art and design should be governed by the same criteria as for other media.
>
> (Winser 1996)

Displays and project books abound with beautifully printed and embellished written and graphic work in schools. However, the potential use of the computer art program as a means of creating original work seems to remain largely unexplored. This is possibly due to several factors, including limited availability of computers and programs, and the implications for pupil time, and, to some extent, the lack of confidence of teachers in guiding and helping children develop their on-screen efforts.

Using the computer for drawing and printmaking, children start with a blank screen and make notes on it just as they do with pencils or paint on paper. Other uses, except word processing, involve working with an already established image on screen. With even a basic graphics program, the child is in control from the start, and able to use the technology to realise ideas and images. Arguably, a child learns more about how to operate the mouse and control of the machine through a graphics program than from working through the set routines of a game. So the type of work suggested in this chapter both enhances the use of computer technology and adds breadth to the children's art educational experiences.

> The aim of worthwhile education is that it nurtures independent inventiveness so that we come to see that everything relates to who we are, where we are. The personal response, the personal discovery, is of prime importance. With computers especially, the students will usually outstrip us in expertise and ease of handling . . . Teaching is not something to be mechanically delivered; learning is not something to be passively received. We know this, so let us not be thrown when we come into contact with the machine. We must not allow ourselves to be used by things. (Nicholls 1997)

To operate a simple program, technically possible for young children, the equipment needed is the computer, loaded with the program, a mouse to operate it, a screen to display the efforts made and a colour printer to make a hard copy or permanent record of the outcome. The program allows the child to choose lines of varying thicknesses, and colours, and qualities, such as brushstrokes or pencil-type effects. The mouse's movements are reflected in the lines or shapes on the screen. These movements need to be fairly subtle, because if they are wild, the cursor goes off the screen. The child needs practise to learn the right amount of wrist and hand movement to achieve the desired effect.

Children can also make enclosed shapes and then colour them in with either solid colour, a variety of textured effects or even wallpaper-style patterns, by clicking on roller, choosing a colour or pattern, clicking in the space to be filled, and the computer magically floods the area with the chosen colour: no messy lines over the edge, no dribbling paint, no broken pencil or charcoal to frustrate. The colour is pure, so the previous colour does not get into the new one, as so often happens when a brush has not been quite cleaned. Click to turn the brush or pencil into an eraser, and unwanted marks can disappear. Or, clicking on 'undo' removes the last few marks altogether, leaving a clean area to rework. More advanced technology allows the use of a digitiser or scanner to grab a piece of work, such as a photograph or drawing, on to the screen. Then, the image can be manipulated, colours altered, lines drawn over, perhaps the ultimate in graffiti art.

Despite its plug, monitor, keyboard and mouse, it is still useful to consider the computer as an extension of traditional, familiar and, to some extent, more user-friendly and often more accessible media. As most of our pupils have keyboard skills, it would seem appropriate to capitalise on them in every aspect of education. Through guided and free

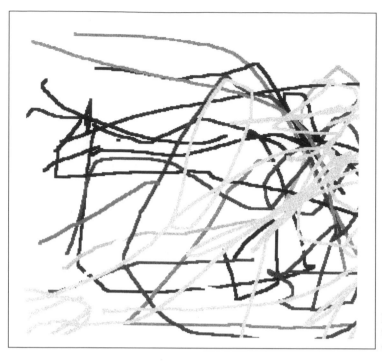

Figure 5.2   *Lines*, computer drawing by a five year
old. Size: 21 × 20 cm

exploration, children can learn what the computer and its programs can do for them (see Figure 5.2). The aim is, as in other media, to provide appropriate experiences, set suitable tasks and give adequate feedback and teaching to enable the children to take ownership of the medium for themselves, and for them and their teachers to see how technology can be useful rather than an end in itself.

Available programs for art and design have particular facilities and limitations, which make the products, on screen or in print-out form (hard copies), different from work in other 2D media. By using the computer as a drawing tool, a paintbrush or a printmaking technique, children develop skills in:

- hand-eye coordination; the hand moves the mouse on a horizontal surface and the result appears at a distance on a vertical screen;
- using different controls to make a range of lines, tones, colours and patterns;
- drawing, painting and printmaking, through their application in a new medium;
- problem-solving, in recognising the limits of line, overall shape and ratio permitted in the screen sizes available;
- trying out ideas in a non-permanent form, which can be modified and adapted with relative ease;
- recognising that there are many options available, that can be tried out before deciding a piece is ready to print, and the ability to save images at various stages in the process for later review and discussion about the process;
- learning about the differences between the light image on screen and the comparatively dull print-out on rather flimsy paper, which is inevitably less satisfactory than a good quality traditional print on paper such as cartridge;
- learning to mix traditional and computer art media, by for instance overlaying the computer print with other media, or vice versa by using a digital camera to transfer an

image onto the screen, overlaying it with marks made electronically, and re-printing the modified version.

In the chapter on drawing, we described the stages through which, conventionally, children pass as they become more skilled and controlled in their drawing. No matter what their age, pupils need the chance to go through perhaps parallel stages in dealing with a new medium. As teachers we should perhaps allow ourselves a similar luxury, to scribble, play and gradually learn what can be done, so as best to select what might be done on the computer in the service of our creative needs.

It is worth noting the public nature of the screen image. Some artwork, and other class-room activities, can progress quietly in a corner, but the screen is viewable from a distance, usually placed against a wall for ease of access and safety. This means that everyone can see what is happening, and the light image draws the eye, so any passer-by has immediate access to the work. For some, this can be inhibiting, at least until controls and techniques have become familiar and easy to operate.

> Visual literacy as an idea places an emphasis on the role and use of visual language and systems. Faster access to line, shape, colour, texture and pattern – used independently or in combination – allows the user to become far more vividly aware of the infinite potential of the language.
>
> (Chambers 1989)

THE CROSS-CURRICULAR POTENTIAL OF COMPUTER ART AND DESIGN

Each of the chapters in this book makes reference to cross-curricular links within the National Curriculum, including computer use. It is important to make a distinction between the different uses of the computer within art and design work, e.g.:

- as a source bank for ready-made illustrations by others, which should be used with great care, as this can inhibit children's own creative endeavours;

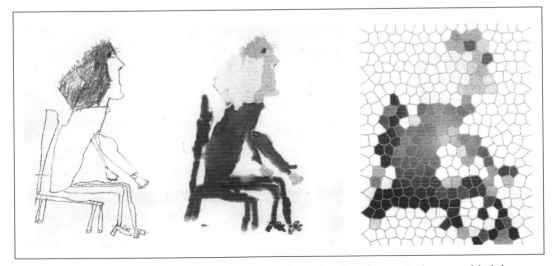

Figure 5.3 *Triptych*, a life drawing, digitised, coloured and with mosaic feature added, by an eight year old. Size: 30 × 15 cm

- as an electronic reference book or encyclopedia, for accessing information about art and design, artists and designers, from all periods and cultures around the world;
- as a 'blank canvas' on which to create original and exciting images, which might be described as drawings, prints or paintings, depending on the applications used (see Figure 5.3).

These different uses link with the Attainment Target in the National Curriculum for art and design, and similarly with the requirements for children to develop computer and keyboard skills in information and communications technology and other subjects.

English

- Using paste-up techniques to enable word processing and graphic elements to be put together, helping children appreciate the interrelationship of words and illustrations in both narrative and non-narrative forms of writing.
- Developing technical vocabulary, through discussing concepts and applications.
- Potential for small group or pair work in creating images and text, which involves co-operative speaking and listening.

Mathematics

- Developing and applying geometric knowledge through use of pattern-making, repeat, blow-up and other facilities.
- Use of geometric and other shapes in creating original images.

Information and Communications Technology

- Developing competence in expanding understanding and skill with different ranges of facilities available through even the most basic art programs.

Design and Technology

- Using the facilities available to plan and design artifacts such as boxes, towers etc., and using a range of typefaces available to embellish models and designs.
- Trying out different colour combinations before finishing off a completed design.

Humanities

- Gaining knowledge and information about art and design, including many historical and geographical settings, and using these to inspire their own art work.

THE BASIC ELEMENTS OF ART IN COMPUTER PRINTMAKING

Line

The width and colour of line is controlled by the toolbox selection; the length, shape and position by the mouse. The line is regular and even, which has advantages in some work, but lacks the different qualities of pencil, or even felt-tip pens, where pressure regulates the intensity or flow. The line on screen is made up of hundreds of small squares, so in curves and ellipses, a smooth arc is almost impossible to achieve in basic programs. To change the width or colour the user has to pause, click, and then return to the image, which can also impede the flow. However, infinite potential is available, and the character of on-screen linear marks can be used to advantage in some work.

Shape

There are, in most programs, predetermined shapes, available through clicking on a circle, oval or rectangle, which can be changed in outline colour, width of describing line, and dimension on screen. While this might seem to make drawing easy, there can be a tendency for children to draw using only predetermined shapes, for instance to make a spider, a house or a person based on circles, rectangles and arcs. This is undoubtedly fun, and helps children familiarise themselves with the controls. But children also need to be able to make freehand drawings with the mouse, including geometric shapes. The ability to make shapes and repeat them, change the scale, colours and ratios, helps children to appreciate both the properties of the shapes they make and their possible function within overall designs and compositions.

Colour

Colour variations and combinations on screen are infinite; altering the colour of one element within a composition helps children see how different hues, tones and shades affect each other when placed together or in close proximity within a design or image. Placing a small area of blue or green (so-called cold colours) on an otherwise predominantly yellow, red and orange composition (of warm colours) can be quite dramatic.

There is the potential to airspray, or create a dotted effect within a delineated boundary, or to flood a defined area with a particular colour from the palette in the program, which delights some children with the clean, crisp colouring-in that can be achieved. This is really helpful when working with designs for artifacts, patterns and abstract work, but possibly less effective when working in a freer mode. The colour can of course be changed, and changed, and changed again, without affecting paper or drawing, which is often not possible on traditional drawing or painting surfaces. Even with so many shades available, it is helpful on occasion to limit the range children work with on screen.

What does not happen on screen is the merging and overlapping of colours, so effective with liquid pigment like paint, pencil or wax crayons. Children need to appreciate this, because with less uncertainty comes less surprise, and often it is the happy accident which becomes a special feature in other colour media.

Pattern

As with colour, patterns can be made and manipulated endlessly on screen. Using editing techniques, repeats are comparatively simple to achieve, and alternative arrangements can be explored. This can be useful as an intermediate stage when planning traditional printmaking, so the effects of full or half drop, overlapping or other tessellation patterning can be explored before setting out to print on cloth or paper.

Some programs contain predesigned patterns, which can be applied like blocks of colour, mixed and matched on the screen, in the same way as conventional collage uses different patterned and textured papers and fabrics. It is, however, more difficult to position patterns, because a horizontal or diagonal stripe will stay like that: its directionality is constant, and a patch of pattern always stays the same way up. Patterns using letter or number symbols can be very effective, with different typefaces, font sizes and colours available for endless repeat and manipulation.

ARTISTS WHO USE COMPUTER TECHNOLOGY

Many practising artists now have websites to display their current work on screen for potential purchasers or galleries. It may be worth investigating whether this is true of any local artists, so children can access their work on screen, and perhaps be encouraged to visit local exhibitions to view the actual work. Museums and galleries may have a website, which can help to plan visits.

The following extract was written almost a decade ago, but still holds true to a great extent today. While fine artists do use computer art and image-making as in Figure 5.4, in practice there have been few significant inroads, applications being more usually in graphic and design fields, including architecture, advertising, interior design and publishing, where it is now taken for granted.

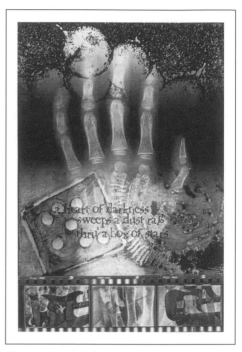

Figure 5.4 *Apothecary*. Colour computer print by Lee Edwards, using Photoshop and a Wacom graphics tablet. Size: 16 × 24 cm

> Computer graphics is in its infancy . . . Artists are still engaged in the process of self-discovery. This new visual medium has many advantages compared with traditional printmaking media, some being unique. Yet the medium has its own problems. Lack of surface texture, constraints on print size, colour differences and general techno-phobia may to some extent explain why computing has still to become an accepted part of art production . . . Perhaps it will be through creative and imaginative explorations and developments of computer printing processes that printmakers will establish computer prints as a standard printmaking medium.
>
> (Mike North 1989)

Some artists work directly on screen, or use technological processes within their work. Sophisticated technology is unlikely to be available in our schools, but children can gain inspiration for their own work from seeing accomplished practitioners' prints.

There are many artists whose past work would seem to have predicted the potential of the computer, such as the multiple prints of Marilyn Monroe and other images by Warhol, Vasareley's or Riley's geometrically designed paintings or Lichtenstein's blown-up comic strips. Even artists who work using the computer still publish images in good old-fashioned books. A visit to a local art school or specialist library will probably repay efforts in providing examples of contemporary work for children to use.

Computers are also used for animation work, although some studios still use individually drawn cells to achieve their moving images. Nonetheless, the potential is there for children to make flip book animations, taking advantage of the ability to print images with small alterations and to change colours easily.

PLANNING

For first steps, try introducing ideas to small groups, trying out each of the controls in turn, and setting tasks they can follow up on an individual or pair basis. Use the controls available in the 'toolbox' on the program to guide your input. For instance:

- turn on the machine and click on the program you require;
- twiddle the mouse around on the work surface, and see what happens;
- click on one of the different sized lines in the toolbox;
- now twiddle the mouse again, and see what has changed;
- do this until you have tried every thickness of line;
- click on 'undo' to clear the screen.

Leave the children to play and try out their own ideas. They discover that they can change colours, and the more adventurous soon try clicking on every icon to see what happens. If you think they are ready to go on to more experiments, you might ask them to:

- click on one of the colours in the colour box on the screen;
- now twiddle the mouse and see what happens;
- click on another size of line and twiddle again;
- click on another colour and twiddle again;
- choose a colour and a line width;
- see how many different lines you can make with the mouse;
- try to make zig-zags, circles, rectangles and other funny shapes in different colours;
- click on a new colour;
- click on the roller icon;
- now click inside one of the funny shapes you have made;
- then click inside another shape, and see what happens.

Similar sets of instructions for each of the controls are fairly easy to plan. Children may need lots of encouragement, or may outstrip your expectations of their capabilities. A checklist of icons can help you record, as you observe them at work, which ones they use with ease and which may need specific input in a later session. Children can of course keep their own record of 'received and understood' achievements.

Extending skills and applications

Because this machine and its facilities essentially provide no less than an additional tool for creating artwork in the classroom, it is worth looking through the drawing and painting activities outlined in the chapters on these topics and adapting them for use with the computer, e.g.:

- experimentation with shapes and lines of different colours and qualities (see Figure 5.5);
- shut-eye drawings, making marks without looking at the tool or the screen and seeing what marks are made, and if they are as predicted;
- observational drawing directly on screen from objects placed in the child's eyeline, or a still-life arrangement, or a mirror to work on a self-portrait directly on the screen.

In short, the computer can complement conventional drawing, painting and print-making media, given the confidence and imagination of the pupils and their teachers!

Figure 5.5 The space ship, computer drawing by a six year old. Size: 16 × 12 cm

CHAPTER 6

Photography

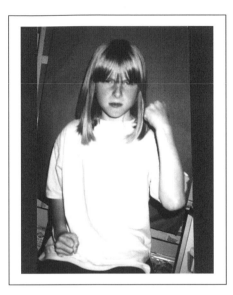

Figure 6.1 *Me. Violent*, photograph planned and posed by the subject, taken by a classmate aged eight.

There are several aspects of photography which concern us in the primary school in considering the making of images, and the use and understanding of the work of experts in the field. We deal in school with both still and moving images. Photography also offers, particularly with still images, the potential to use others' work to manipulate, recompose and rearrange, to make new images in montage (collage) form, or to use other media on top of a photograph or photocopied image to change its appearance and meaning. This is less accessible for moving images, because editing facilities are rarely available in primary schools, although selecting extracts for viewing by fast forwarding on the video player can be seen as similar: a modification or edit of the original is achieved.

> In making and using images for different purposes children will become visually literate in the same way that they acquire literacy through practice in the use of descriptive, transactional and expressive language. Children need to be visually literate to function effectively in a society where visual images enter our lives through the mass media – publications, newspapers, film, television – where so much information is presented to us through visual means in our everyday environment. (Clement and Page 1992)

For children, photography is a familiar and almost mundane technology (see Figure 6.1). Most know what a camera is, how it works and what it does. Some may be able to identify different cameras and describe their functions. Many children already understand something about the stages of the photographic process: putting film in the camera, taking the photograph, having it processed, excitedly looking at the results. They may also understand something about the relationship between taking photographs and light.

In this chapter we look at using still and moving images as separate aspects of photography in school, although ideas for one type of work may well translate into work in another.

STILL IMAGES

The still camera

'It is well known that children recognise photographs before they can understand the written word' (Jayhem and Walton 1987). Knowledge about photographic processes, equipment and products means that photography is approached by children with confidence and enthusiasm. A camera is a common domestic appliance, and as children see it used regularly by those they know are not experts, they judge it to be technologically undemanding. These positive responses, to a medium with so much expressive and communicative potential, can be invaluable in the classroom. On the other hand, this familiarity can create difficulties for teachers in locating photography in the arts. The National Curriculum requires children to investigate and make, to be practically involved in the process of photography, and to develop knowledge and understanding of the medium. Children investigating and making in photography can be:

- involved in alternative ways to express and communicate ideas and feelings;
- developing skills in selecting, arranging, organising and decision making;
- designing and making images;
- responding to and evaluating images from the locality, from past and present and from a variety of cultures;
- using strategies for collecting and recording information for future evaluation;
- investigating different ways to illustrate stories;
- making a record of an activity or capturing a moment or event where no other lasting record is possible, e.g. puppetry or drama event, sports day etc.;
- experimenting with composition, images, tone etc.;
- developing their confidence and self-esteem;
- developing understanding of process;
- developing negotiating and collaborating skills.

Developing knowledge and understanding of photography involves:

- looking at photography as an art form in itself;
- considering the work of photographic artists, processes and genres;
- looking at work of artists who use photographic images: photo-montage, collage, panorama, mixed media.

Working in this way:

- helps children appreciate the characteristics of the medium;
- shows the diversity of photographic images;
- demonstrates the relationship between the audience and the product and the way that

images are manipulated to produce an effect and response;
- develops visual literacy and visual perception;
- helps develop a critical attitude to the use of photographic processes.

Developing a critical attitude to reading and taking photographs is important in helping children to understand better this most common of visual technologies. Through personal involvement with cameras and photographic images, and having time and encouragement to evaluate their own and other people's work, children learn about the potential of the medium. It can be used imaginatively in other ways, for instance:

- taking photographs of children on their birthdays;
- taking photographs to record the process of work in school as well as the products, for instance during rehearsals for a play, or of physical education sessions which are otherwise rarely observed by parents and visitors;
- recording stages of growth of plants and animals kept in school.

Photographs also help children to see their own efforts from others' points of view, to record process as well as product, and to appreciate the literal point of view of another. This device, much used in special schools, has a place in mainstream schools too. With a little additional input, the now fairly routine use of photographs to document the life of a school can be elevated to an 'art' status, as suggested in some of the ideas given below.

The photocopier

The use of the photocopier as a camera has been exploited in most imaginative ways in some schools. This is of course fairly expensive, but it enables multiple copies to be made of a particular image, copies to be made of drawings or other 2D work at different stages, and allows copies of otherwise precious photographs to be handled, and perhaps modified, by children (see Figure 6.2). With more sophisticated machines, the facility to enlarge and reduce images can help with planning layouts. Older primary children, working in sketchbooks towards a major composition, can use photocopies of their work to plan the final layout. Photocopies of images from books relevant to the research in hand might be pasted into sketchbooks for reference. On occasion, a copy of a sketch of work in progress might accompany the final work in a display or exhibition.

Links between photography and traditional printmaking are now well established. One school we know makes photocopies of children's hands at the beginning of each academic year, not for fingerprint files, but to compare sizes from year to year, and to compare with traditional hand-prints.

The photocopier has in many ways taken over from the use of light-sensitive paper for producing images. Suggestions offered for work with still photographs may also be tackled with the photocopier as a camera substitute or in a supporting role.

Figure 6.2 *Me. Stroppy*, photocopy of photograph taken by a classmate by an eight year old.

Colour photocopies remain prohibitively expensive for most primary schools, but they have a quality of colour and texture that, like computer print-outs, can actually add interest to an image. (If the budget allows, children might select just one image to be colour photocopied for their art and design record files.) Before using the computer to scan images, consider whether the photocopier could do the job just as well.

Slide and overhead projectors

Not so much in evidence these days, but with great potential, is the slide projector. The advantages of a facility for a large group to focus on a single light image is evident in art and image-making as much as in any other curriculum area. Apart from the use of slides of works of art, often available from local libraries, to view and discuss, there is the potential for children to make their own slides as easily as colour prints. Incidentally, glass slide binders can be used to project in large scale items such as strands of thread, a fingerprint or even a drawing with a china marker made direct on the glass. For a project on 'ourselves' with infant children in one school, a lock of each child's hair was (with express permission from parents!) made into a slide, and compared and contrasted with great interest, since the variations were quite extraordinary.

Photographs and other images can also be copied onto special overhead projector transparencies. This facilitates critical discussion of, for instance, newspaper or magazine images, especially as a part of the image can be concealed at any point. With the advent of computer technology, it is unrealistic to hope for an overhead projector as standard equipment in every classroom, although its uses within art and design education are many. Photocopies of illustrations and texts onto transparencies enable children to use and share almost any text in black and white, or in colour if this is added afterwards with felt-tip pen. (Use colour pens on the reverse of the photocopied image, or it wipes off the copier ink.)

When groups are planning a video production, or a series of photographs, they can draw the story-board directly onto an overhead projector transparency, for ease of viewing and sharing ideas before the photography begins. With water-based pens it is easy to erase and modify on the spot, and to reach general agreement fairly early on in the process. (This is also helpful for other large-scale planning, such as a frieze or a class book.)

MOVING IMAGES

Video

Television broadcasts feature, it seems, more and more home movies, illustrating news items, embarrassing clips of people falling into ponds in full wedding dress, and security camera shots which record motorways, shops and even quite modest homes. Children are therefore quite familiar with video as a medium, and often well able to manipulate equipment at home to record or play favourite programmes, films or family videos.

Encouraging critical use of video in school is not easy, although it has been observed that active involvement in producing programmes helps children to articulate and develop their understanding of how it works. Programmes which show the out-takes (e.g.

hilarious incidents of emus biting cameras), also demonstrate the role of the editor in the process of making dramas, documentaries and news programmes.

Making videos in school requires children to understand and become familiar with the technology. The teacher needs to be very clear about the learning intentions for the work, which parallel those outlined above for still photography. The equipment is much heavier and more expensive than cameras, so health and safety considerations must be rigorously observed. A tripod is essential for camcorder use.

The video camera in school can become a worthwhile tool for evaluation, for instance when children are preparing for a performance. This might be for a short presentation of work to the class, or a more ambitious parents' event. If possible, set up a tripod and record children at work occasionally, to share the making process with class colleagues, and so that children can experience the dual aspects of being both creator and presenter.

Animation

This type of film is probably familiar to most children through cartoon films, advertisements and sequences within conventional films such as Pink Panther movies. Time-consuming and costly to produce, nonetheless primary school children can achieve simple animation by using the photocopier. Although computer graphics are the mainstay of professional animators these days, some studios retain the image-by-image photograph or celluloid transparency to make animated cartoons.

Perhaps the simplest way to achieve animation is on the overhead projector, where a basic image, for instance of an animal's body, can be overlaid with transparencies depicting a progressively longer tail, or the top transparency can be manipulated by the operator to make the tail move on the screen. Once the technique has been demonstrated to children, they are able to use the idea to great advantage in story illustration, often using conventions of classic cartoonists as models for their work.

Multiple copies of a basic image can be copied, e.g. a torso without arms or legs, to which can be added the limbs in movement sequence, image by image. Pasted into a book or stapled together, the images make a simple flick book, which, when pages are viewed in rapid succession, gives an impression of movement.

THE CROSS-CURRICULAR POTENTIAL OF STILL AND MOVING PHOTOGRAPHY

English

- The use of photographs in illustrating literature.
- The use of photographs as starting points for discussion or writing.
- Creating narrative histories, e.g. photographs of family events such as weddings, anniversaries, holidays.
- Media studies.

Science

- The study of light.
- Obtaining and considering scientific evidence.

Information and Communications Technology

- Work on photographic imaging where technology is available.
- Using the computer to generate text to accompany photographic images.

Design Technology

- Studying products and their applications.
- Planning how to use materials, equipment and processes, for focused practical tasks.

Geography

- Using photographs as secondary sources to obtain geographical information;
- Collecting geographical evidence photographically.

History

- Investigating different interpretations of history through the way it is represented photographically.
- Historical enquiry from photographic resources.
- The history of photography and the way it has influenced and been influenced by the work of artists.

Physical Education

- Taking still or moving photographs, including outdoor and swimming lessons, to record the body movements and sequences for later discussion in class and as possible reference for drawings or paintings.

Religious Education

- Using photographs as sources of information about different religious practices.
- Photographs as starting points for discussion or writing around a theme.

THE BASIC ELEMENTS OF ART IN PHOTOGRAPHY

Pattern

Recording patterns in natural objects or geographical features, such as on coral or a shell, on water or a cloud formation, helps children to focus, first while taking and framing the image, and later when it is printed, because they have an association and relationship with both the object and the image they have made of it.

Colour

The type of film and the camera used generally dictates the quality of colour in the photographs or film produced in primary school. Experiments with varying exposure times and different filters are usually not appropriate for primary children. However, colour can become a focus if children are asked to select or construct a composition with a particular emphasis or theme based on colour and colour combinations.

Tone

This can be explored through the use of black and white film in particular. With colour film, recording in photography an example of, for instance, a still life arrangement, then photocopying it in black and white, can help children identify how tonal values work. (It is quite important they go through the process themselves, so they are aware of the original, the colour representation and the photocopy.)

ARTISTS WHO USE PHOTOGRAPHY

> A distinction may be made between works of art created before and after the advent of photography. Prior to the camera, artists commissioned to produce a 'likeness', or naturalistic representation of a person or place, were reliant on accurate observation and 'photographic memory' of their subjects, noting details meticulously in sketchbooks.   (Peter 1996)

The work of artists who use photographic images or processes may be less familiar to children in primary school. However, many artists currently use them in their work, and some photographers view their work as being very much in the fine arts tradition. There are many ways of using photographic processes in art making, too many to list here, but the following suggestions provide a starting point for further consideration:

- Using photographs to construct visual images, in combination with collage or montage techniques, or even the use of photocopier and fax reproductions, as with Hockney's more recent work.
- Manipulating or distorting photographic images, to obtain unusual visual effects, as employed by Scarfe and Steadman.
- Using materials such as light sensitive paper to create image, tone or texture.
- Using photographs to make a permanent record of temporary structures, such as the work of Goldsworthy and Long, artists who create sculptures that by the nature of their construction, their situation or the material from which they have been made, are temporary; further photographs can exploit the different effects caused by contrasting weather conditions or variations in light.
- Using photographs to document the process of making art.
- Taking photographs as a personal response to experiences or situation.
- Using photography within printmaking, such as photographic screen-making.

Figure 6.1 *Keep Out of Reach (1998)*. Photograph by Kamina Walton. Size (of container): 15 cm high

- Using photographs to document a process, event or state, such as self-portrait images, the progress of a train or other vehicle.
- Using photographs as visual resources or memory prompts, to support developing ideas and work, as a substitute or accompaniment to the sketchbook.
- Using photographs scanned on to the computer screen as a basis for composite images.

All this provides a rich background of experience and exciting new possibilities for classroom work in photography. The development of sophisticated graphics computer technology has provided unlimited opportunities for artists, as touched on in the previous chapter. The use of video is now almost universal, and the moving image is more and more dominating the modern art scene, in lieu of, and complementary to, more conventional static 2D and 3D work.

Historically, there are also famous photographers such as Beaton, whose work provides an indication of the values and attitudes of his time. Children today will be very familiar with the concept of the papparazzi, and can discuss the ethical issues involved in photographing famous or ordinary people without their consent. There is also an issue of whether or not 'the camera never lies', a challenge older children might take up with some interest, given a task to prove that perhaps it can.

Bookshops, particularly second-hand ones, often have bargain books with photographs around a particular theme. Among our collection are books containing stunning photographs of black American women who have impacted on the development of the country, American Indians photographed earlier in the century, fashion photographs, travel books about particular countries or cities, etc. Such books may inspire an illustrated guide to the school, its locality or the local town or city.

Fine artists have been using, manipulating and distorting the photographic image for decades, perhaps most notably Warhol, whose photographic screenprints of multiple images of Marilyn Monroe (1967) emphasised the packaging of a screen icon. In the fifties, Blake and Hamilton also used photographic collages to depict symbols of the decade, which may interest older children studying the fifties as part of a history theme. Other artists who worked in this way are Schwitters and Hausmann, whose work is challenging and disturbing and cynical. It may be useful to look at these artists when working with children on a photo-montage task, described below.

Where the moving image is concerned, most children are more than familiar with movies, cartoons and film drama, through cinema, video and television viewing. Encouraging an understanding of different genres and their purposes is arguably as important as the parallel work with books. To do justice to this aspect of photography in education would take a tome larger than this, but a beginning might be made through discussing films and television programmes in terms of the creators, such as the writers, designers, producers, special effects departments and their work, as well as dwelling on the content, storylines, etc. Television programmes about how films are made, for instance *ET* and the work of Disney, may be useful for children to view.

The more children understand about the intentions and skills of professional photography and the many genres it embraces, the better they are able to judge their own work critically, and the better they can appreciate its potentials and limitations.

CURRICULUM PLANNING

There are of course financial and resource implications when planning a curriculum for photography; take account of the equipment available in school and the ongoing cost of processing. The following activities are for use with standard technology. Where schools have access to more sophisticated equipment, e.g. polaroid or digital cameras, most can be adapted to suit. They all acknowledge the fact that most children will have taken photographs themselves or know how it is done.

SUGGESTED CLASSROOM ACTIVITIES

Still photography

Although familiar from family photographs and commercial photography in advertising, commercial portraiture (passport or school photographs), medical photographs such as x-rays, illustrations in fiction and non-fiction books, news and sport, children still benefit from a step-by-step approach to the skills and techniques available, and from adopting a critical attitude to their own work. The first step is to introduce the camera, exaplaining to the children that a photographer must:

- get used to the restricted view seen through the lens;
- decide on the best distance away from the subject, moving in closer, moving farther away;
- stand still and hold the camera steadily.

This leads on to exploration of the use of a viewfinder, (already in regular classroom use to support compositional work in painting, drawing and printmaking), to identify possible shots in a selected area. Children can be asked to:

- make quick sketches of the area defined by viewfinder;
- use a camera without the film to practice pointing and standing still.

Extending first experiences will involve:

- taking long shots and close-ups of detail;
- developing a critical approach to own photography;
- evaluation of the photographs of others to improve own technique.

Other possibilities at this stage might be: photographing areas of a display, e.g. a display of teddy-bears. Choose to take a picture of a favourite bear or the best bit of a particular teddy; photograph a familiar or favourite part of the classroom or school; select a subject for a photograph, such as a playground feature, and take photographs of it from different distances and angles, perhaps measured out in advance, e.g. from the front, sides and back at distances of 5, 10, 15 and 20 metres. When these are processed, discuss them and select 'best' examples. Give reasons for your choices.

Further development

- Look at a group of photographs on a theme: holiday snaps, family portraits or groups, news pictures etc. Discuss, evaluate and select the best, giving a rationale for the choice.
- Take a series of bad photographs with a chosen focus.

Further projects using still photography

The immediate environment

- Look at a collection of about ten photographs of school to identify the position and angle of the photographer. These can focus on particular aspects of building to be used in another curriculum area, e.g. building materials, doors or windows. Discuss and evaluate the photos and choose the best, according to your criteria.
- Discuss how photographs of school can be used, e.g. as illustrations for a school booklet, or to accompany an application for funding to decorate areas of dilapidation in school buildings. How might these two aims affect the types of photographs taken? Groups can work on either brief, and later compare and contrast how they managed to take images of the same place to make it look very good or drastically in need of repair, according to the intended audience. What criteria did they use to select location, camera angle, framing etc.? What did they choose to leave out?
- Plan, take photographs for, and make a panoramic montage of the school for display in the school entrance hall. Remember what is at one side of the viewfinder for each photograph when you take the next one, so the photographs will join together.
- Decide to record a particular time, for instance between 9am and 10am in the morning, so you get shots of everything that happens during this time. Or, take shots every 20 minutes or so in a given location, such as the school hall or the classroom. This gives an idea of the school activity, the children's work at different times of day, or whatever other priority you set for the decisions about what to photograph and when.
- Think about what you see when you come into the school. From outside the main entrance to the classroom, there are different points of view, and different objects and landmarks which attract attention. Take photographs to represent these, and decide why they are significant. Then think about anything you might like to change.
- At playtime, take photographs of different parts of the playground as children play. Then sort the images and arrange them to make a picture of playtime. What does the picture not include? How might you use other media to include things you have left out?
- Dress up and pose for a sequence of photographs illustrating a story set in the school.

Taking photographs in different conditions can enhance children's understanding of shades and tones, light sources and other conventional qualities of 2D work. The following suggestion may help them to appreciate these qualities, not only in photography, but also in drawing and painting.

- Set up an arrangement of objects, on a table with a light cover, by a window, and a camera on a tripod facing the window. Set the 'distance' control on the camera and take a photograph. Then, take a further series of photographs, as follows:
    - hold an opaque white sheet of card or cloth in front of the window as a background;
    - substitute a black sheet of card or cloth in front of the window;
    - substitute a net curtain, or other translucent material, in front of the window;
    - change the white cloth on the table to a dark one and take the same series as above.

Then, move the camera and tripod to the side of the arrangement, so the light from the window is to the side of the camera. Take a similar series of photographs. Place a strong light (the overhead projector may be ideal) on one side of the arrangement and photograph, then take another shot with the light on the other side.

When the photographs have been developed, place them in order of best to worst, and identify which conditions were best to photograph the arrangement. (Using a child as a model may be easier to organise, draping dark or light cloths over the shoulder.)

Portrait and portrait studies

Self-portrait

- Study of a set of studio portrait photographs from a range of historical periods and cultural backgrounds. Discuss the aim of the photographer, the setting, facial expression and pose and the impression of personality or self (see Figure 6.4).
- Scrutinise a further set, showing people in an outdoor setting. Discuss as before. Select favourite photographs, group them, and justify your choices.
- Plan a studio self-portrait. Decide on detail that will communicate information about interests, hobbies, personality, etc., such as clothing to be worn, setting, props, pose and expression. This might be 'as I am', 'as I will be', or 'as I want to be'. Photocopies of the portraits can be modified with colour and drawing (graffiti), to change or improve the original image.

- Arrange for a friend to take photograph. After processing, discuss and evaluate the result, according to which aspects you think are like you, which might be more flattering, and how the camera angle, focal distance or setting might be changed to make it more satisfactory. Then adjust and modify the setting, the pose or the camera angle, and take another photograph.
- Try the same procedure, but with the intention of creating a portrait that misleads the viewer, giving a completely inaccurate impression of the subject. How does the way you use the camera influence the portrait?

Figure 6.4 *Me. Excited*. Photocopied photograph reworked in collage and felt-tipped pens by an eight year old.

Portraits of others

- Plan a montage portrait of a friend. The montage can include a range of photographic images and other visual material that conveys information about the personality, interests, skills, enthusiasms, preferences (music, food, clothes) and possessions of your friend. Look at the work of artists who have used this approach, such as Hockney. Search out photographs that you can use from wherever you can find them, and arrange to take photographs yourself of anything else you need.
- Find a series of portraits of a favourite popstar, sports personality or other famous person. Look at the portraits, and decide what characteristics they show. Group the photographs according to your own criteria. How does this study help you to make your own photographs?
- An extension of this may be to use newspapers. On a day when a particular person, perhaps the Prime Minister or a show-biz personality, is making headlines, look at how the different newspapers illustrate the stories. They might use the same photograph, or different angles and shots by different photographers. Why did the editor choose one photograph and not another? Are all the images flattering? How do the images match with the way the story is told in the paper?

- Children themselves might take the photographs for the school entrance. As part of a project on the school, they could include familiar school visitors such as local religious representatives and others associated with the school, like the swimming pool instructors. Each portrait can be planned to illustrate the relationship of the individual with the school, and highlight traditional aspects of portraiture within particular settings.

Photo-montage

- Collect photographs from magazines and papers on a particular theme e.g. portraits, faces or individual features; a particular colour range; feathers; leaves. If possible, arrange to take additional photographs you need for the final montage. Cut, arrange and mount on a background, to create an exotic and complex image.
- Make an impossible picture using photographs of people and objects of different scales and sizes, e.g. a car in a tree, a child carrying a house, a montage using a child's own picture surrounded by favourite pop and television personalities. Such images are popular in advertising features, and a collection of these can inspire subjects and arrangements. The use of strange juxtapositions of objects and people featured in much 'surrealist' work, the humour (if not the full significance) of which invariably appeals to children.

Using light sensitive paper

To use this technique, a darkroom or temporary substitute is necessary, and some knowledge of how to process. The teacher needs to be familiar with this process, and the chemicals used must be handled with extreme caution, especially if children are present when the actual processing is done. A friendly photographer may well be prepared to help introduce this technique to children. First experimental images can be followed up with more carefully composed and arranged compositions, to extend the children's understanding and control of the medium.

- An otherwise completely blacked-out room is lit by a red photographic light to enable you to see what you are doing.
- Photographic, light-sensitive, paper is used, opened from its packaging in the light-safe environment.
- Objects are arranged on the paper, such as natural objects, pieces of paper or even a hand, and the paper is briefly exposed to full light (ie. the normal light of a room, or a light bulb).
- Once exposed, the paper is processed, fixed and washed in the usual way for prints obtained from negatives.

Work based on artists' approaches to photography

- Study the work of Goldsworthy and Long. Using natural materials, design a similar, temporary, work to emphasise their characteristics, surface texture and colour. Make the design and take photographs.

Film: moving photography

Through television and visiting the cinema children will have watched news reports, documentaries, animation and fictional narratives. They may have personal experience of using video camera. The immediacy of the video, both for making and for watching films more than once, means children can respond, evaluate and modify their efforts with comparative ease once they are familiar with the technology. A colleague gets the children to draw the camcorder on its tripod with an operator. The close scrutiny necessary for accurate drawing helps children to notice and identify the different controls and their functions as they record them on paper. Children need to try:

- using a video camera without film to practise manipulation and operation;
- getting used to holding the camera and moving it steadily;
- getting used to the restricted view seen through the lens;
- using facilities, operating zoom.

First experiences will also involve taking long shots and close-ups, and evaluation of their own and others' photographs to improve technique. The children may then:

- Make a series of sketches with the video, trying out the different controls, such as zoom, and seeing how well close-up shots work. This will almost certainly be a fun session, when children play up to the camera, and enjoy posing, no matter how familiar they are with the camcorder's use in other settings. View the film immediately, at least once for fun and then several times to make notes of different technical aspects, such as how steady the operator is in achieving zoom or close-up, how well particular sequences are framed, how the sound affects the image and vice versa, and other features identified in the pre-film discussion.
- Record on video a short television advertisement, or the introductory sequence for a familiar programme (such as an Australian soap) to view with the children. Ask them to represent it in storyboard form, to help them appreciate how planning decisions are made, and to help their awareness of well-known conventions in making video sequences, such as how the product name is highlighted, or how characters are introduced in a setting appropriate to their roles in the drama. Children can then develop these ideas through, for instance, making a video short to introduce themselves, or as a promotion for a product they know, or to communicate a strongly held opinion they want to put across, such as keeping the playground litter-free.
- Make a short video film to introduce the classroom to a new child. Make a storyboard to prepare for taking the video, and work out roles within the group. View the product immediately, and evaluate according to the aims for the video: does it do its job? If possible, retake the video, taking account of points raised during evaluation, and implement improvements suggested.
- Plan and shoot a short film using a video camera with the sound switched off. (See also ideas in the chapter on collage.)

CHAPTER 7

Bookmaking

Figure 7.1 *Rabbits.* Sewn book with block-printed cover, designed and made by a ten year old. Size: 45 × 45 cm

The history of books and bookmaking reflects social and political history: the publication of the first Bible, and the burning of books at various times were significant political acts. Almost any local museum will have examples of ancient books, illuminated manuscripts being part not only of Western European traditions but also of the Middle and Far East. Calligraphy as an artform is a subject we do not cover in this book, but teachers have ready access to information from any local stationery store, where calligraphy pens come complete with instructions on how to make beautiful letters with exotic inks.

Bookmaking has a very special place in the primary classroom, from the basic stapled pages of a first storybook, to well crafted and designed books that are themselves works of art. Children can be led to examine the nature of books through a display of different types, especially very old books for children with engraved illustrations and beautiful frontispieces. If parents are asked to bring a special book for a display, the resultant temporary collection may include examples of precious photograph albums, a school prize, a Mills and Boon story, old sets of encyclopedias, a tiny hymnal, or even an old school textbook or copybook. These can inspire children's own designs, and give an added dimension to the concept of 'book'. A bookmaker or binder may be able to bring and show examples of the many types of binding, papers and endpapers, spines and covers.

Books, files and folders are part of everyday classroom life, e.g.:

- individual story or topic books written by children;
- story books written by groups of children working together;
- anthologies of children's prose or poetry;
- collections of work arising from a topic or theme;
- books to record trips in photographs, paintings, drawings, written work etc.;
- albums of photographs.

Commercially produced scrapbooks, folders and files are cheap and effective to use. Plastic binders are a good way to present collections of children's work, either as individual pockets or actual books made from bound pockets, now available in sizes up to A1. Other available binding processes include plastic strips, old-fashioned file strings with metal tags (treasury tags), metal rings (rather like key rings), staples, split pins, and spiral binding machines. Zig-zag books stand up easily for display purposes (as in Figure 7.2).

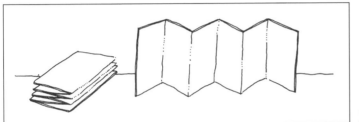

Figure 7.2 Zig-zag book

Hand-made books are easily made, inexpensive, attractive and always much valued by the children. Book-making offers children the experience of:

- following a sequenced process, through verbal and written instructions, leading to an end product;
- finding out about the qualities of different materials, card, paper, adhesives;
- measuring and cutting out accurately;
- designing, planning, organising, taking decisions and making choices;
- working collaboratively;
- considering illustration and decoration;
- scrutinising the format, layout, design of published books;
- making an item that gives pleasure and status to the bookmaker and in consequence raises self-esteem.

THE CROSS-CURRICULAR POTENTIAL OF BOOKMAKING

English

- Appreciating the nature of the book and its conventions, such as cover, layout, author and illustrator information, blurb etc.
- Recognition of different types of books for different purposes, such as story, information, reference books etc.

Mathematics

- Estimating, calculating and measuring components for the book and its covers.
- Deciding on overall shapes and appropriate proportions for the pages and covers.

Information and Communications Technology

- Possible use of computer generated prints for endpapers.
- Use of computer print in special scripts for titles and contents lists.
- For older children, using data processing to make index pages for topic books.
- Research for information about books and bookmakers.

Design Technology

- Designing bookjackets to conform to conventions of commercial publishing.
- Examining different types of books to see how they are made, bound and presented.
- Looking at different materials used for special books, such as rag and card books for babies, photograph albums with protective interleaves, special bindings for sacred texts used in worship.

Geography

- Studying formats and materials used for different types of books in different parts of the world, e.g. how some books read from back to front or from top to bottom (from the Western point of view).
- Using and studying books from other parts of the world, such as storybooks for children from the place currently being studied.

History

- Study of the history of the book and its significance within different cultures.
- Comparisons between books today and those of the period being studied, e.g. illustrations and layout of children's books from the Victorian era, tablets of ancient Greece, or papyrus in ancient Egypt, and of different bookmaking techniques and materials used.

THE ELEMENTS OF ART IN BOOKMAKING

Almost all the elements of art, colour, texture, form etc., are criteria for decision-making and choices for children regarding, for instance, the texture, colours and shapes of paper and card, types of threads, if used, and other binding materials, as well as the combinations of cards and papers used for covers, pages, endpieces and spines. There are many similarities between making books and following procedures for making other artifacts, as outlined in the chapters on collage and sculpture.

ARTISTS WHO MAKE BOOKS

Artists have their work published in books, and some have, like Hirst recently, published a limited edition of a special volume that not only illustrates work, but is also regarded as an artwork in its own right. There is also a tradition of hand-made one-off books as works of art, of all sizes and shapes, made with many different materials, and bound in various ingenious ways. The format of the books themselves can make particular statements about their contents which may be purely visual and/or text-related. For instance, a heavy wooden book with a studded leather spine and a padlock closure contained images related to imprisonment; a white book of hand-made paper, delicately sewn with silver metallic thread, opened up to make a box, with beautifully calligraphed poems in metallic ink on each face, and which contained icons related to the text.

Like puppets, masks and other cultural artifacts, the book has its own distinct and fascinating history, and its development in different cultures reflects the time, place, available materials and predominant values of that time and place. Bookmaking is both an art and a craft, as well as being nowadays part of our everyday lives in mass production. Books play an important part in the lives of all the children we teach, and in designing, making, embellishing and completing their own books, they acquire both valuable skills and precious artifacts.

MAKING YOUR OWN FIRST SKETCHBOOK

A first sketchbook is a treasured possession. It can be any shape or size, contain any sorts of paper (preferably plain, and of good quality), and be a posh, shop-bought artists' book or a home-made assembly. Knowing how to make books is a useful and satisfying skill (see instructions later in this chapter). On the other hand, making an instant book can be great fun and children then have a book which is indeed their very own. Have available a wide range of papers cut into similar sized pieces, such as:

- sugar paper in different colours;
- cartridge (which will be limited due to cost);
- squared paper;
- tracing paper;
- photocopy paper;
- textured paper (eg. pieces of textured wallpaper);
- brown paper.

Lay them out on a long surface for children to walk past and select. There may need to be a limit on the number of pages but the child should decide whether to have all the same or a range of different colours and textures. Also have available:

- pieces of card of appropriate size for the cover, which can be folded and stapled to hold the pages in place;
- masking tape to strengthen the spine and protect fingers from the possible ravages of staples;
- staplers and people to staple.

Once children have made the first sketchbook, and used it well, they may be able to go on to more sophisticated ways of bookmaking for future work.

Making a sewn book

The card and paper should be prepared by using the guillotine to ensure accurate edges and square corners. Your materials are:

- two stiff cards for covers
- decorated or coloured paper for covering the card covers
- paper for pages
- narrow strips of paper for reinforcing pages
- strip of bookbinders cloth or similar material.

Method

Decide on the size of your book. This will depend on what you intend to put in it, but also consider choosing a size that will fit into a large size of card without leaving unusable offcuts. Decide on the number of pages. Too many will make too bulky a book. Choose the colour and type of paper for the pages: mixed colours, white or coloured, sugar paper or cartridge etc. Then follow this procedure.

- Cut the paper for the pages in double-sized sections, not as single pages as they will be folded over during the book making process.
- Cut a 10 cm strip of paper the same length as your pages on the fold edge.
- Cut two pieces of card for the covers, slightly larger than the paper pages. Write 'spine', 'top' and 'bottom' along the correct edges of these card covers. Then measure along the edge of each cover that will be towards the spine of your book. Add 4 cm to this measurement and jot down.

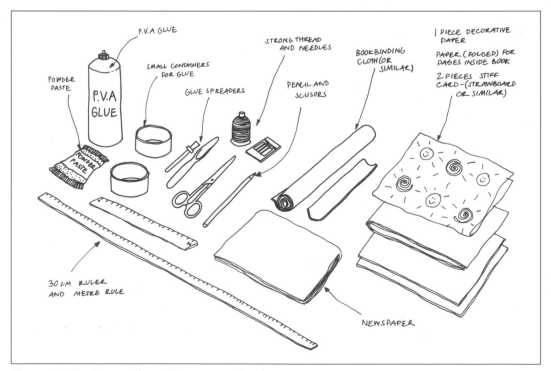

Figure 7.3 Equipment for making a sewn book

- Cut a strip of bookbinding cloth or similar material 10 cm wide and the same length that you jotted down (the length of the spine of your book plus 4 cm).
- Select some decorative paper for the covers of your book. This needs to be larger than your book covers by several cm. all round.

Work on clean newspaper. Follow the directions illustrated in Figure 7.4.

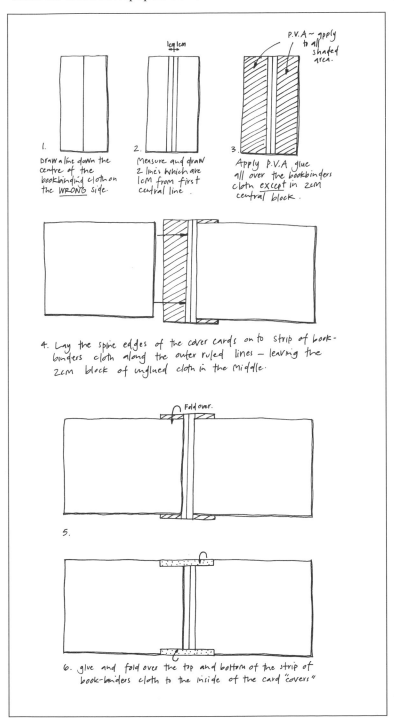

Figure 7.4 How to make a sewn book

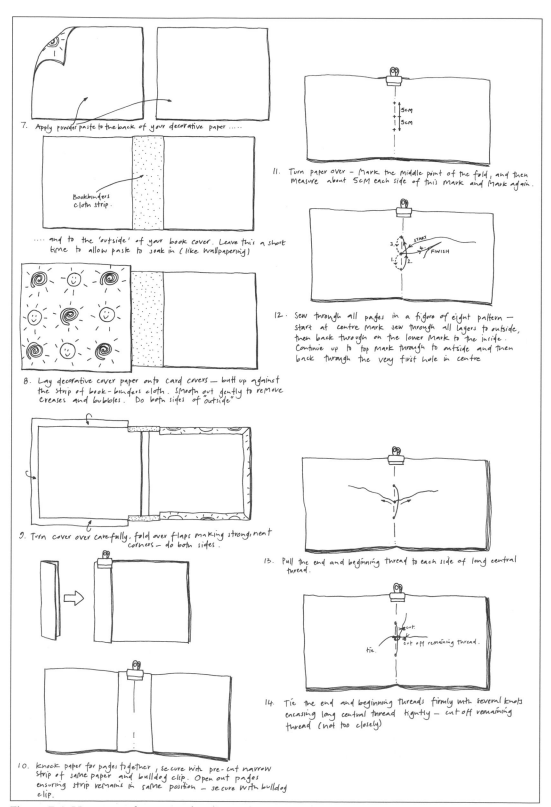

7. Apply powder paste to the back of your decorative paper .....

Bookbinders cloth strip.

..... and to the 'outside' of your book cover. Leave this a short time to allow paste to soak in (like wallpapering)

8. Lay decorative cover paper onto card covers — butt up against the strip of book-binders cloth. Smooth out gently to remove creases and bubbles. Do both sides of "outside"

9. Turn cover over carefully, fold over flaps making strong, neat corners — do both sides.

10. Knock paper for pages together, secure with pre-cut narrow strip of same paper and bulldog clip. Open out pages ensuring strip remains in same position — secure with bulldog clip.

11. Turn paper over — Mark the middle point of the fold, and then measure about 5cm each side of this Mark and Mark again.

12. Sew through all pages in a figure of eight pattern — start at centre mark sew through all layers to outside, then back through on the lower mark to the inside. Continue up to top mark through to outside and then back through the very first hole in centre

13. Pull the end and beginning thread to each side of long central thread.

14. Tie the end and beginning threads firmly with several knots encasing long central thread tightly — cut off remaining thread (not too closely)

Figure 7.4 How to make a sewn book (cont.)

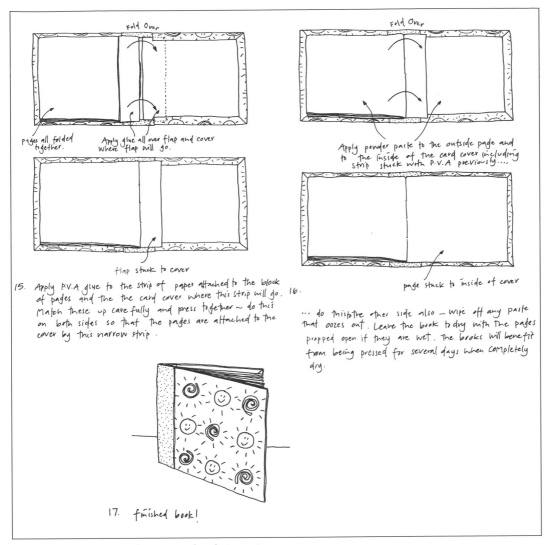

In the diagrams:

Fold Over

pages all folded together.

Apply glue all over flap and cover where flap will go.

Flap stuck to cover

15. Apply P.V.A glue to the strip of paper attached to the block of pages and the the card cover where this strip will go. Match these up carefully and press together ~ do this on both sides so that the pages are attached to the cover by this narrow strip.

Fold Over

Apply powder paste to the outside page and to the inside of the card cover including strip stuck with P.V.A previously....

page stuck to inside of cover

16. ... do this to the other side also — wipe off any paste that oozes out. Leave the book to dry with the pages propped open if they are wet. The books will benefit from being pressed for several days when completely dry.

17. finished book!

Figure 7.4 How to make a sewn book (cont.)

MAKING A BOOK AS AN ARTIFACT

Once children understand the basic methods of bookmaking, they can perhaps take a more imaginative approach to the task, by designing a book inspired by ideas of artists and designers as a major project. For this type of work, the teacher also needs to be resourceful and imaginative in the range and type of materials on offer to inspire the work, as well as on ideas to give the children as starting points. Lay out the materials and tools carefully, to enable children to select and make considered decisions, and encourage them to select what they want to use, take that back to their workspaces, and use tools and equipment provided in the same orderly way.

Almost anything that comes in fairly flat, sheet form is useful, such as plastic offcuts, plastic carrier bags opened out, balsa, thin ply, any sort of cardboard or corruflute, fabrics, papers of all types, including transparent and translucent, and natural materials which can be woven to make sheets such as grasses and reeds. Large leaves might also feature, like those from the overgrown rhubarb plant. Fabrics may be used for spines or covering, especially ones dyed by the children themselves. Offcuts from the paper cutter may inspire a long, long, thin, thin book, and the spare prints from a printmaking session can be valuably recycled for decorative finishes.

Binding materials might include rings and strings, split pins of different sizes, threads, cottons, wools, thin wire and raffia with large needles for sewing, and different types of sticky tape. Double and single hole punches, including a leather punch to make several sizes of hole, scissors or craft knives can be used to cut holes for fixing papers together.

THE JAPANESE SKETCH BOOK

For this method of making a simple book from one sheet of paper, we are indebted to a colleague. Use a large sheet of paper, preferably cartridge, strong enough to be folded as required and to be used on both sides for drawing. It needs to be minimum A4, and can be as large as A2, but it should be a standard A size. The idea is to cut and fold one piece of paper in a particular way, to work like a real book with 16 sides. Follow the directions in Figure 7.5.

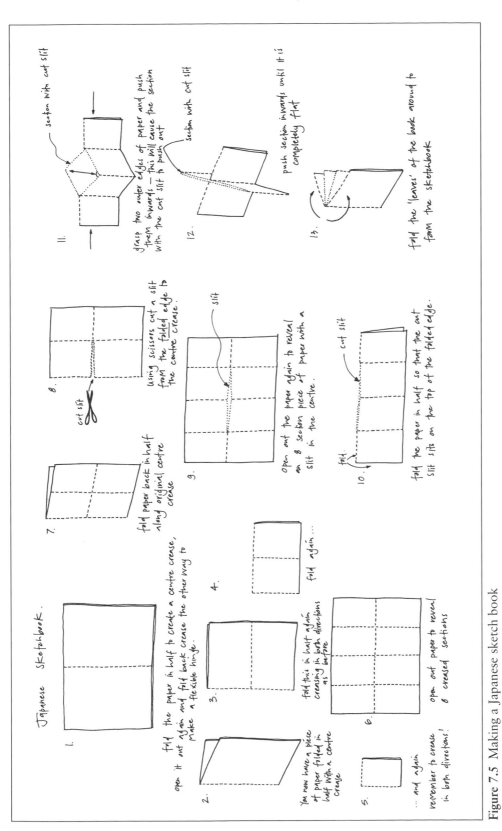

Figure 7.5 Making a Japanese sketch book

CHAPTER 8

Collage

Figure 8.1 Card and paper collage by a seven year old. Size: 15 × 10 cm

Collage involves gluing layers of material and/or paper onto a backing to make a pattern or image. It has been used by artists in many cultures, notably in Europe. In school, collage links work in 2D and 3D, in using fabrics and papers, in sculpture and, occasionally, moulding. It offers potential for the teacher and children to focus on particular skills, such as gluing and cutting, and on particular elements of art such as texture and composition. A collaged surface can be either the first stage or the finishing process for paintings, drawings, and box modelling.

Too often in schools, we see collage mosaic pieces used as a colouring-in exercise for an outline drawn by an adult. Children are merely occupied, and rarely learning. The effect may be pleasing in some respects, but children are given a message that they are not able to produce outlines of a sufficiently high quality. Perhaps this is the seedbed from which later uncertainty grows.

Stained glass windows, using black card and transparent plastic papers, are also a form of collage. If this effect is desired, try to work freely with transparent collage pieces arranged onto a white backing then apply the card over the top to give the appearance you want. It may be helpful to cut the white backing to the size of the window panes you want to cover, so children are working from the start to the exact dimensions, and the overall finish will be neater and more satisfactory. Remember to use modern examples, readily available in books about stained glass in the craft section of the local library, as well as the more traditional 'church' glass children may find familiar.

THE CROSS-CURRICULAR POTENTIAL OF COLLAGE

English

- Discussion, decision making and evaluation of the work in hand.
- Research into the subject matter of the work.

Mathematics

- Estimating area and length when cutting paper or fabrics.
- For murals and windows, calculating overall size to fit a particular space.
- The use of patterning in overall composition and in patterned papers or materials as part of the collage.
- 'Tile' arrangement, as for a patchwork or mosaic, when individual pieces of similar sizes are fixed together to make a composite piece of work.

Figure 8.2 *Flower*. Card and fabric glued collage by a seven year old. Size: 21 × 26 cm

Information and Communications Technology

- Use of collage technique with made and predetermined patterns in the graphics program memory.
- Using computer print-outs as elements of a traditional collage design.

Design Technology

- Suitable uses of glues and adhesives.
- Techniques for cutting, attaching layers, ensuring that the glue does not disfigure the surface layer.
- Use of collage or découpage techniques as a finish for constructions.

THE BASIC ELEMENTS OF ART IN COLLAGE

Texture

Each component of the collage has its own texture, so interesting contrasts can be made by juxtaposing for instance very shiny and quite matt materials, or very rough and quite smooth. Bubblewrap, plain polystyrene, crumpled tissue or the addition of glass beads, sand and seeds can add to the range of textures. Making a base layer of highly textured materials such as corrugated card, and sticking on flimsy fabric or paper can give particularly interesting, and often unexpected, textural qualities. Paper off-cuts, left-over prints and rubbings add further possibilities (see Figure 8.2). Paper can be given added relief qualities by rolling it around pencils, scoring, scrunching and tearing.

Colour

The range of colours achieved through the layering of different papers and fabrics, especially tissue, crepe and transparent plastic papers, translucent nylon, nets and fine fabrics, is vast, and can include vibrant effects not possible through the normal range of paints and inks used in primary schools.

Composition

Selecting and placing the materials in a pleasing arrangement allows children to try out different compositions for themselves, and large collaborative pieces can be worked on flat before being displayed vertically. Selecting, discarding, juxtaposing different elements within the composition, overlapping or butting contrasting materials or colours, are all part of the process of composing a whole from its components.

Shape and pattern

Each component of the collage has its own shape, and needs to be placed in relationship with others. Collages can be based on particular shapes, perhaps geometric, perhaps irregular, or a combination, to make a pattern. Fabrics can be sorted according to pattern, so the children can make informed choices about where and how to place them.

Figure 8.3 *Camouflage*. Collage with tissue paper, felt pen, pen and ink, by a group of eight year olds. Size: 54 × 36 cm

ARTISTS WHO USE COLLAGE

Many artists have used a collage or montage technique within paintings, which have the feel of being made from an assemblage of images, as well as in actual collaged work. The

Surrealists, for instance, achieved very interesting effects, making the viewer look more closely at everyday objects in unconventional surroundings. Cut-out paper shapes were perhaps most famously used by Matisse, whose bold flower shapes and body forms, and brightly coloured geometric shapes arranged in a spiral inspired by a snail's shell, have adorned many walls in reproduction. In the sixties, record covers and other art made use of cut paper techniques, familiar from the Beatles' *Sergeant Pepper* album. Artists who used photographic collages are also mentioned in the chapter on photography. Computer imaging has also offered new possibilities. Mixed media relief work is also favoured by artists and sculptors (see Figure 8.4).

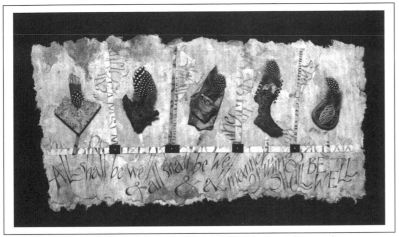

Figure 8.4 *Collage on bark paper (1996).* Mixed media work, using found objects, by Eleanor Glover. Size: 50 × 25 cm

Découpage, from the French word for cutting, was skilfully used in 18th century Europe to decorate furniture, boxes and other items. Cut-out images are pasted onto a surface, so they appear as if they are painted directly on when carefully varnished. Children can use magazine pictures, cards and catalogue photographs to make assemblages of images, colours and patterns to decorate 2D or 3D surfaces. This is quite a sophisticated technique, which requires some skill and dexterity to achieve satisfactory results.

Patchwork, quiltmaking and appliqué work associated with fabrics also have close connections with collage, although here the pieces are more likely to be sewn or embroidered in place rather than glued. Mosaic is used more often in school with paper than ceramic tiles, and therefore included here. We are familiar with the mosaics of ancient times, but they are also in everyday use on tabletops and swimming pools, and for architectural details, as in the work of Gaudi in Barcelona.

Stained glass has been used in design work for centuries, and is still a popular medium with artists. Examples of domestic use are to be found in almost every area in the U.K., in front doors and partitions. Yellow Pages list suppliers and designers, who may be able to come and talk with children about their work. Many art schools run courses, so there is another source of expertise. Books on Art Deco invariably have examples of fine work using stained glass for domestic artifacts such as bowls and vases as well as doors and windows. The more types of example children are shown, the more adventurous their work is likely to be.

ORGANISING COLLAGE IN THE CLASSROOM

The classroom comes to resemble a good haberdashery for worthwhile collage work, where children can examine, select, and test different materials for particular purposes. To build up collections requires ingenuity, resourcefulness and sheer determination, qualities which are second nature to primary teachers.

It is important to offer the children an appropriate starting point for the task, visual resources and books for research and inspiration, and varied materials, to stimulate the imagination and to develop skills during the completion of the task. There may be a temptation to over-direct the children, to encourage them to use your best idea for representing an animal's coat, or a cloudy sky. Do resist this, and leave the children scope for their own decision-making, imagination and efforts. The more varied the resources on offer, and the better they are presented, the more children will be able to surprise you with their ingenuity and creativity.

Ideas for suitable materials, glues and their storage are to be found in the chapter on sculpture and box modelling. In addition, you might offer paper and card off-cuts and samples, and magazine pages, which have a dominant colour or colours, torn to irregular shapes and stored in small boxes according to main colours. Children can also create their own textured papers, using printmaking techniques, marbling, rubbing or any processes described in the paint chapter. Children can usefully do the sorting and sifting into the boxes as a preliminary activity, considering the potential of each.

Whole-class teaching may be best for introducing ideas, the task and the materials, and to show children artists' work which depicts or communicates ideas about the topic or theme of the work.

All the suggestions below might be used for mosaic work as well as collage. Try to get children to work directly with the pieces, rather than drawing out first. Card and paper off-cuts can be torn into smaller pieces for mosaic, and each piece does not have to be a geometric square. In fact, irregular shapes often inspire a freer approach.

SMALL-SCALE WORK

Non-representational work can be inspired by abstract themes, concepts and ideas, such as colours, textures, the weather, emotions, landscape. You might try the following in an A4 or A3 format, with children working individually or in pairs.

- Use only three colours to make a composition on your page. Choose fabrics, papers, sweet wrappers or anything else you can find, but use only three colours, including the background of the work. The colours could be contrasting, like red and green, or close to each other, like orange, brown and red. If you are not sure about a particular shade, talk it over with a friend. Some reds, for instance, look very like orange, or purple, or brown. See how they look next to each other. Try not to make a picture of anything, but place the colours in an interesting and pleasing arrangement.
- Choose one of the following: trees, water, ice, earth, sky, sea, rocks. Make a collage using a limited range of colours to give an impression of the title. Look at photographs and other artists' work to inspire you before you start, especially when you are decid-

ing which colours and textures to use. For example, the earth is not always green or brown, and the sea is only blue when it reflects a blue sky. So you do not have to stick to the usual colours. Be adventurous, and use colours you feel are right for the impression you are trying to create.

- Imagine you are looking through a window at a favourite place, or use a photograph to remind you of a holiday, a visit or another view that inspired you. Choose materials to depict the elements of the view, and then make it look as you would like to remember it. Many artists have used a 'through the window' device to make paintings and drawings, because the frame and the light make interesting effects. Look at some of these paintings or photographs before you begin to work on your collage, to get some ideas which may help you with designing your own view.

- Try at home, with your family, to make a patterned collage using bits and pieces from around the house that can be spared, like bits of washing up cloths, green scrubbers, food packaging, paper towels. Be sure to ask permission before you cut or use anything. Spread out the stuff you have collected, and see what sort of ideas you get for making the arrangement. Then glue it down, or bring it all to school to use in a collage session.

LARGER PROJECTS

Collage self-portrait

The tradition of portrait-painting as a representation not only of the physical features but also as a record of character, past achievement and future hopes, is well established through work over centuries in Western and Eastern art. Many artists use their work to explore personal themes, and, like some novelists and poets, draw on autobiographical events to inform their art. This type of task is very appropriate for a class working on biography or autobiography as a genre in English, an 'ourselves' project, or a study of the work of particular famous people in history, geography or religious education.

Children too use personal experience to inform stories and drama, and at its extreme, art therapy encourages the use of graphic representations of self and experiences as a vehicle for exploring feelings, events and influences on patients' lives. It is appropriate here to state very firmly that therapy is a professional area on which primary teachers impinge not only at their own peril but, more importantly, at severe risk of endangering the pupils they seek to help. If a child seems to display inappropriate behaviour, e.g. obsessive or destructive tendencies, during an art-making session, the teacher's duty is to refer to an appropriate agency, not to try to provide classroom therapy.

Displays of artists' self-portraits can include postcards and books about artists and their work. Portraits of others by artists can promote discussion about the nature of portrait and of self-portrait. The word means self portrayal, or an image of oneself, which can be almost anything the self-portraitist wants it to be. It may be in everyday mode, dressed up for an occasion, or in a fantasy role. Children can decide why the artists chose to depict themselves in particular ways, what clues there are as to character, hopes, ideas and self-image through the clothes, the setting and the props included.

Children can also look at the many different approaches to portraiture, including photographs of themselves and of family occasions. Using any historical family portraits, of grandparents or earlier generations will offer many clues about how the notion of portrait has changed, particularly since the advent of photography.

Portraits made of others, notably Van Eyck's *The Arnolfini Marriage*, group portraits by Rembrandt, various royal portraits through the ages, also offer insights into how artists have composed, selected and included or excluded items related to the character or characters depicted. Settings also provide clues as to the lifestyles, habits, concerns and interests of the person depicted.

Over a period, children may collect together examples of objects or illustrations which they feel are of significance to them personally. Then, using a mirror and making as many sketches as they can of themselves from different angles, they may gradually piece together the elements of a composition which will be a self-portrait.

A sketchbook can be used to record significant events and ideas over a period of time. This cannot be an 'instant' session, since it requires considerable reflection, discussion, collection of 2D items or sketching of 3D items of value, mementos or photographs. A letter home to explain the project is helpful, so that a precious family photograph does not get spoiled in the enthusiasm.

Here is an opportunity to explore the notion of personal research as a major factor in the 'artistic process'. Children may collect items such as:

- photocopies or original photographs of themselves at different times in their lives;
- photographs of important people in their lives, family, friends, television personalities or pop stars;
- mementos like tickets to a theme park, bus or air tickets for significant journeys;
- packaging of favourite foods, or the inevitable McDonald's souvenir;
- birthday, feast day or other cards from special occasions;
- pictures of pets past and present;
- dried flowers or leaves from a special place;
- scraps of fabric from once-favourite clothes;
- historic pictures of important family occasions;
- postcards of special places;
- covers of favourite magazines or books, photocopies;
- items from magazines about favourite television programmes.

These can be stored in wallets for sifting and arranging later. They could also be used to illustrate a written autobiography, but in this case we consider the visual self-portrait. This may be organised chronologically, or not, but a process of selection is needed, to prioritise which items can be fitted usefully into the given area of paper or card. The arrangement might be tried out on the photocopier first.

Children can also photocopy and then adapt a picture of themselves, to have new clothes, or to superimpose visual representations of their wishes and dreams. (Further references to these ideas are in the chapter on photography.)

Evaluation

How do people who do not know the subject well interpret the picture? How well have children managed to prioritise and arrange their resources? How does the composition work? Have they been able to use ideas garnered from looking at artists' work? How well does the finished picture fulfil the original brief?

The teacher and the pupils need to decide how to present the final pieces. If they are large, it may be appropriate to display a few at a time, as they are finished. Certainly such work provides plenty of opportunity for class discussions, and offers much insight for family members who come to call.

Friezes

Current topic work may be depicted in a large collaborative class frieze. If this is about the Egyptians or Greeks, for example, children can study and analyse examples of the art of the time and place, and consider the pigments, compositions and conditions under which the originals were made. Ancient Egyptians, for instance, worked crouched in very small caverns on occasions, using only light reflected from outside through a series of mirrors.

The composition of large friezes needs careful consideration of the size and scale of items to be placed on the finished piece. An overhead projector can be used to help place elements of the design together.

The first layer of colour may be with paint, using large applicators to give a thin layer over the entire surface, after which a collaged layer can be applied to the dry paint with pva glue. More ideas are given in the painting chapter for additives to paint which may enhance the textural qualities of the finished piece.

Large-scale collages depicting people

Teachers sometimes are tempted to draw outlines for children particularly when the scale is larger than they feel children can cope with. In this case, we may be forgiven for breaking the 'no template' rule in art education: children themselves become templates.

In movement, dance or drama sessions, children explore and experiment with the shapes and limits of their body movements. These can be linked with the topic in hand, e.g. during warm-up, they can imitate rich Victorian ladies wearing constricting skirts and corsets, or less affluent traders carrying loads on their heads.

Such moments can later be frozen, as a child lies on a large piece of paper, and other children draw around the outline made as the basis for a painted or collaged composition. The way the body is arranged on the paper is itself an exercise in composition; limbs and head may be moved to a central, or not so central, position.

Another way of making large-scale work from small beginnings is to trace or photocopy a sketch onto an OHP transparency which is projected onto a large piece of paper taped to a wall. Adjust the focal length until the sketch is the right size, then trace the outline directly on to the paper. The children's own work is then the basis for the composition. This also works with silhouettes of complete children, such as heads in profile. The same technique can be used with a slide projector, for example using photographs taken of a local street or a particular building. Such processes are often used by artists, notably for theatrical sets when small-scale designs need to be interpreted in very large formats.

At this stage, it is helpful to pin the drawing on a wall or lay it on the floor to discuss. It needs to be looked at from a distance. Decisions can be made about what else will be included in the final picture, how the person will be dressed, what the background colours and textures may be.

Figure 8.5 *Tiger*. Tissue paper and sugar paper collage by a seven year old. Size: 46 × 36 cm

Children can use skills previously learned about mixing large quantities of paint, and a range of exciting large applicators such as foam sponges attached to sticks with an elastic band, painter-decorators' brushes and rollers etc., quickly to achieve an overall colour base to the collage.

CHAPTER 9

Sculpture and Box Modelling

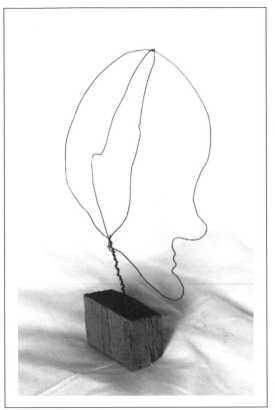

Figure 9.1 *Head*. Sculpture in wire and wood by a student. Size: 20 cm diameter

Children can learn about three-dimensional construction and building, sculpture and modelling through art, craft, design technology, science or mathematics. This chapter can be used in conjunction with those on modelling, collage and clay, since many of the principles outlined apply equally across relief and 3D work. Objectives of teaching 3D construction and modelling were usefully outlined by the Arts in School Project Team (1990):

- to increase awareness of tactile sensations;
- to develop awareness of texture, shape, scale and size;
- to develop manipulative skills;
- to develop a sense of spatial awareness;
- to work cooperatively;
- to encourage language development;
- to encourage an element of problem-solving;
- to encourage children to express emotions in a creative sense;
- to enrich visual and tactile awareness.

Sculpture and modelling of all types involve consideration of the piece in the round; children need to see, feel and experience 3D art and artifacts. However, we must not forget that children have lived in three dimensions since birth, and that learning takes place from initial sensory explorations from which abstract concepts are formed. They know that some things are rigid, some flexible. They know that it is possible to change the form and shape of solid things, objects and artifacts.

Sculpture is concerned with building; selected components are put together and joined firmly to make a new form. Sculpture is also be created through a process of demolition; a block of material is transformed by cutting away or carving. Children learn to distinguish between basic form and its surface decoration; between loadbearing components and superficial details. As with all areas of art and design, experimentation is vital, so children learn potential solutions to design problems. Making art involves the selection and choice of what is useful and relevant from the range of ideas presented or discovered.

The value of sketchbooks becomes very apparent, even in the early years. Children can make notes of research, sketch from life or freeze frame video, collect images and gather ideas which may (or may not) inform the final piece, such as observational drawings from different angles.

THE CROSS-CURRICULAR POTENTIAL OF 3D WORK

Each topic or theme within the National Curriculum boundaries has its own conventions, history, cross-cultural implications and potential for ingenuity and creativity. The following list indicates the range of artifacts which may be the products of work described in this and other, related chapters:

- sculptures representing 'abstract' concepts or real people or artifacts
- masks and puppets
- costumes
- hats
- crowns
- carnival and theatre designs
- body adornment
- shields
- kites

- bridges
- dolls' houses
- animal models
- architectural models
- rooms in boxes
- geographical models
- pop-up cards
- musical instruments
- mathematical models (eg. nets).

Here is a real interface between art, craft, design technology, science and maths, together with English, in articulating the aims, discussing possibilities, describing processes and using reference texts. Time is the most limited resource at the teacher's disposal, but the potential for true cross-curricular learning means that at different stages of the project, different subjects will be highlighted. It is up to the teacher to make explicit, in planning and to the children in introductory sessions, the range of skills and knowledge they are gaining, developing, consolidating and applying.

Much 3D construction work in the primary school is linked to a current project or topic, often located in a particular geographical or historical setting. Maps of different scales, for different purposes, topographical maps, weather maps, tourist maps, local road maps, and in different formats fold-up, pop-up, atlases, are fascinating, and encourage children to seek information in different ways. Maps provide visually recorded information, and children can find out about the climate, landscape and location of monuments, castles, etc. from good maps. This enhances the research process, since architecture, cultural artifacts and items of daily use are almost always products of the time and place in which they are made: an important concept for children to grasp. (Maps can also provide direct inspiration for design work, especially in collage.)

THE ELEMENTS OF ART IN BOX MODELLING AND SCULPTURE

Form

In sorting, classifying and selecting materials, children consider form and its elements. In deciding to modify, cut, tear or carve boxes, tubes or corks, children work out through hypothesis, trial and error how components will fit together. They also need to work out how to fix the structure to serve its purpose.

Colour

Applying or using colour in 3D construction work consolidates ideas and skills developed through painting, collaging and other media. Colour in 3D works in some ways very differently from 2D: the way light falls on different faces will affect its appearance and tones. Colour may be intrinsic in the building process, if coloured materials are used. Or, it may be applied with paint or decorative finish materials once the basic structure has been completed. These options will influence the choices made throughout the construction process.

Texture and pattern

Deciding how to achieve particular finishes requires knowledge and understanding of how texture and patterns work when viewed from different angles. Ingenuity is a great asset; texture can be achieved with paper confetti, sawdust, sand etc.

USING THE WORK OF ARTISTS, DESIGNERS AND CRAFTSPERSONS

Craftspersons, designers, sculptors and artists from many cultures and in many traditions have used the principle of building up and cutting away to make artifacts (see Figure 9.2). Sculptors Paolozzi and Picasso have been influenced by the work of artists and craftspersons such as North American Indians, Inuits, Australian Aboriginals and Africans. Children can begin to appreciate ideas and principles represented in such sculptures and artifacts. There is little to be derived, however, from just copying them.

Makers of museum dioramas, dolls' houses, model railways, theatre set and costume designers, carnival costume-makers, puppeteers, milliners, jewellers and others employ the skills of the box modeller in their work. A feel for materials, an understanding of their potential uses, and above all an ability to improvise and to 'see one thing in another' are evident in the work of accomplished practitioners.

Sculpture trails have been erected in both urban and rural settings, and provide fine examples of modern sculptures at first hand.

Architects such as Aalto, Gaudi and Rogers, have made models to demonstrate their plans. The relationship of form and function, between buildings and their purposes, is a unifying theme. The need for shelter is universal, whatever the climate, for living, for working and for leisure pursuits, for privacy and for personal comfort. Dwellings and other shelters have rarely been developed without aesthetic considerations, from thatch decorations of rural England and parts of Africa, to ornate embellishments of church bosses and ancient Egyptian temples. In particular cases, importation of materials was seen as a sign of wealth and status.

Figure 9.2 *Wooden figure with letter forms (1995).* Carved sculpture by Eleanor Glover. Size: 38 cm high

The notion of appropriate technology should be considered, alongside fitness for purpose, use of available materials and the caution over the use of non-renewable resources. Thus the same materials may be used for the basic structure as for embellishments. Wood, granite, marble, straw, and other available materials have influenced the development of particular styles of architecture, evident for instance in parts of Africa and in the distinctive mud-brick buildings of Santa Fe. We need to exercise caution lest we promote a stereotyped idea of how buildings look in different places: mud huts, igloos and teepees are only one aspect of the cultures we associate with them. A balanced view must be offered to children.

The form of a building is, in general, influenced by its intended use, in scale, number and size of doors and windows, and the intentions of the owners or commissioners. These constraints seem to be universal, as do exterior clues to interior functions, such as Town Halls, places for religious worship, commerce or education. Children can work out the function of even unfamiliar buildings from the exterior. They might sort postcards into groups, according to function, size, geographical location or materials used: compare types of windows or doors and work out why they are appropriate, and look into the significance of decorative features. The recent proliferation of Do It Yourself programmes on television may have given children an awareness beyond that of previous generations.

The roles of architect, builder, designer, engineer, surveyor or electrician are still rather vague for most children. Through the study of architecture, children can also be taught about the roles of these experts in different times and places. Debates about traditional and modern architecture still rage. Why identify a public lavatory as a listed building?

Were similar arguments about the old and the new always around, in olden times and faraway places, or is this a recent development?

PLANNING, RESEARCHING AND RESOURCING

Children work best when given a challenge to meet, a task or a brief. The degree of choice offered depends on the materials available and the task in hand and the intended context for the work. Of most importance is how the child learns through doing, articulating ideas at each stage, and considering options available. The primary teacher's skill lies in matching task, tools, materials, creating a stimulating learning environment, ensuring consolidation of previously encountered skills and concepts, and in introducing appropriate levels of challenge throughout.

To tell children 'how to make' implies that there is only one way (ours), which encourages dependency: they learn how to make an item but may not have subsequent opportunity to apply skills in their own way. Working collaboratively, children share skills, work on different elements of a project and negotiate when problems arise or decisions are to be made.

An important element of task-setting is to define appropriate parameters within which the children will work. What materials are provided, and how they are set out, also affects the quality of the choices made and the standard of finished work. Prior to embarking on an ambitious product, children need to research aspects of the design brief in several areas:

- the nature of the artefact: how it works and how it will be used;
- how other people have approached a similar task;
- the subject-matter;
- the qualities of different materials which might be used for the artifact.

For instance, bird masks will inspire, or be inspired by, work on birds, using direct observation, books and other documents, CD Rom, video recordings as well as the study of masks. Stimuli can also come from reading stories or poems, or extracts from information books, carefully chosen as part of English provision, presenting work in different genres on a similar theme. Extracts from adult fiction can be appropriate: a description of a building, a hat, a bridge or an event, such as Christmas portrayed in the poem by Dylan Thomas. An initial display of visual stimulus, prepared by the teacher, from source materials around the given theme, inspires research.

Children need to work out what materials are of a suitable weight, strength, colour, textural quality and plasticity to perform the function required; which are suitable for the basic structure, and which best for embellishment. In arranging the layout of the room, the teacher offers both options and boundaries, which may on occasion be challenged by particular children. Such challenges can then be discussed in the light of the brief set, and the learning intentions outlined. In a free-for-all, or too restrictive a setting, it is difficult to focus, challenge and develop ideas.

Long, medium and short-term plans are necessary, in line with the school's policies and schemes of work. Consider the overall aims, and how much time is needed for each stage of the process. Consult school and LEA health and safety documents.

Aims

These should consider children's development, continuity, progression and consolidation of existing knowledge and understanding, prior experience and current needs.

Intentions

Children need to be very clear about the intentions for the task set, which can usefully be framed in terms of a design brief to be met rather than a predetermined product to be copied. Set criteria carefully, and ensure that children are aware of which elements are essential and how much leeway they have in their interpretation of the brief.

Resources

Storage and access to appropriate materials is the key to successful modelling (see Figure 9.3). Having a wide range of choice can be inspirational to some, daunting to others. A limited range can elicit quite ingenious responses.

Organising the classroom to ensure good studio or workshop conditions is the teacher's responsibility; high quality results are rarely achieved in cramped conditions, and space is an important factor in ensuring focused, on-task work. Always consider how work will be stored or displayed between practical sessions. A classroom plan helps.

The teacher, and any other assistants who will be working with the children, should try out the brief beforehand, to see how long it takes, what space is needed and what

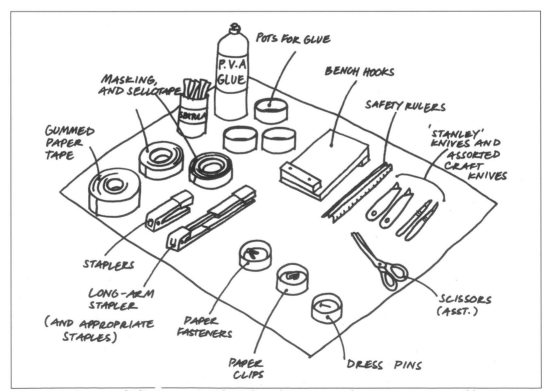

Figure 9.3 Suggested 'display mat' with tools and equipment for 3D session (per table)

resources are essential. Tasks should be challenging and thought-provoking, but there is a fine line between this and frustration.

Timing

Introductory sessions need to be fully planned to give credence to the holistic nature of the work in hand, and to show evidence of the cross-curricular links which apply. If a kite-making workshop is planned to bring together and complement work on forces, materials, festivals and stories or poems, introductory sessions can be planned separately under science, technology, or English, in the same way that a movement session based around the movement of a kite would be separately planned and assessed.

The finish of a model or sculpture is very important, so children can take pride in their work, and so that it does not fall apart at the seams. Models need to last after all the effort they represent and masks should be worn and puppets played with. So children need to be taught ways of achieving durable and well finished work, and have enough time to get it right.

Evaluation and assessment

To evaluate adequately, children need to enjoy looking at and thinking about their work. Time is needed for intermediate appraisal, perhaps the day after the practical session, with each group presenting and describing the piece as it stands, and answering questions or taking suggestions from classmates.

The original brief can be written out for everyone to read. Children can refer to the criteria, and explain how they decided to interpret the brief, and their reasons for departing from it if they did. It may well be appropriate for the teacher to make notes during the feedback sessions to place on file.

Displaying finished items provides opportunities for evaluation and assessment. A booklet for comments could be made for children to note their responses to the work. If photographs have been taken during the process, children can sort them and make captions to explain how they worked. Photographs of the products, preferably taken by the children themselves, can provide a permanent record, especially if placed in a book alongside written comments and samples of materials.

CLASSROOM ORGANISATION

Health and safety

A major contribution to health and safety considerations is the maintenance of good working practices. Safety rules need to be written up in an appropriate place, carefully explained to the whole class, and emergency routines rehearsed (see glue guns). A major rule is, if in doubt, don't! Children will need regular reminding: stop the class every 20 minutes or so to recap on work to date and to give reminders where necessary. If you only ever stop them to nag, they will ignore you.

Teachers must ensure that children work safely and efficiently. This is not difficult, but requires meticulous planning, so children are able to work more independently and to a higher standard. There is a strong argument for specific teaching, e.g. about how to use glue sparingly, how to use a spatula, how to cover the edges but not the work surface, how to twist or manipulate the material being cut (rather than the scissors) when going round corners. There are also routines to be learned about how to set out the workspace, ensuring that tools are in good order and keeping them clean, and keeping working space uncluttered. These can be taught in groups through demonstration and experimentation, as part of the research process. It is difficult to teach one or two children the use of a knife with a straight edge and an edge clip while everyone else is also working on unfamiliar techniques.

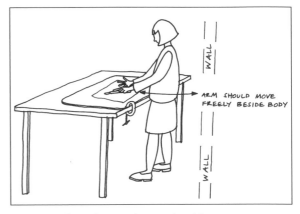

Figure 9.4a Electrical safety

Channels of potential movement influence the room plan for the session. Define areas for sitting down and standing up. Keep work surfaces uncluttered,

Figure 9.4b Safety at the work table

replacing tools as you go. Tape electrical leads to the floor (see Figure 9.4a). Clear debris into bags taped to the table, to be collected later. Allocate tables or work surfaces for particular purposes, so children take only what they need to their own tables and replace when finished reference materials, to encourage on-going research, materials, tools, adhesives and 'fixers', glue gun, woodwork.

Materials: storage and access

Make sure that the container has inside only what it says on the label. Even recycled materials should be treated with respect. Children's Scrapstores are a good source of both materials and storage containers, and local retailers are often happy to recycle packaging etc. for schools to use. Present the various materials as clearly as possible. Here are some ideas (see Figures 9.5 and 9.6):

- transparent carrier bags on hooks, carefully labelled;
- boxes with lids: shoeboxes, of uniform size, can be stacked efficiently;
- lids display a selection of items on a table-top, with the larger container under the table for access;
- trays in classroom units are useful for smaller items;
- vegetable racks allow easy access;
- large plastic containers hold small items like corks;
- small transparent bags hold a selection of sorted fabric scraps: the contents can be easily seen, and only a small amount is in use at one time;

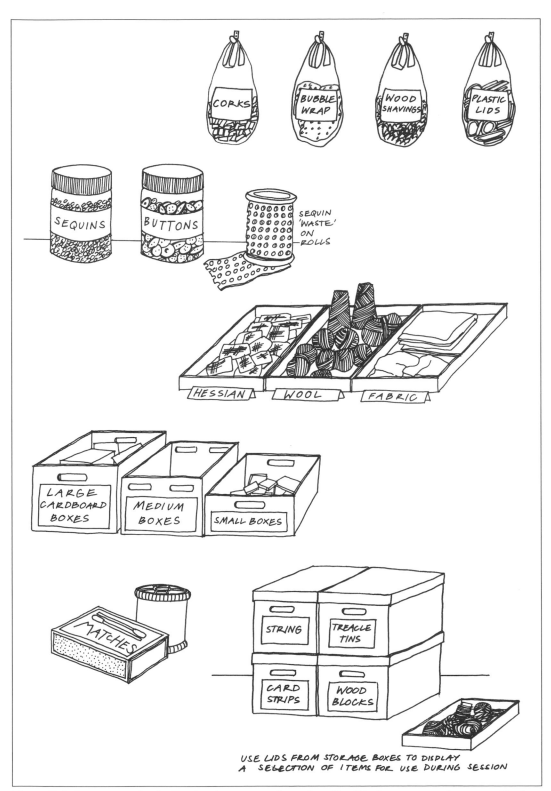

Figure 9.5 Storage methods. Storing buttons and sequins. Use lids from storage boxes to display a selection of items for use during session

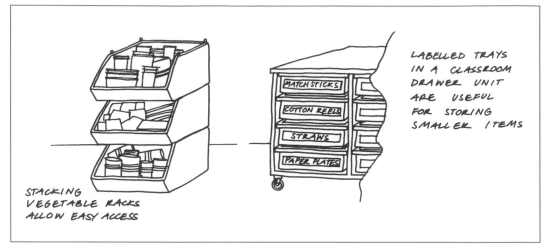

Figure 9.6 Trays and racks

- cylindrical containers, boxes or spare waste baskets hold paper rolls, sorted according to type.

Some schools dedicate a central storage area and allocate helper time to maintain a stock of items for this type of work, often donated by parents, for all classes to use. When the treasures arrive, discard any toilet roll middles, or polystyrene packaging which you think children might cut into. Children can sort them, perhaps using plastic hoops, and make labels, as a mathematical sorting activity and/or a science materials task. This checklist may help you to collect and organise resources.

To model

Sticky back plastic pieces, small assorted paper strips, egg cartons, coloured cellophane, tracing paper, kitchen paper, newsprint, tissue paper, squared paper, crepe paper, metallic paper, corrugated paper, gummed paper, bubblewrap, paper plates, small card pieces, tubes/cylinders of different sizes, paper/plastic straws, boxes (sorted by size), plastic containers, plastic bags, paper bags, pieces of leather, hessian, wool and other fabrics, corks, cork tile pieces, mosaic tiles, cotton reels, matchboxes, matchsticks, wood shavings, assorted lollipop sticks, sawdust, small dowel rods, buttons, sequins/sequin waste, wire bits, pipecleaners, coathangers, stripped cable, plastic/polystyrene plates, foam shapes and pieces, plastic lids, polystyrene packaging (do not cut!).

To cut

Scissors, craft knives, stanley knives, wire cutters, cutting boards, edgeblocks, hacksaws (see Figure 9.7).

To join

Bulldog clips, paper fasteners, split pins of various sizes, sellotape, masking tape, bookbinding tape, string (various), pva glue, wallpaper paste.

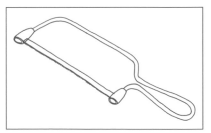

Figure 9.7 Junior hacksaw

Cutting

Plan the room for pupils to stand against a wall rather than in the middle of the room, so passers-by do not bump into them and you can keep an eye on them. Always provide a cutting board or workbench, if possible with an edgeblock. Ensure that the tool is aligned with the arm/hand, so the elbow rests against the body: if the tool slips, it will stay clear of the body. Never cut at an angle across the body: the cutting movement is made parallel to the side of the body in a pulling motion. Try not to turn the body or the tool while cutting; always turn the item being cut (see Figure 9.4b).

Glues and adhesives

Read instructions on the container with the children before use: manufacturers usually know best. If there is a hazard sign on the box or tube, do not use it with children, ever.

Gloy, Bostik paper glue, cold water paste (powder)

Mostly supplied in liquid form, these are economical and easy to spread, especially powders, which can be made up in large quantities. Use for paper and thin card only, when joints are not loadbearing. They are safe to handle, non-sniffable, easy to remove from clothes. Drying takes at least 30 minutes.

Glue-sticks, glue-pens etc.

These are easy and safe to use, quick and clean, for small scale, lightweight mounting and sticking only. They can be affected by heat if work is displayed above a radiator. They are non-sniffable and usually easy to remove from clothes.

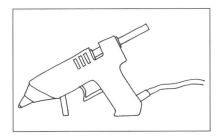

Figure 9.8 Glue gun

Glue guns

These electric tools (Figure 9.8) heat up glue sticks inserted in the gun, and are easy to use. They give excellent adhesion on a range of materials. Always use with a circuit breaker and provide a safe work area. The glue dries immediately and is non-sniffable. There is some risk of burning if hot glue falls on skin but lower heat guns are available for use in school. Glue guns should always be supervised. If the supervisor is distracted, children stop working. If the supervisor is called away, children leave the table and pursue other activities until they can continue. Remember to switch off the guns! Leads should be taped very firmly and very obviously to the floor to avoid stumbles and to draw attention to the presence of a potential danger.

Bostik, UHU, Copydex, Balsa cement, Pritt Multi-Glue, Superglue

These are versatile, strong, ideal for use on porous surfaces, but messy and difficult to remove from clothes. Drying times vary; some impact adhesives take about 20 minutes. Packaging may carry a danger symbol, because of dangerous and addictive fumes. They are unsuitable for children and therefore should only be used in the classroom by adults. There must be adequate ventilation. Read instructions carefully.

Marvin Medium, Copydex Childsplay, pva etc.

These are versatile adhesives for card, leather, fabric, wood etc., easy to use, relatively cheap, safe and non-sniffable. They wash out from clothes with cold water (hot water tends to set the glue hard). They take about 15 minutes to set. When gluing difficult surfaces, the impact adhesive method helps to ensure a firm bonding, particularly useful for box modelling and fabric joins where sellotape, masking tape or ordinary glueing are inadequate. Follow these steps.

- Place the glue, decanted into a coffee jar lid or small carton, on a mat to avoid spillages. A spatula can be made from a triangle of fairly thick card, and discarded after use.
- Coat each surface to be bonded with a very thin layer of glue.
- Wait (this is the difficult bit) until the glue begins to get tacky after a minute or two, and is almost transparent. Place the two surfaces together, and hold in place firmly until the joint has dried, if necessary, with a clothes peg or G-clamp.
- Leave to dry. The bond will be firm and withstand a certain amount of pressure.

To fix a cylinder to a flat piece of card, cut a fringe around the edge. The process is shown in Figure 9.9. Alternatively, place a series of pieces of masking tape (not sellotape) around the edge to form the fringe.

To fix yoghurt pots or other plastic to another surface, stick paper over the plastic first with a pva-type glue for better adhesion.

1.

2. cut a 'fringe' on cylinder using scissors.

3. fold out fringe to give a flat base to cylinder.

4. Place cylinder onto paper/card to which it is to be fastened and draw a guide-line for gluing.

apply glue to fringe

P.V.A.

5. Apply glue to marked out section of card and to fringe of cylinder, allow to almost dry and then press together to join

Figure 9.9 Fixing a cylinder to a flat card

STORAGE AND DISPLAY OF ONGOING AND COMPLETED WORK

At planning stage, consider how many structures will need to be accommodated on worktops during practical sessions and in storage space when half-finished. Bear in mind that work takes several sessions to finish, and that some will be completed before others.

Displays of finished 3D work are, on the whole, best done simply, to give the form and colour of the artifacts due attention against a neutral background. Fussy settings may mean the work has to fight the background; let it speak for itself. A plain fabric placed over a trolley, with a small screen or pinboard behind is usually adequate. Photographs, sketches and resource materials can be displayed alongside.

BUILDING UP USING WOOD

Wood is readily available in different forms: some pliable, such as shavings, some solid, some finished, some unfinished. Using wood to form structures and sculptures helps children appreciate its qualities, and encourages them to look closely at the grain, the bark, the colour and texture (see Figure 9.10).

Sculptors use wood in two basic ways: carving out and building up. Carving is difficult for younger children with anything more resistant than balsa, and is probably best done with softer materials such as damp clay. Building up, on the other hand, is relatively easy, once children have learned how to join wood to wood, or other materials, efficiently. Impact adhesion or a glue gun are best. Suitable tools and materials to provide include:

- hammer, bradawl, hacksaw, screwdrivers;
- nails and screws;
- glue guns;
- pva adhesive;
- pieces of balsa in a range of shapes and sizes;
- wood shavings;
- sawdust;
- wood strips and dowels (lollipop sticks, matchsticks etc.);
- small blocks of wood;
- larger blocks of wood;
- pieces of ply.

Figure 9.10 *Figures*. Mixed media and wood by students. Size: 12 and 13 cm high

A useful preliminary exercise is to sort bags of miscellaneous pieces according to the criteria children decide, which might include size, planes, smoothness or roughness, quality of grain etc. Drawing a section of a piece of wood to follow the lines of the grain or the texture of bark also encourages close observation and study. Children might also look at, or create, photographs of wood in different forms.

These can form part of a display of wooden pieces and artifacts such as bowls and tables, along with sculptures and woodcarvings of animals or masks, including the work of local craftspersons. The display can also include magazine photographs, books about sculptors and other woodworkers. Children can see how wood is used in the building of bridges, houses, places of worship etc., both for structural and decorative purposes. A visit to a local woodyard or DIY store may be arranged, and the local tree surgeon may come to call, bringing samples of tree roots, sections of trunk or branches. Most schools have a skilled carpenter as a friend or neighbour.

Inspiration for the children's own work comes from a growing knowledge and understanding of materials, appreciation of what skilled woodworkers can do and make, and ideas presented through research about the artifact they are to make. Building up using wood can be a lengthy process, but such time is well spent, since greater skill means increasing independence and more satisfactory outcomes. Techniques may be taught by one child to another, or parents may be able to participate in the process. The use of a saw, a bradawl or a screwdriver needs to be taught with the care and attention devoted to the use of a pencil or pen. Wood can also be used with other 3D materials to make frameworks or armatures on which to build with materials which are not self-supportive.

Below are suitable tasks to set to investigate the potential of building up with wood:

- a tower for watching animals in the wild;
- a box to hold a very precious key;
- a sculpture to go high on a hill you know;
- a structure using as many textures as possible;
- a structure to represent anger, delight or another emotion;
- a structure to represent flying or swimming.

WIRE, CHICKEN WIRE

It is not difficult to provide a range of wire of different grades and gauges for children to use to bend into wire sculptures with fingers or tools, for instance:

- old coat hangers can be unbent and reformed;
- redundant electrical cable from skips can be stripped of its plastic coating: the wire underneath is a lovely copper, and the earth wire will probably be thicker and heavier;
- the plastic coating itself may provide a good colour range; emphasise that this is for model-making, and no longer appropriate for electrical circuitry.
- chicken wire can be obtained in various gauges, some covered with plastic, in squares or in honeycomb form with different sizes of holes between the wires. It is quite expensive. Teach children to use pliers correctly to cut and bend the wire. Put small pads of masking tape on sharp corners. Gloves may be necessary.

Strands of wire can be used for 3D drawing. Some children actually find it more satisfactory to draw in this way than in 2D, as the wire can be bent and rebent until the desired effect is achieved. Rubbing out is not necessary. Observational portrait or figure work is particularly satisfying, e.g. a profile and a full-face outline joined together, either left as it is, mounted on a wood block base, or to use as an armature for papier mâché moulding. Wire figures can be twisted into various shapes to represent different movements, based on observations of classmates, or inspired by photographs of athletes, dancers, sportsmen or women (see also Figure 1.5, p. 10).

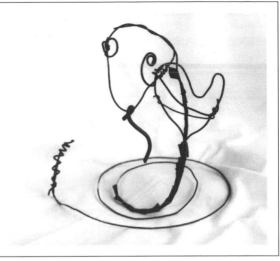

Figure 9.11 *Snake*. Sculpture in wire and plastic by a student. Size: 18 cm high

Wire is used in Carnival costume-making to form the structure for e.g. wings and headdresses. This technique, used for the most elaborate constructions, can be tackled by children as long as they are strong enough to handle the gauge of wire appropriate for the scale of the work in hand.

- Draw the outline to the size you need on paper.
- Use pieces of heavy gauge wire to form the shape. Placed the wire on the paper, and bend it to follow the line of the drawing.
- Bind pieces together with smaller pieces of thinner wire.
- Cover this armature with fabric, cut roughly to shape. Carefully glue it to the frame, leave to dry, then trim. Glue raw edges over the wire.

POINTS TO REMEMBER

The following points summarise this chapter, and can be used as a checklist for planning and assessment for teachers and children.

- Identify clear objectives for learning. From the outset, encourage adequate planning and establish clear criteria and aims with children, such as the scale, finish or surface required, materials and equipment available.
- Recognise and exploit the potential of cross-curricular work in your planning: give each area appropriate emphasis within the whole. Adopt a realistic approach which does not stifle creativity but which allows time for necessary investigations to build up sufficient experience.
- Research the work of sculptors in books, in your locality and through the internet. Try to find examples photographed from different angles.
- Plan for progression and set challenging tasks which match pupils' manipulative skills, abilities and potential.

- Describe work according to the product, rather than as junk modelling, e.g. mask-making, box sculpture etc.
- Provide safe areas for children to work in, where tools are in good working order, with sufficient elbow room and adequate storage. Regularly reinforce instructions about using equipment and tools safely. Use a circuit breaker with electrical equipment.
- Provide experience of a wide variety of tools, materials and adhesives to stimulate decision-making and choosing.
- Be eclectic! Collect, and encourage children to collect, interesting manufactured and natural items like bones, wood and pebbles, suitable for re-use in this way.
- Be selective about the materials you provide, e.g. cartons that are not too flimsy or too difficult to join together.
- Provide quality resources to support work, such as books, artifacts, video, computer programs.
- Give advice and help with the construction and use of appropriate materials as required, *but* resist the temptation to impose your ideas and restrict the problem-solving process with your solutions.
- Encourage ongoing evaluation of process and product; remind children to evaluate work in terms of the criteria laid down at the design brief stage, to discuss these between themselves before presenting their products and evaluating with the whole class.
- Take photos of the process for later evaluation and assessment, for displays and in records as evidence.
- Always expect quality performance. Never undervalue or underestimate children's abilities, especially younger or so-called 'less able' ones.
- Use and enjoy the artifacts! Share with others in and outside the school. Invite visitors to the exhibition. Present the work in assembly. Show off!

CHAPTER 10

Modelling

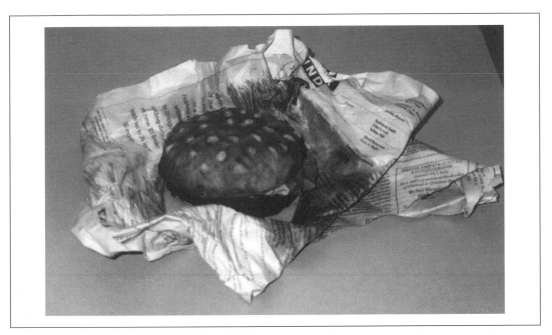

Figure 10.1 *Hamburger.* Salt dough model from observation by a student. Size: 15 × 15 cm

The pliable materials, plasticine, play-dough, papier mâché and mod-roc (plaster impregnated bandage), dealt with in this chapter have many features in common with, but provide no substitute for clay, which has its own chapter. Newspaper has been included along with papier mâché. Distinctions between this and chapters on sculpture, clay and collage are blurred, since a combination of techniques is often appropriate.

We recommend that children work with a range of mouldable materials, a range of rigid materials and with clay independently, in order fully to investigate the properties of each. This helps children and teachers to decide which medium is most appropriate for the task in hand. For instance, play-dough and salt dough is not best suited to models with legs, and even plasticine will topple if there is not a firm base. Wire, wood or boxes can be used under papier mâché as an armature on which to work, which may give more stability.

This cheap and often underrated set of resources for making needs to be well presented in the classroom. Planning needs careful thought, since without direction or tuition, children may tend to fall back on the same limited ideas we experienced in our own primary education, little gardens and baskets of eggs. These might be fun, but alone are not sufficiently challenging or stimulating for today's children.

Principles of planning and resourcing outlined in other chapters apply equally to moulding materials. They are easy to mould and can be finished to look like wood, metal and other much less pliable materials. Thus quite authentic golden crowns, iron helmets, silver jewellery and other artifacts can be made in plasticine or papier mâché, inspired by topic research about cultures in familiar and unfamiliar geographical, historical or fantasy settings.

Children can play with design ideas on a small scale, such as jewellery, miniature artifacts, story characters, transport models or even musical instruments (see Figures 10.2 and 10.3). For large-scale work, applications to be described such as newspaper rolls as armatures, can be adapted for other work in design technology, such as bridges, frames for furniture or boats.

Designing and making body adornments offers opportunity to explore symbols and motifs, to research a variety of ancient and modern artifacts, and the range of media employed to interpret and realise the designs. Women have always played an important part in this area of design/craft.

Children can start from a favourite personal item, e.g. a ring or bangle, a watch or hairslide. By sketching it, and perhaps making notes on why it is significant, they can begin a process of accumulating illustrations and photographs to keep in sketchbooks for reference. They can also research jewellery of the Vikings, the Ancient Egyptians,

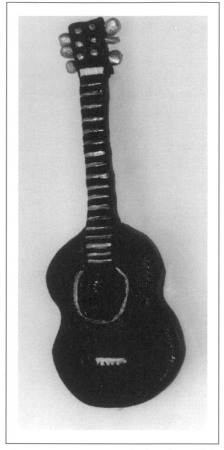

Figure 10.2 *Guitar.* Salt dough model, gloss painted, by a student. Size: 15 cm long

the Elizabethans or the Celts. They might research motifs, flowers and animals, which figure in the designs. Publications like *National Geographic* offer superb photographs, as do newspaper magazine articles on fashions, festivals and designers.

Figure 10.3 *Necklace.* Pulp papier mâché artifact by a student. Size: each face 5 × 3 cm

The use of jewels to make a public show of wealth exists in almost every culture, for example, among the Pharaohs of Ancient Egypt, in the South Asian tradition of gold jewellery for the woman's dowry. The Royal family wear extravagant, costly examples of wealth to demonstrate their glittering heritage. Bet Lynch, late of the Rovers Return, Coronation Street, used her outrageous earrings to comparable effect.

Many artists have employed their skills to design and make beautiful items of adornment, notably Mackintosh and others associated with Art Nouveau. The designs and materials used in jewellery often reflect and complement current fashions in clothes, tableware and furniture. In the 1960s in Europe and the USA, there was much flamboyance in the way young people dressed, their jewellery (flowers) and the way they decorated their homes. Mary Quant and other designers wielded great influence on the current stylistic trends. Punk fashions with safety pins emanated from the catwalk fashions of Vivienne Westwood in the seventies. Children might research a particular designer as part of their history research as well as for their art work.

THE BASIC ELEMENTS OF ART IN USING MOULDABLE MATERIALS

Texture

These materials have an intrinsic texture which changes as they are worked and as they dry. The texture and the consistency are interdependent. The finish of pulp papier mâché depends on the recipe, so how soggy the paper becomes dictates how smooth the final texture is. There are advantages to a fairly lumpy texture or consistency, as it has interesting surfaces when dry. The texture of strip and paste papier mâché depends on the size of the torn strips and how carefully they are layered. It is possible to achieve a very smooth, even finish but the definition of layers in finished work can be an advantage. Using small squares, rather than strips, gives a different sort of finish. Dry papier mâché can be sanded down, but this needs a dust mask and painstaking care, so it is not appropriate for most primary school children. Modroc, which can be applied to dry papier mâché, has its own bandage-like texture, which can be smoothed over with wet fingers or a sponge. Plasticine comes in ridged blocks, with a textural quality which disappears as it gets used, moulded and formed into balls. Like play-dough and salt dough, it can be textured using fingers or tools to dig in to the formerly smooth surface. Apart from plasticine, all these materials can be coated with varnish to make a glossy surface. When play-dough dries, the salt tends to dull the finish, and colours fade.

Colour

Colour is intrinsic to plasticine and play-dough, and suggestions are given below for making often pale and insipid colours more exciting and tempting. Children enjoy helping to make play-dough and they then have an opportunity to create different colours from the outset. Colours of each material can be merged (but not plasticine with play-dough!) to make a marbled effect or even new colours.

With other materials, colour is more usually applied after modelling, when the piece is dry. Powder paints, readimix, inks and other dyes can be used for different effects. Colour can also be applied with coloured paper, fabrics or using découpage as a final layer.

Form

Relief work is possible in all these media, but it is valuable also to explore the 3D nature of each. Working on one side of a form affects the other faces or angles. A turntable is a useful device, but children can also be encouraged simply to keep turning their boards around as they work.

Shape

With pre-coloured media, shapes can be cut in different colours and arranged together like tiles or mosaic. Shapes can also be added as relief: small balls, strips, triangles or other shapes can be applied like collage. Cutters are fun to use, preferably of geometric rather than picture shapes.

Pattern

By applying surface decoration, or cutting pieces to lay together, which may even tesselate, pattern is made through tile or mosaic techniques with plasticine and play-dough. Pattern can be painted or glued on to other materials as part of the design for the finished piece.

ARTISTS WHO USE MOULDABLE MATERIALS

Artists who work in play-dough are, we confess, a little thin on the ground, although salt dough is a recognised medium in the craft world, for items such as Christmas or harvest decorations and mock food display foods in restaurants and shops.

Plasticene is famously used in the Wallace and Grommit productions and others in the animation field. Video clips of such work can inspire the children to make their own complex and interesting designs from plasticine, and may even encourage a similar approach

Figure 10.4 *Monica*, papier mâché sculpture by Elza Scoble. Size: 40 cm long

with play-dough. The history of plasticine has been well documented in books and on television.

Papier mâché is a technique much used in 17th and 18th century for embellished furniture and picture frames. It literally means 'chewed paper', dating from the time when old women without teeth literally mashed woodpulp or paper to produce material which was then moulded and shaped with the addition of glue. Once dry, it was coated with various substances and painted or gold-leafed to make items such as Rococo mirrors, wall and ceiling embellishments and mouldings, which have the appearance of very finely carved wood. Nowadays, use hands or the food processor to achieve the same result. Many artists use both pulp and strip and paste papier mâché to make sculptures and objects (see Figure 10.4).

The application of the techniques in puppetry, mask and costume-making, and preparatory work for sculpture and architecture, is also possible through books about sculptors and artists.

CLASSROOM MANAGEMENT AND ORGANISATION

Children may work directly on the table-top, but a heavy plastic mat, or large ceramic tile prevents the material from sticking and serves as a board for later display of work. We now consider each medium in turn, together with ideas for initial experiments. Some may apply to more than one medium, although each needs to be explored in its own right.

Plasticine

Available under many brand names, this is the original and best-known description of this material (see Figure 10.5). It comes in a wide range of colours, which can be kept vibrant if it is stored in different small containers with lids, with a spare for mixed colour. Since it hardens quite quickly, put it on a radiator or in a warm place for a day or so before use. A few drops of petroleum jelly will, apparently, keep it soft.

Figure 10.5 *Skull masks*. Plasticine models by students. Size: 5 cm

Play-dough

The term covers many types of pre-cooked, coloured dough. Use plenty of colouring to make strong, attractive colours. Brusho inks work particularly well and even black, brown and vibrant oranges, greens and purples are possible. The ingredients are:

- 2 teacups plain flour;
- 1 teacup salt;
- 2 teaspoons cream of tartar;
- 1 cup tap water;
- 2 tablespoons cooking oil;
- colouring.

The method: In a large pan, mix all ingredients except colouring and stir to a smooth paste. Divide the mixture, and add different food colourings, inks or Brusho to make a strong colour. Stir continuously over a medium heat until it sticks to the spoon and comes away from the side of the pan. Remove from the heat and leave to cool. Knead for about five minutes. This keeps in a sealed container in the fridge for a week or so. Each colour can be wrapped in clingfilm which looks very inviting. If children in different classes make different colours to share, everyone has an exciting range.

Salt dough

Colouring may be added to the wet ingredients before use, but this recipe is best for modelling without added colour and painted after baking. The proportion of flour to water may vary, so adjust as necessary to make a firm but pliable dough. Sculptures can be painted and/or varnished if required, but sometimes the effect is very pleasing without additional colour. The ingredients are:

- 4 cups plain flour;
- 1 cup water;
- 1 cup salt;
- optional: a teaspoon of glycerine.

The method: Mix the dry ingredients together. Add water (and glycerine) gradually. Knead. Model on a lightly floured surface. Leave to dry out slowly, on a rack to ensure air circulation, in a warm place. Then bake in the oven at a very, very low temperature for a long time, several hours if possible, to give more permanence.

Initial exploration with play-dough, plasticine or salt dough

A table lay-out for plasticine is shown in Figure 10.6. The following tools can be used with plasticene, play-dough or salt dough:

- rolling pins or thick dowel rods, with bits of wood to achieve an even layer;
- commercially produced wood or plastic modelling tools;

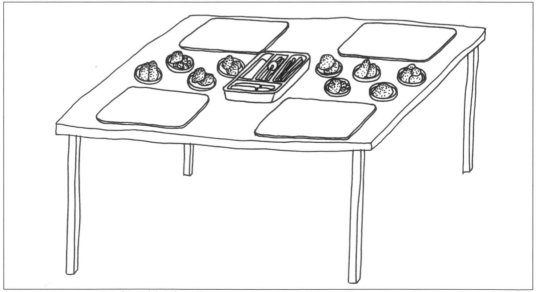

Figure 10.6 'Laying the table' for plasticene

- old blunt kitchen knives;
- craft knives for older or more dextrous children;
- forks and spoons of different sizes (plastic may suffice);
- pastry cutters with geometric shapes in different sizes;
- pizza cutters for older children (they are sharp);
- spatulas, worn-out biros, old combs: any items which will make patterns and textures.

Not all these ideas work with all media. These are good starting points with children of any age, although the younger or less able need more supervision and guidance. Older children may be able to read the tasks for themselves, and adapt and modify ideas according to their skills and abilities. They may add more ideas of their own. As they experiment, children learn more about the qualities, potential and limitations of the materials.

Aims for introductory sessions can be identified in terms of understanding texture, pattern, relief, colour, pliability and conservation of volume, as well as the use of tools and imagination. In all 3D art, children learn about the application of mathematical concepts as an intrinsic part of making (see Figure 10.7). Unlike clay, which dries out as it is worked, play-dough and salt dough and plasticine retain their pliability because of the oily content. Directions to the children might be:

- Hold a lump in your hand. Squeeze it through your fingers. Roll it back into a ball. Squeeze again. Pat the ball between your hands, to make a big pizza. Put it on the table and roll it up into a sausage. Squeeze the sausage to make it very long and thin. Now coil it round and round to make a catherine wheel.
- Squash it back into a ball. Pat it to a pizza. Roll it out with a rolling pin. How big can you make it? How thin can you make it? What shape does it make?
- Cut the edges straight, and make a rectangle. Now you have a tile. Dig your fingertips into the tile and make marks. Do the marks stay on the surface, or disappear? Pinch it all over to make a different texture. What does it remind you of?
- Roll it out flat again with the rolling pin. Roll it the other way, like a swiss roll. Coil it back into a catherine wheel. Squeeze it and make it back into a ball. Dig your fingers into the ball so it has little holes all around. Make it smooth again.
- Use a fork to make marks in the ball. Can you make little holes, smaller than your fingertips? Can you make lines all over it with the fork?
- Roll the ball out, so it is flat and makes a tile. Use pastry cutters to cut shapes out of your tile. Make lots of the same shape and pile the shapes up. What does this remind you of? How many layers did you make?
- Use different colours to make a pattern when you pile them up. Is there the same number of each colour? Which colours look best together? Take the layers apart and make them into bigger balls again.
- Take two small balls of different colours. Squeeze them together in your hand and twist to make them look like marble. Keep working until you make a third colour from the first two. Can you separate the colours now?
- Roll out your new colour. Take a shape cutter. How many shapes will you be able to cut from your flat piece, do you think? Cut out as many as you can. Try to make each shape look different, by pinching, digging or using a fork. Cut the same sort of shapes from what is left. Arrange them in a pattern on your board.
- Roll out two colours. Use the same cutter to cut shapes out of each colour. Put the

shapes of one colour into the holes in the other colour. Will they fit? Did you have enough to fill all the holes? Put the colours back together again, and roll them out to similar shapes and size. Try this time to cut the same pattern in each colour with the cutter. Fill up the holes again and see if the patterns are the same. Use a smaller cutter of the same shape, and cut small bits from the middle of your shapes. Use these to fill up the holes in your shapes.

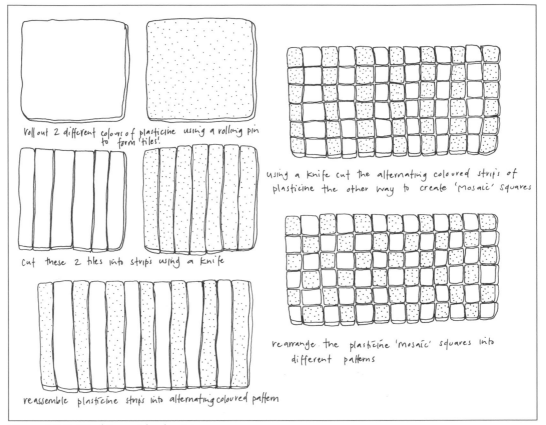

Figure 10.7 Working with plasticine

Pulp papier mâché

The glue in this mixture makes the paper fibres stick together and to its base as it dries. This material is very heavy when wet, and takes a very long time to dry. Paper pulp can be painted wet, but dries to a rather dull and lacklustre finish. Powder paint, including metallic, can be sprinkled dry on to the wet surface. The ingredients are:

- 1 large newspaper;
- 1 tablespoon cooking oil;
- 3 tablespoons pva glue;
- 3 tablespoons wallpaper paste;

- water;
- optional: a few drops of disinfectant to stave off mould if it is to be kept; check no child is allergic to it.

The method: Tear the newspaper into small squares, about 30 cm, and soak in water overnight. Boil it up with plenty of water for about 20 minutes. Whizz it in a food processor. If you are not prepared to sacrifice your food processor, boiling will take considerably longer. A potato masher helps break down the fibres. Once the pulp stage has been reached, it requires additional effort to squeeze out the excess water to achieve a workable consistency. Preliminary sieving needs to be followed by squeezing quite firmly through the hands. This is a time-consuming process, and less than enjoyable for those who resent their hands being covered with grey fibrous matter. Add other ingredients and mix well.

Alternatively, soak the torn-up paper in pre-mixed paper paste. Stir thoroughly and add more and more paper pieces until the paste has been completely absorbed. The substance should keep its shape when squeezed. Add pva glue, and disinfectant.

Pulp papier mâché: trying out relief

Tools

As for play-dough, plasticine and salt dough (except the rolling pin), plus:

- moulds to work on: sieves, colanders, plastic plates or bowls, which may need to be covered with cling-film to avoid the pulp sticking to the surface;
- boxes, strong cardboard cylinders to use as bases;
- card cut to various sizes and shapes to experiment with;
- knives, scissors to cut and shape bases if appropriate.

Cover the table with newspaper, and set out a formica or similar board for each child, a bowl of pulp, and a series of small cards, about 15 cm, of different shapes.

- Take a handful of pulp, squeeze it into a ball. Make a number of balls of different sizes. Roll them back into a large ball.
- Make the pulp into a sausage shape. Make it very thin and see how long it gets before it disintegrates.
- On the cards, use pulp to make different textures, some around the edge, some in the middle. Turn the base as you work, and try to achieve smooth and bumpy effects. You might stick little balls down close together.
- Try digging your fingers into the pulp and see what happens. Can you make a pattern? Does it stay on the surface?

Strip and paste papier mâché

Torn paper strips are pasted with a brush or dipped into paste, and draped over a base or mould. A wet layer can be followed by one or more of dry paper, which absorbs the paste from the previous layer. As it dries, it takes the shape of the mould or armature, and provides a smooth or textured surface to paint, depending on how the paper has been laid.

This method is ideal for finishing off models or sculptures made from boxes, because it helps to reinforce the structure of the model, adding strength and stability. It is especially useful for covering plastic yoghurt-type pots on models, because it provides such a good surface for gluing or painting.

For a large shape paper can be crumpled on to a card base of approximately the right size and shape and secured with masking tape. Pasted paper strips can then be applied in layers and moulded with fingers to the required finish.

Masks and bowl shapes can be made over pliable moulds, such as old plastic plates or balloons. A layer of varnish, clingfilm or dry paper directly on the mould will allow the papier mâché to be removed once dry. With a final layer of white newsprint or modroc, the overall form can be more easily determined than with newspaper, making it cleaner and easier to paint. Tissue or other coloured papers add interesting texture and colour.

Strip papier mâché: working with boxes

Materials: Provide boxes and moulds as listed above for pulp papier mâché, but not scissors (torn paper is best). Wire pieces can be bent as a working base shape. Set out:

- trays of torn-up newspaper, white newsprint, tissue paper of various colours;
- paste;
- card boxes and tubes of various sizes, eggboxes;
- masking tape (not sellotape).

Then follow these steps:

- Assemble some boxes and tubes, and fix together with a little masking tape. Dip newspaper strips into the paste, and lay them over the structure to join several components together. Repeat, until the whole structure is covered.
- Place a layer of dry newspaper over this, then another wet one, until the paper is very soggy and you can pinch and squeeze it to make different textures on the surfaces of the construction. Then cover with very small strips of white newsprint to finish. Smooth rough edges with your fingers, or leave them as a textured finish, if you prefer.
- Leave to dry. In a few days, use it as a sampler to try out surface decoration. Try: pva glue mixed with powder paint; magazine cut-outs glued over parts; a layer of modroc; cut-out bits of card glued on firmly to make a pattern of shapes all over the surface.

Modroc

Modroc is also used on broken limbs. Bandage is impregnated with plaster of Paris which is dipped in water to activate the plaster, and used in approximately the same way as papier mâché strips. While occasionally appropriate in primary schools, modroc creates a lot of fine dust in use, and the user should always wear a protective mask. Children with respiratory problems should definitely not use plaster in any form.

No special tools are required. Make sure there is at least one bowl of water and one container of modroc placed between each pair of children so they do not have to lean over each other. Make sure sleeves are rolled up and that clothes are covered. Plaster will wash out, but it can prove difficult to remove, especially from knitwear. Try out the ideas given above for strip and stick papier mâché.

Newspaper rolls

A newspaper, rolled diagonally and fixed with masking tape, makes an effective and strong tube, like a very large drinking straw, which can be cut to required length, joined to others and formed into a structure to support embellishments as desired. However, large piles of newspaper can, in some conditions, self-combust. Store it in large trays, like those for fruit in supermarkets, to avoid mountainous piles. Quantities can be obtained from local libraries when they dispose of back issues, or from newsagents.

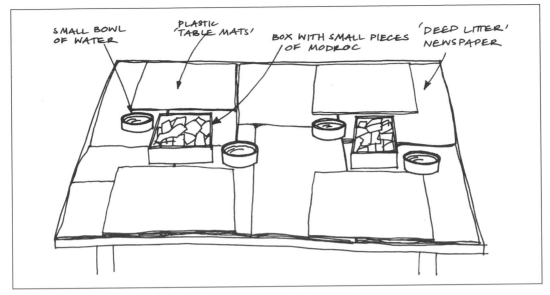

Figure 10.8 'Laying the table' for using modroc

Figure 10.9 *Moving Figures*. Newspaper, tape and paint models by ten year olds. Size: 35 cm high

Experimenting with structures

These starting points encourage children to learn how structures work, and experience how much space can be occupied by a (once) flat piece of paper. Each group of about four children needs:

- a pile of newspapers, broadsheet and tabloid;
- a plentiful supply of masking tape;
- elastic bands;
- a generous space in which to work;
- a piece of card on which to support the structure.

Tearing is more satisfactory and immediate than scissors: the hands are sometimes undervalued as tools. The task set can be very simple, giving children maximum opportunity to experiment: make a person, a piece of furniture, an enormous plant, an animal, a shelter or a teapot. Older groups can try to portray an idea, emotion or concept in sculpture, which may result in either figurative or abstract realisations, e.g. strength, sadness, happiness, tension, power, love.

Once structures are made, perhaps in a fairly limited time, and discussed, decide if they are finished or if further work is to be done. This type of spontaneous response to a challenge may result in a dispensable structure, the purpose having been served in the immediate making and discussion, with no further place or reason for its existence, although taking photographs may ease the pain of parting.

Children can evaluate the learning they feel has taken place, by considering how well they met the given brief, how technically accomplished their structures were, and what skills they have acquired or developed in the process. A list of points made, pinned on the classroom wall, serves to highlight achievements made, and boost confidence, as well as providing the teacher with assessment data.

Rolled newspapers as armatures for figures or animal sculpture

The following suggestion is based on the work of sculptress Folake Shoga, who uses an ingenious and cheap form of armature to make a full-scale model. The process takes a long time, but implications for reinforcing work in e.g. maths, science and design and technology, are enormous. Folake makes a basic armature from strips of cane, but it can be accomplished on a small scale with newspaper rolls, padded with balls of scrunched up newspaper taped in position and covered with strips of pasted paper. The model may stand (difficult) or sit (easier!) or lie down (cop-out!). It is possible to make a giant by doubling dimensions, but large armatures need considerable strengthening. It could be fun to have groups working on different parts of the body which are then assembled, to see how well they all fit! Photographs of the model from different positions and angles, or drawings in sketchbooks help children work out body mechanics as the sculpture develops. (See smaller versions in Figures 10.10 and 10.11.)

Cut rolls to the required length for a particular person's arm, leg, hand etc., and fix together with tape or elastic bands. Double to make them thicker and firmer. Scrunched up balls of paper can be taped to represent fat, muscle etc. The head will need to be made out of a large ball of newspaper. It is sometimes hard to work out how to bear the weight of the head on the neck, how to bend the knee or indicate the waist. Quite a few anatomical features of a real figure are found mirrored in the construction with newspaper.

The basic structure can be covered with pasted strips of paper, tissue, foil or other papers for special finishes. It can be dressed using real clothes, though dressing a rigid structure is not as easy as dressing a real person: another aspect to debate.

Research and practical work helps children understand how sculptors work, such as Rodin, Degas, Frink, Giacometti, Moore, Hepworth and Gormley, especially if their sculptures are viewed from more than one angle. Videos about artists and their work are helpful.

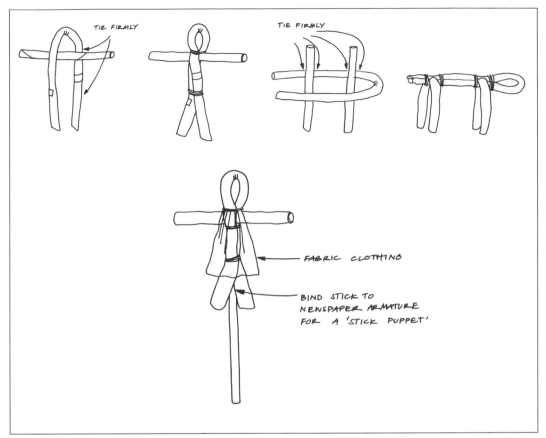

Figure 10.10 'Newspaper roll' armatures

Figure 10.11 *Moving Figures*. Newspaper, tape, string and wood sculpture by a student. Size: 20 cm high

CHAPTER 11

Puppets and Masks

Figure 11.1 *A Christmas puppet*. Gold card, decorative finishes, by a nine year old. Size: 75 cm

Figure 11.2 *Homage à Picasso*. Mask using bubblewrap, card and stick by a student. Size: 45 cm high

The making and use of puppets and masks, both functional and decorative would seem to be almost universal, and within the experience of almost every child and adult, regardless of cultural or geographical roots. Puppetry and masks clearly link with drama, in theatres and outdoor settings such as carnivals, festivals, celebrations and religious observances. Puppetry and masks are very effective for formal dramatic work, but can also provide props for role play, or to transform routine dance and drama sessions.

The impact of puppets and masks can be very powerful, since they can in the hands of skilled operators frighten, amuse, provoke, disorientate, entertain and delight. Thus research into aspects of puppets, masks and their place in the performing arts will include keying in to the design and traditions associated with the inanimate artifact and the place it takes as an animated component within the masque, production or carnival.

The materials and the quality of the artifacts are influenced by the way in which they are to be used, the story they tell and the traditions of decorative and fine arts prevalent within the culture they represent.

Puppets and masks therefore need to comply with minimum standards of wear and tear, since eventual use dictates how durable and perhaps weather-proof they need to be. This also influences the scale, from the enormous masks of the USA carnival parade or the giant-sized puppet costumes of characters from the story of Divali, to the tiny puppet designed to fit a child's finger. The way they are dressed is influenced by the tradition within which they operate, and of course on the available resources.

Puppetry, mask-making and performance have traditionally been important aspects of primary school life, offering unparalleled opportunities for exploring and contrasting literature, storytelling, decorative and even political influences on the art form. Children need opportunities from a range of experiences to create their own artworks and performances, and to recognise that this is a valid part of the research process. The product is no less individual and personal for being based on other examples, and need never be the straightforward reproduction of a given model.

On a rather negative note, perhaps one of the least inspiring sights in a primary classroom is of row upon row of almost exactly similar puppets or masks made on paper plates or from a given template. When a matching set is required for a dance or movement session or performance, there is a space for this type of work, but if artifacts are made to someone else's formula, they can hardly be afforded the status of art products.

Mask-making, and its possible applications within puppetry, is much enhanced if basic skills are well taught, then used and applied in the creation of a unique artifact. Thus mask-making or similar longer-term design and make projects represent the culmination of a thought-out process. When children learn how to design and make, and gain more independence, the product is the more valuable, satisfactory, personal and meaningful. Teaching puppetry, costume construction or mask-making provides opportunities for children to:

- experience the process of planning, preparing for and giving a performance;
- work in a group as a team, to develop ideas and put these into practice;
- use simple techniques, both verbal and non-verbal, to communicate ideas;
- develop self-confidence and raise self-esteem through using the puppet or mask as a vehicle for self-expression.

THE CROSS-CURRICULAR POTENTIAL OF PUPPETRY

While this list focuses on puppetry, there are similar potential links in the uses of masks for drama and dance, especially if a narrative is involved.

English

- The use of written and spoken language, through improvisation, producing a script and enacting the drama.
- If appropriate, accompanying publicity materials to invite people to the show.
- Use of information books for research into puppets.
- Use of stories for inspiring the characters, plot and setting for the drama.

Mathematics

- Predicting and planning for timing and programming.
- Predicting and measuring the amount of materials during the making of the puppets and the set.

Science

- Consideration of different materials, e.g. transparent, translucent and opaque.
- Light, through placing and manipulating lights and spotlights.

Information and Communications Technology

- Use of CD Rom to research puppets in different cultural settings.
- Use of tape recordings and sound effects for the performance.

Design and Technology

- Application of learned techniques through making puppets, sets and theatres.
- Application of design and make processes throughout.

Humanities

- Historical and geographical research, through reading about traditional puppet forms from different cultures.
- Potential use of geographical and historical themes within the research, design and make process for puppets and sets.

Creative Arts

- Music, through the production of an accompanying sound track.
- Design and production of accompanying publicity materials.
- Dance and movement through manipulation of puppets to imitate body movements.

ARTISTS WHO MAKE MASKS, COSTUMES AND PUPPETS

Puppetry and mask-making are art, design and craft forms in their own right, and the traditions and customs of each deserve special consideration. Mask-making offers opportunity to study the depiction of the face in many stylised forms, e.g. in Noh Theatre, African ritual, and in local May-day rituals. The work of face make-up artists, for theatrical performances, can prove fun and interesting for children to see. Looking at good photographs of animals can also inspire, especially in the *National Geographic*, which often publishes excellent images of animals from different angles.

Mask and costume making also apply the principles familiar to many of our pupils through local carnivals and celebratory events, particularly the Notting Hill Carnival,

Figure 11.3 *Whistle for it*. Notting Hill Carnival costume, designed and made by Lucky Thomas with help from Carla. Photographer: Nick Strangelove. Size: 3.5 m diameter

based in the Trinidadian tradition (see Figure 11.3); the Rio Carnival and Spanish street processions; Rama and Sita figures which feature in Divali celebrations, and the Chinese New Year dragons. All these are well established community, national and international cultural occasions, which depend on the application of a wide range of skills, knowledge and techniques, often passed from generation to generation through clubs, societies and groups which come together for the purpose. This is exemplified in the Bridgwater Carnival celebrations in the West Country, where millions of hours are spent by thousands of people, each of whom contributes in different ways to making the procession a success.

Puppetry is and has been, a strong element of cultural representation, perhaps epitomised in the very English Punch and Judy, which has its roots in the French and European traditions as well as the Victorian English sea-side. Puppets have been used throughout centuries to tell stories, often with a religious or moral message, to give information, and to inspire mirth, laughter, fear and excitement. It is a powerful medium in many ways, and even has links with the street effigies with political significance, not least Guy Fawkes and the ritual burning of his form, nowadays an excuse for entertainment rather than having the political and religious meanings it once held for its audiences.

In most communities where such events are held, designers, makers and performers are valued for their making and design skills: these contributions are professional or amateur, but nonetheless skilled.

The masks of Africa, and those made by Inuit and American Indians have inspired many Western artists, including Paolozzi, Picasso and Matisse, whose work can provide useful examples and starting points for mask-making with a range of materials.

PUPPETRY

There are four main types of puppets, hand, rod, shadow and string. These can be made from a range of materials; often the simplest things can be the most effective, such as newspaper, paper, card, paper/plastic bags, boxes of all kinds, fabric, recyclable materials, foil, buttons, natural materials, clay, plasticine, wood, wool, string or thread, string etc. Puppetry need not be purist. A shadow puppet performance can have rod, stick or glove puppets appearing above and around the screen, and sock puppets can creep up on string puppets very effectively. A mixture of commercial and home-made puppets can be useful, especially if an experienced puppeteer comes with them to work alongside the children.

Hand, sock, glove, bag puppets

Puppets can be built around the hand itself, by decorating the hand with felt pens, or by putting the hand inside a decorated bag or sock or glove.

Rod puppets

Hand-held rods are attached to parts of the puppet and manipulated to give movement. Rods are usually operated from below and obscured by draped fabric or clothes. There is a strong tradition of rod puppetry in China, Indonesia and Turkey.

Shadow puppetry

Puppet shapes are made from opaque and transparent paper or card and attached to sticks. These are operated in front of a light source, behind a translucent screen. Parts of the puppets can be hinged to imply movement. Traditionally shadow puppetry is used in China, Indonesia, Egypt and Turkey.

String puppets, marionettes

Movement is through the manipulation of strings attached to parts of the puppet.

Theatres and screens

These can be easily constructed for rehearsal and performance from furniture or easily obtainable materials. Children can help with the design and construction, using large cardboard boxes with the sides cut out or one table upturned on top of another, as shown in Figures 11.4 and 11.5.

Light sources

Any light source can be used to illuminate a puppet theatre or screen for shadow puppets, such as natural light from a classroom window, an office lamp or an overhead projector.

Sets can be made on overhead projector transparencies, and projected from behind on to a white backdrop. This is very effective, but needs rehearsal to ensure that there is

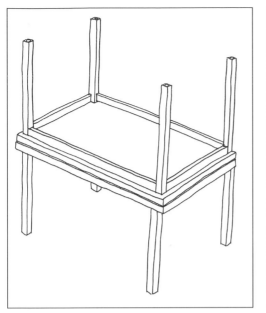

Figure 11.4 One table upturned on to another

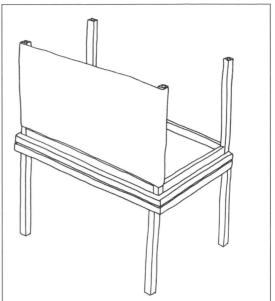

Figure 11.5 Stretch fabric over the legs and secure with pins or sew to make a screen for shadow puppets – to be lit from behind

enough room to project at the right focal length to fill the space behind the stage, and to make sure no shadows are cast between the light and the screen.

TEACHING PUPPET-MAKING

Most children have experienced puppetry through television and live shows, but it is important to remind them of the principles before beginning work on a particular project. A good starting point is to make a display of puppets of different types in the classroom, which will be fairly easy to organise with the simple ploy of asking as many people as possible to contribute puppets to the display. Books to give additional information about puppets and puppetry are available from libraries.

As far as possible, allow the children to use and play with the puppets. Show them how they can draw on their hands to make the simplest, most accessible form of puppet. Putting a sock over the hand and using fingers and thumb will provide further sophistication. Videos of puppets are readily available, incorporating shows, practical demonstrations and the work of experts in the field.

Once children have played, investigated how different types of puppets work, and had opportunities to watch others using puppets (to get the feel of how to convey ideas to an audience), the process for making and producing a puppet play follows well established procedures, each stage of which requires separate and distinct lesson planning by the teacher as well as full briefing of any supporting adult helpers. The stages are:

- discussion of stories: characters, plot and setting;
- handling a range of materials to decide what might be suitable for a particular purpose;

- deciding in groups who will fulfil which function, and play which role;
- listing requirements, and/or collecting materials from display to make puppets and set;
- time for making different elements, puppets, set and any other props needed;
- intermediate rehearsal with puppets;
- rehearsal of scripts and lines, to ensure clarity of voice from behind the screen;
- finishing off of practical work;
- final rehearsals;
- performance.

Intermediate rehearsals can be video-taped. Children then have an opportunity to see how their efforts look from the other side of the show, and to gauge how well their voices carry from behind the screen. The appearance of their own heads amongst the puppets, or the bird falling apart as it 'flies' through the sky, can be treated with good humour, as children also note what modifications are needed for a more polished final performance. This in turn may be videoed, for appreciation of the performers, and for posterity.

TEACHING BASIC MASK-MAKING

An introductory exercise

This work is best done in small groups, although a whole class session will work with sufficient resources and adult help. Children need to look at a variety of visual resources depicting hats, masks, face paints etc., to give them ideas about the nature of a mask, and how the face can be masked. They can quickly try various ways of using their hands to cover parts of their face, and make up faces to disguise their features. To make an instant mask, each group needs:

- card or heavy paper strips (e.g. paper trimmer off-cuts) of different colours, textures and weights, although a limited selection of colours may be effective;
- scissors, one pair per two children;
- staplers with the right size staples;
- masking tape;
- pencils.

An adult may need to be the stapler assistant, but should try to follow instructions from the children rather than dictating how to make the mask. Staples should be covered with a piece of masking tape, especially if sharp wire will make contact with the head or face. Children need to be reminded of the health and safety aspects of the work, told about the types of materials they can use, how long that have and who can help them. However, avoid giving them a model to work towards, since they should have some ideas from the visual resources, and from trying out shapes with their hands and fingers.

Task

The task is to make a mask, in a given length of time, using only available materials. It must fit your head, and stay in place (with hands free) if you move around with it on. You must be able to see through it, but it should disguise your features.

A good starting point is a coronet, although a face frame works well too. Children can work in pairs to measure and mark the card strips to make the base shape. This can then be embellished and decorated using other bits of card, cut and stapled in a contrasting pattern or fringed for hair or beards. Eye holes may be cut, or slits left between strips of card; children soon realise they only need a little aperture to be able to see through. For once, children with glasses may be at an advantage, since these can be part of the structure, with due precaution. Once made, the masks should be worn, for an ad-hoc parade, or for props for a dance or drama exercise.

This type of session offers teachers the opportunity to assess children's design and technology skills, their ability to measure, form and fix paper and card, their ability to work safely within a structure and to carry out a design brief effectively. Their ingenuity and adaptation of resources is often quite startling, and solutions may be attempted which would be missed if following a fixed design.

Evaluation might be done in pairs, including how well the design brief was met; overall effectiveness and wearability and comfort, plus a comment about whether and how the visual stimulus used inspired them to try out a particular idea for themselves. While such work is not very durable, the effects of the exercise can be long-lasting. In particular, it offers children the chance to learn about distinguishing the basic structure of a piece from its decorations or embellishments, and realise that the prettiest decoration is only as effective as the structure it is decorating.

Mask-making using modroc or gummed paper strips

This is a technique which can be used in primary schools but only with the utmost caution, and an adult–child ratio of at least one to two. It is included here because many people know about the process and consider using it in class, but it should never be attempted except under the most favourable circumstances. Student teachers should never do it without a qualified teacher in the room. Do not do this on anyone else if you have not had it done on you! Do not do your first mask on a child – practice on an adult first.

Nostrils and mouths must be clear at all times. There is a very real danger of fatal suffocation if the airways (nose and mouth) are covered. The model should be warned that the process takes quite a long time and that s/he will need to keep both face and body very still for the period. Have a mirror to hand to show the model how the work is progressing. Children should never be permitted to carry out the whole process unaided. Check regularly that the model is happy with proceedings; if not, stop immediately and abandon the mask.

If after all these warnings, you still want to make a modroc mask, the process described below should be followed in detail. Substitute brown gummed paper strips for the modroc if you can, although it is more tricky and fiddly to use; even when wet, the paper strips are not as pliable as modroc.

Process

Tie hair back from the face, and cover hairline with a scarf, securely tied. Cover all clothes carefully. Ensure the overall is tucked inside the neckband or collar. Cover face and neck with a generous layer of vaseline, or the mask will stick to the skin and pull at facial hair – painfully. Pay particular attention to eyebrows and hairline, even though the model is wearing a scarf.

Set out a small bowl of water and small strips of pre-cut modroc, or brown paper, about 10–15 cm long by 2–3 cm wide.

Dip strips in water one by one and place carefully on the face, overlapping slightly, in this order:

- around the chinline up to the hairline to make a frame around the face;
- across the forehead over the eyebrows, avoiding eyelids and eyes;
- across the cheeks between the nose and mouth, taking care not to block nostrils or cover the mouth;
- across the cheeks, over lower part of the nose, avoiding nostrils;
- down from centre hairline to tip of nose;
- across bridge of nose under eyes.

This will give the basic coverage, and further vertical strips can be added to fill in gaps, except for eyes, nostrils and mouth. Another layer can then be applied in the same way if the model is sufficiently patient and forbearing.

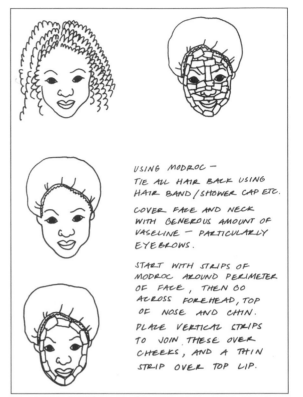

USING MODROC —
TIE ALL HAIR BACK USING HAIR BAND / SHOWER CAP ETC.

COVER FACE AND NECK WITH GENEROUS AMOUNT OF VASELINE — PARTICULARLY EYEBROWS.

START WITH STRIPS OF MODROC AROUND PERIMETER OF FACE, THEN GO ACROSS FOREHEAD, TOP OF NOSE AND CHIN. PLACE VERTICAL STRIPS TO JOIN THESE OVER CHEEKS, AND A THIN STRIP OVER TOP LIP.

Figure 11.6 Using modroc

The model then needs to sit still until the plaster has dried, usually about 4–5 minutes for a single layer. Test if it is time by gently lifting the edge of the mask – if it is dry, it will be relatively stiff. Then, gradually and gently ease the mask from the face and place carefully on a surface to dry.

Wash the model's face immediately in warm, soapy water and dry carefully.

After about 15 minutes, the mask can be worked on further. Layers of modroc can be added, e.g. to cover the mouth and nostril apertures, and the eyes, if appropriate. Brown paper masks will benefit from an extra layer of white kitchen paper, applied like papier mâché strips.

Once completely dry, the mask can be painted and decorated with conventional water paints, although a little pva glue in the paint will add a slight sheen to the finish. Hair, fabric for clothes or headgear, jewellery etc. can be added if it is to be a human model, or other features if it is to be turned into another sort of creature, such as an animal, spaceperson or monster. Attached to a stick, such masks can also make good puppets; glue some fabric around the neck to indicate a shirt, dress or cloak.

CHAPTER 12

Clay

Figure 12.1 *Miners*. Biscuit fired clay models by ten and eleven year olds. Size: 10 cm high

Wherever you are, it is almost certain that you will see something made of clay: plates, cups and other domestic items, bricks, tiles and building materials, ornaments and jewellery. It is very easy to provide a display of clay objects and artifacts to demonstrate to children the many uses of this wonderful material and its universal application in practical and decorative forms throughout the world.

When clay is dug from the ground, it is muddy, almost liquid, and oozes between the fingers when handled. In a short time, as the air dries out the water content, it becomes more malleable, and can be rolled between the hands, patted from palm to palm, squeezed into a ball using the whole hand and then reworked again and again.

Children and their teachers need first-hand experience of these qualities, to see how the consistency, and consequently the modelling potential, changes as it dries or is made wet again with damp fingers. It is remarkably absorbent, and dries out very quickly, or can be kept damp in an airtight container.

Once formed and completely dry, it can be fired (baked) in a kiln at a very high temperature, so it keeps its form, although this process, biscuit firing, will not make it watertight. For this, a glaze, effectively powdered glass, needs to be applied to the surface and the clay re-fired so the glaze fuses, like molten glass, into its surface, providing a watertight seal.

Working with clay has a special role to play in children's artistic and aesthetic development. It is easy to manipulate and very responsive to touch; it can be formed into an infinite variety of shapes and decorative features; its form continually changes, but can be transformed permanently through firing. No other material offers this potential, which is why artists and potters, designers and manufacturers have used it throughout the ages and across the world. It has a wealth of historical and social traditions associated with it, offering experiences to children that support their learning about the art of others, and to inspire their own.

Clay is readily available beneath our feet, although of course not all forms of mud have the potential of the type of clay bought in processed form from suppliers. Considered a basic play material in schools for younger children, clay has also been regarded as messy and difficult to organise: this is not necessarily so. Well organised and resourced, with challenging tasks offered, clay is a worthwhile and most satisfactory medium which children and adults find stimulating, pleasurable and rewarding.

Other modelling media offer similar potential in some respects, e.g. play-dough, plasticine and salt dough. Each has its own qualities, some in common with clay, but there is, frankly, no substitute for the real thing. Harder materials can be used for carving, e.g. soft wood, salt in blocks, soft plaster. The benefits of clay, however, far outweigh the others for general classroom use in primary schools since:

- it is relatively cheap to buy;
- it can be used in the classroom with a minimum of specialist tools and equipment;
- it can easily be recycled;
- its plastic state permits a continual changing of form thus encouraging personal discovery and expression;
- as a three-dimensional medium, it demands a specific mode of thinking;
- it encourages the development and use of problem solving strategies;
- it promotes the understanding of spatial relationships;
- it links across the curriculum, promoting the use of language, the application and development of mathematical concepts, scientific and technological ideas while providing a wealth of historical and geographical material for consideration, and provides a context for exploring the multicultural nature of art and crafts.

Children need to understand the qualities, potential and limitations of materials they work with. This is especially true of clay, which is infinitely forgiving as a medium, but also makes certain demands. They need sufficient time for structured play, so they can be more independent, and achieve more satisfactory results. At least one session is needed to introduce or revise basic techniques before making a specific piece. Clay can be reworked many times, if treated with care, so children should be encouraged to discard 'draft' experimental work.

THE CROSS-CURRICULAR POTENTIAL OF CLAYWORK

English

- Developing descriptive and technical language through interactive displays.
- Recording children's discussion, so their own words are used in labelling.
- Writing up accounts of processes.
- Researching the work of artists and craftspersons using clay.

Mathematics

- Investigating the difference in weight between wet and dry clay.
- Comparing surface area with its mass: a ball can be rolled out very thinly, shaped to a cube or cuboid; a stubby thumb pot can be stretched to a very thin and fragile form.
- Developing geometry through tile design: patterns, tessellation and irregular shapes.
- Using slabs to make cylindrical, cuboid, or irregularly shaped pots;
- Consolidating concepts of capacity, surface area and solid forms in designing pots.
- Incising surface patterns: regular or irregular, symmetrical or asymmetrical.
- Using scale and comparative size in model-making.

Science

- Calculating how much water clay holds, and how much is lost during drying/firing.
- Articulating principles of solids and liquids changing form during making, firing and glazing.
- Understanding temperatures and processes of change when clay is in the kiln.
- Understanding principles of dustbin kiln firing.

Information and Communications Technology

- Using computer imaging to design a clay artifact.
- Accessing computer design programs for tiles and mosaics, to investigate tessellation.
- Using CD Rom to research aspects of clay and its use.

Design and Technology

- Recording domestic, decorative and architectural uses of clay.
- Considering the form and function of a range of items and fitness for purpose of specific materials, e.g. the relative advantages of ceramics, metals, plastics, glass, wood etc. for specific items such as teapots, plates or drinking vessels.

Geography

- Investigating universal applications of clay: body adornment, vessels, architectural features and domestic items.
- Comparing these with artifacts familiar to the children.
- Studying different finishes and glazes used according to the geological features of a particular region.
- Finding out how different types of clay are transported from one area to another, according to needs, e.g. the use of Cornish china clay both for production of clayware and for medical purposes.

History

- Using displays of historical and modern artifacts from the local region and throughout

the world to examine the universality and durability of the medium.
- Studying narrative on Greek vases.
- Studying the significance of Ancient Egyptian and other African tomb clayware.
- Obtaining archaeological evidence from Roman and other pots, mosaics, jewellery etc.
- Studying developments in design through the ages.

THE BASIC ELEMENTS OF ART IN CLAYWORK

Line

Children use clay as a drawing medium, manipulating it into shapes and forms with as much ease as they would depict these with a crayon. The malleable and responsive qualities of the material encourage this free and creative use. Surface decoration on claywork also involves the use of line. Fingers or tools can be used to make incised or engraved marks. Thin coils or strips added to the surface can create linear texture, pattern or images. (A layer of clingfilm over clay before drawing on it will prevent the clay surface from being dragged.)

Colour

Clay comes with its own colour, red, buff and grey terracotta being most common in primary schools. Using several different coloured clays in combination extends the decorative opportunities available, as long as they are able to be fired at the same temperature if necessary (see Figure 12.2). Colour can be applied to the surface of clay in the form of glazes or slips, although many of the associated processes are complicated and costly. There are commercial paint-on colours available for Newclay. Most claywork has to be fired twice to obtain a glazed surface.

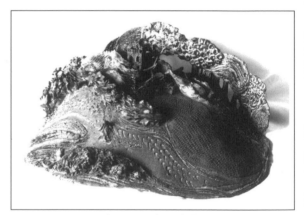

Figure 12.2 *Landscape*. Glazed clay model by a student. Size: 60 cm high

Texture

The tactile experiences associated with using clay contribute significantly to children's learning about texture. The texture of the clay itself can be liquid and mud-like, plastic and pliable, hard and cheese-like or dry and crumbly. This continual changing of form is a source of discovery and interest. Texture can be added to the clay surface by smoothing or roughening, incising or engraving. The finished item can be rough as rocks or smooth as silk, or any combination, depending on the clay and how it has been treated.

Form, shape and space

Clay is a three dimensional medium and so working with it promotes a particular mode of thinking. Building up a model or pot from component parts, or alternatively cutting away from a lump to reveal a shape, demands specific cognitive processes and encourages learning about scale and proportion and spatial relationships.

ARTISTS AND CRAFTSPERSONS WHO USE CLAY

Working in clay offers unique opportunities to introduce children to the work of artists, craftspersons and designers (see Figures 12.3 and 12.4). Children need, if possible, to touch and hold it, to feel the surface texture and appreciate the many surfaces that can be achieved, and to appreciate its 3D nature. Most local colleges have examples of students' work, and may be willing to give some to schools for a resource collection. If possible, acquire examples of how different techniques have been used for both hand-building and thrown pots made on a wheel. Local museums have examples of pots and vessels from different times and places, although it is rarely possible to handle them. Books about artists and craftspersons from many cultures can be found in the art, history and archaeology sections of good libraries. Illustrations can be blown up on a photocopier to complement a display of real clay objects.

While tiles and relief work can be rather like working in 2D, the basic material is solid, malleable, carvable and able to have different surface applications. Looking at artists' work and examining the techniques used, as well as describing and discussing the effects achieved, encourages

Figure 12.3 *Clock piece (detail).* Clay sculpture by Abigail Leach. Size: 30–35 cm

Figure 12.4 *Untitled.* Matt glazed moulded clay bowls by Yani Nichols. Size: 25 cm diameter

children to be more adventurous in their own work. Experimenting with different ways of working helps them appreciate the finer qualities of artists' work they view. It is unrealistic and limiting for children to copy another artists' work. However, looking closely at the elements contained within a piece of sculpture or researching a vessel made by someone else does promote ideas and inspire the imagination.

Figure 12.5 *A field for UWE*, work inspired by sculptor Anthony Gormley's *Field for the British Isles*, clay figures, dustbin fired, by students. Size: 20 cm high

TYPES OF CLAY

Different types of clay can be bought through art suppliers or from local potteries. It comes in large plastic bags, weighing 12.5 or 25 kilos, which should be airtight. The terms earthenware and stoneware denote the temperature range at which the clay needs to be fired. Otherwise, they can be treated in the same way. The type and texture you need depends on what you want to do with it. The following terms are descriptive rather than technical: children can find their own words as they investigate different consistencies and textures. The main types are:

- *Earthenware:* This is usually used for red terracotta clay, although it can be grey/pink or white in colour. It is dense in texture and the most common type found in schools.
- *Stoneware:* This is usually white, or rather grey clay of which other types are porcelain and china clay. Each has its own properties. Buff stoneware is most likely to be found in primary schools.
- *Newclay:* This is white clay with tiny nylon fibres and a non-toxic drying agent added during processing, which bond the finished work when dry, almost as if it has been biscuit fired. It is expensive, and for the clay enthusiast, is not nearly as satisfying to use.

CONSISTENCIES OF CLAY

Muddy: Almost like thin cream, with a high water content, this clay oozes through the fingers. Slurry is even runnier, used to join two clay surfaces. Slip is also of a cream-like consistency, sometimes coloured and used for surface decoration. The term slip is often erroneously used in school for slurry.
Soft: This is rather like uncooked pastry, malleable and able to be rolled into a ball. If the thumb is pressed firmly into it, to make an indentation, it becomes a thumb pot. Rolled into sausage-like strips, fixed to a base, it becomes a coil pot.

Medium hard: In consistency like warm plasticine, this holds its shape and can be rolled out like pastry into tile shapes, or slabs which can be joined using slurry to make a slab pot. It is also suitable for moulding, modelling and some carving purposes.

Leather hard: This is tough, difficult to tear by hand, but can be cut like cheese with a cutter or knife to make slabs or tiles, and is suitable for carving with a sharp tool. It can be burnished with the back of a spoon, a smooth stone or pebble, to give a sheen like polished leather, or otherwise textured to achieve a decorative matt surface.

Dry: Completely dry made items are ready to fire. Test by holding it to the cheek: if it is cool, it is not totally dry. Bone dry clay will feel warm to the touch. If dry clay has not been fired, it can be reconstituted with water to make it useable.

PREPARING CLAY FOR USE

If you are fortunate enough to have clay straight from a new and unpunctured bag, it should be medium soft, ready to be torn or cut into appropriate sized pieces for use. If, when you cut it, there are Emmental cheese-like holes, it will need to be wedged to get rid of the air bubbles which can prove disastrous in a kiln. The air inside the bubbles expands as it heats, and the whole pot shatters, probably damaging everything else in the kiln at the same time. To wedge the clay, cut it into thick pieces, roughly 20 × 15 cm. Slap each piece hard, edge down, onto a board, lift and repeat about 20 times, each time slapping a different edge onto the board. You may also knead the clay rather like kneading bread. Test the clay by cutting across it with a wire. There should be no holes in it.

Always check the state of clay a few days before you need it. Never assume that everybody else is as careful as you in ensuring that it is put away ready for re-use. If your bag or bucket of clay is solid as a rock, do not despair. Reconstitute. Put on a dustmask, and put the clay inside a bag which will withstand the battering you are about to give it. Break it into pieces with a hammer. Let the dust settle inside the bag, then carefully place the bits into a medium sized bucket. Pour over just enough water to cover it, and leave to soak for as long as it takes for the dry clay to absorb the water and become moist, which could be several days.

If you can, use a plaster bat (see below), a wooden board or a large pad of thick newspaper. Ladle the clay on to it, and let it spread out. It resembles mud, but do not worry if it is runny. Leave it to dry out sufficiently to roll it into small balls. Line a plastic bucket with a plastic bag. Put the balls into the bucket, lay a damp towelling cloth over them, twist the bag to make an airtight seal and put the lid on.

The clay will now be ready to use when you need it. In future, always ensure that clay to be reused is placed in a ball in a separate bucket, lined as above. Spray it with water to keep it moist; enough for the clay to absorb if it has been dried out. Seal and cover the bucket or bowl (see Figure 12.6).

You can make a plaster bat by pouring liquid plaster-of-Paris into a large box, to a depth of about 5 cm. Leave it to dry, remove the box, and you have a bat, on which the clay can be left to dry out. Never let even a grain of plaster get mixed with clay if it is to be fired. It will blow up in the kiln.

CLAY IN THE CLASSROOM: PRACTICAL ADVICE

Working surfaces

Clay can be used directly on any formica-type surface, but in schools it is best to cover the table with layers of newspaper. On top, put small formica boards cut from old shelves, hessian, or plastic cut from heavy duty bags. Hardboard pieces work well: the texture on the non-shiny side adds interesting patterns to rolled out clay. If the clay is quite wet, a small newspaper will absorb the dampness. It is best to have a range to choose from according to the condition of the clay.

Encourage children to keep their hands over the working surface, so any bits stay on the table top. A thick newspaper 'mat' on the floor may be advisable in certain less predictable situations. Any small discarded bits of clay can be rolled together and kept damp in a plastic container. This minimises the amount left to clear at the end of the session, and the clay is kept in a more useable state. Make sure during clearing up that no clay goes down the sink. Leave cloths to dry the hands, and put crumbs in the bin. Unless a clay trap is fitted, the sink will get totally blocked.

Water

The clay table need not be near the sink; indeed sometimes this is really not advisable! Provide a damp sponge in a saucer to wet fingers, or to smooth over the clay's surface if necessary. A water spray is useful. For joining, a small quantity of slurry, liquid clay, can be applied with fingers, or with a brush kept for the purpose.

HEALTH AND SAFETY WHEN USING CLAY

When it is dry, clay is quite powdery, and toxic, so the greatest care must be taken so that no one inhales it. No children or adults with any respiratory problem should clear up after a clay session. Good procedures include the following:

- Make sure clay stays on the work surface and not on the floor.
- When children finish work, carefully wrap and remove work in progress, prepare spare clay for recycling, remove all tools, and gently roll up the newspaper so any dust is enclosed and does not float on the air.
- Carefully wipe remaining clay particles from the surface or floor with a slightly damp cloth. Sweeping causes the particles to rise into the atmosphere which can be harmful, but if necessary, wrap a slightly damp cloth over the bristles first.

STORAGE

Claywork in progress is very fragile, and needs to be handled with care. Any work to be kept damp for the next session can be put on a wood or formica mat, on a piece of newspaper to help retain moisture and prevent the clay sticking to the mat. It should be lightly sprayed and tucked up snugly in a damp cloth, then wrapped in a sealed plastic bag, or in

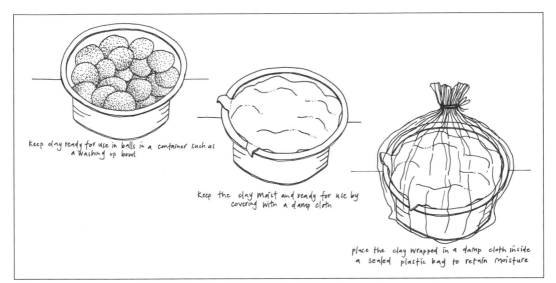

Figure 12.6 Ways of storing clay

an airtight container. Plastic cartons can be stacked to take up as little room as possible. Keep them away from the heat, and make sure the lid is firmly on. Check from time to time to ensure the container remains damp inside.

TOOLS AND EQUIPMENT

Fingers are the best tools for starting off. Special tools are available, but improvisation is easy, as long as the tool serves its purpose and is not too sharp (see Figure 12.7).

Cutting and carving: the tools for this are:

- blunt knives;
- spoons of different sizes, to carve, or to dig out the insides of a solid piece before it dries;
- cheese cutters: two pieces of wood for handles linked with nylon thread, or wire, which cut into the clay; these are strictly for adults, since children can easily wrap the thread around their wrists with disastrous, even fatal, consequences. Never have these out where children can idly pick them up to play with.
- cutters: pastry cutters and coffee jar lids to cut rolled clay into shaped tiles.

Modelling: this can be done with:

- spatulas or lollipop sticks;
- commercial wooden or plastic sets;
- blunt knives;
- small and large metal or wooden spoons;

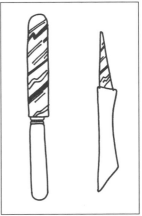

Figure 12.7 Knives. Old round bladed table knives are good for cutting clay and much safer than the traditional potter's knife shown on the right.

- small pieces of wood, smoothed and perhaps shaped;
- kidneys: commercially produced kidney-shaped rubber pieces, used like sponges, to smooth the clay surface.

Texturing: rolling out on a textured surface will give a surface finish to the clay; almost anything can be used to press into fairly hard clay, to make patterns or indentations, e.g.:

- forks;
- round and square short dowel rods;
- cogs;
- small lids;
- strong matchbox sleeves;
- empty glue-stick containers and biros.

Rolling out: for rolling out use:

- old wooden rolling pins (clay sticks to plastic);
- sections of metal pipe, thick dowel rods;
- wooden blocks: to roll the clay out evenly, place the clay between two long thin strips of wood of equal size to roll on so clay is rolled out to an equal thickness. If the clay being rolled or flattened is placed on hessian or heavy cotton mats, the texture imprints on the clay.

Sieves and colanders: are useful to drain excess water from very wet clay. If soft clay is pushed through a sieve or colander, spaghetti-type strips emerge which is texturally effective and great fun to do. Garlic presses work well too.

Turntables: small turntables are expensive, but enable work to be turned around. Put a sheet of paper under the clay so it does not become too difficult to remove.

Cutlery trays: plastic cutlery trays are useful to store and present tools for easy access and checking at the end of the session. One tray between four or five children will usually suffice.

Water sprays: plant sprays are helpful to stop the clay drying out during work, or to dampen it prior to storage.

TEACHING TECHNIQUES

Whether the artifact is a pot, a vessel, a model or a sculpture, basic ways of working with clay will be used: building up, shaping, cutting out, pulling out, digging in or carving. Terms below are not technical but descriptive, to help children articulate their intentions and actions. Children need demonstrations and practise with all of these techniques, using clay of varying consistencies, to become familiar with how to use them as appropriate for the task in hand. The pine cones in Figure 12.8 are observational work, demonstrating different approaches to making clay models.

Figure 12.8 *PineCones.* Biscuit fired clay models by seven year olds. Size: 8 cm high

Building up: starting with a shaped ball or a base, other pieces of clay are stuck on, using slurry and cross-hatching to ensure a firm join for ears, handles, wings etc.

Shaping up: with a final overall idea in mind about how the clay will finally look, the ball or other shapes piece of clay can be pummelled and pushed into roughly the right shape before work begins on the finer points of the artifact. Hands are the best tools for this, although 'proper' tools may be used as well.

Cutting up: clay can be cut with knives or torn with the hands. Only adults use wire or cheese-cutters for cutting.

Pulling out: a ball of clay is pinched and pulled out, usually between thumb and fingers, to make the desired form. Its plasticity depends on its consistency, and damp fingers help keep it moist.

Carving, digging in: the basic form having been shaped, fingers and tools are used to cut into the surface to sculpt or model, or to add interesting textures. It can also be carved with appropriate tools for overall shaping or modelling, or for details.

Joining clay

The fragility of clay, as it dries and during firing, puts pressure on delicate work. When pieces of clay need to be joined or stuck on, for handles, features of a face or limbs of a creature, it is vital that a sufficiently strong bond is made between the two pieces of clay. If not, each piece dries independently and the whole thing falls apart. Teach techniques to join clay effectively to avoid later disappointment.

Always use clay that is suitably damp and plastic. Encourage children to identify when clay has become too dry, when the surface begins to crack, and to return it to the bottom of the clay bin and replace with damp workable clay.

Join large areas by pressing firmly together, e.g. the legs on a model animal to the body, and smooth with a tool or the fingers if appropriate.

For more delicate pieces, use slurry. Roughen both edges to be joined by making small crosshatch incisions on each surface, and apply slurry to both with a sponge, brush or fingers. Then press firmly together. For small pieces, this will suffice. For larger pieces, you may need to use a tool to smooth the join to ensure a firm bond. A supporting coil of clay pressed around the join and smoothed works well.

Thin and fragile pieces are nevertheless apt to break off when dry. Looking at artists' work, particularly sculptures, will inform the children of how the limitations of clay bearing its own weight has been taken into account, especially for equestrian and human models. Make sure that long thin bits are supported appropriately, or redesigned if necessary. This is best learned through experimenting on non-precious items, rather then on the carefully worked piece.

If clay does break while drying, it can be repaired by painting each surface with vinegar and then pressing together. Only do this when the clay is bone dry. Remember to crosshatch both surfaces before moistening with vinegar.

INVESTIGATING CLAY

The following ideas can be worked through with a group as a starting point for a session, after which children can apply the techniques to more considered work:

- Take a ball of clay and work it in your hands, squeezing, pulling and pinching. Flatten the ball onto your clayboard. See how many different textures you can make on the surface using only parts of your hand – fingers, nails, palm, fist, knuckles. Each makes a different mark when pushed or poked or pressed into the surface of clay.
- Smooth the surface of the clay flat again. Select from the marks you made previously, arrange them into a pattern. Repeat this, using contrasting marks.
- Make your clay back into a rough ball, by patting and squeezing it to shape between cupped hands. Roll it out the longest possible sausage you can make. Roll up the sausage into a very smooth and regular ball. Notice if the clay has changed in any way as it has been used.
- Roll the clay flat. Cut it into several pieces, one large and several small, with straight edges. Decide where to join the small bits on to the large one. Mark the place with a tool. Roughen the edges with a tool, a fork or a knife, to make a crosshatch pattern. With a sponge, wipe the rough edges to make them damp. Carefully place the smaller pieces perpendicular to the larger piece on the rough damp marks you have prepared. Press each one down gently, and use another tool to smooth the edges. Hold up your construction to see if the bits stay on. If they fall off, try again. If not, roll the clay back into a ball, and make a new construction to practise the technique.
- If the clay is a bit dry, dampen your fingers from the sponge to moisten it. Then try these ideas again, and see how long the clay stays usable and soft enough to work.

CONSTRUCTING POTS

These are basic hand building techniques used for clay vessels or pots, or as the basis for a model or sculpture: thumb pots, coil pots, slab pots, and moulded pots. Children find these ways of working endlessly adaptable, and come to appreciate how artists and craftspersons make their work. A description of each type of pot is followed by instructions which can be used with children, and ideas for extending the technique. (We do not here discuss the use of the potter's wheel, because this is usually best left until children are older and can cope with the machine. Film of a potter using a wheel may nonetheless fascinate primary aged children.)

Thumb pots

The clay is rolled into a ball, and the thumb pushed in to make a hollow. The edges can then be worked on, as the pot sits in the hand while you extend it by pulling it out between thumb and fingers. The clay can be worked to a very thin layer. Keep dampening fingers keep it moist if it starts to dry out and crack. The procedure to be followed for making a thumb pot is shown in Figure 12.9, and some successful pots appear in Figure 12.10.

The process of making a pot in your hand will determine the shape and size, but after the initial operation the pot can be adapted or transformed in any way you wish.

- Make two thumb pots, roughen and dampen the edges, put them together and smooth the join. Squeeze gently to develop the shape. Decorate the surface.
- Make a perfectly symmetrical thumb pot. Pinch and pull the sides until the shape is transformed.
- Join two pots together to make a hollow shape as a base for a model.
- Combine a number of thumb pots make a composite pot.
- Look at pots, books and other items on display to identify a favourite ceramic vessel shape. Work to create your own version in clay, keeping the general shape but change some aspect of it to make it asymmetrical.

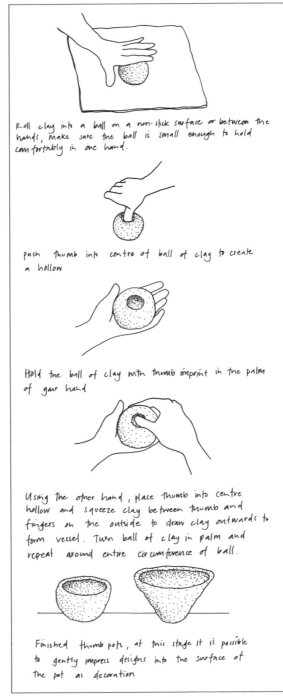

Roll clay into a ball on a non-stick surface or between the hands, make sure the ball is small enough to hold comfortably in one hand.

push thumb into centre of ball of clay to create a hollow

Hold the ball of clay with thumb imprint in the palm of your hand

Using the other hand, place thumb into centre hollow and squeeze clay between thumb and fingers on the outside to draw clay outwards to form vessel. Turn ball of clay in palm and repeat around entire circumference of ball.

Finished thumb pots, at this stage it is possible to gently impress designs into the surface of the pot as decoration

Figure 12.9 Making a thumb pot

Figure 12.10 *Thumbpots.* Melted wax resists glaze on pots by eight year olds. Size: 7–10 cm high

Coil pots

Traditionally, coils are sausage-like shapes, but can equally be made of flat strips, long and not too thin. They do not have to be regular in size, nor do they have to be placed regularly. Gaps can be left, or a thick coil can be followed with a thin one. As long as the pot holds its shape, and conforms to what you want to make or try out, there are no rules. Coil work can prove very strong, once the basic techniques and skills have been acquired. Figures 12.11, 12.13 and 12.14 show interesting examples of the coil pot method. In Figure 12.12 the way to make a coil pot is demonstrated.

Remember to roughen the edges and dampen, to take the first coil. As each coil is added, roughen and dampen the top edge. Press each layer together lightly as you work, joining them at different points on the circumference – this is important because joins on top of one another will be weak.

When you are satisfied with its size and shape, consider the surface texture. A coiled surface can look attractive, or you can use a tool to smooth each coil downwards into the one below. For a smoother surface, hold the pot in one hand and gently tap the surface with a spatula or ruler as you turn it around in your hand. If a water-tight pot is required, smooth the inner surface as indicated above before drying.

A small group of children can make a composite pot on a fairly large base. Each child makes a series of coils, to add in turn to the pot. They learn from each other, remind each other of the 'roughen and dampen' routine if necessary, and are more adventurous when working in a group, perhaps to make an abstract construction of different sized coils. The pot can then be discussed, dismantled, and turned back into smaller balls.

Figure 12.11 *Coil pot.* Textured biscuit fired clay work by a student. Size: 45 cm high

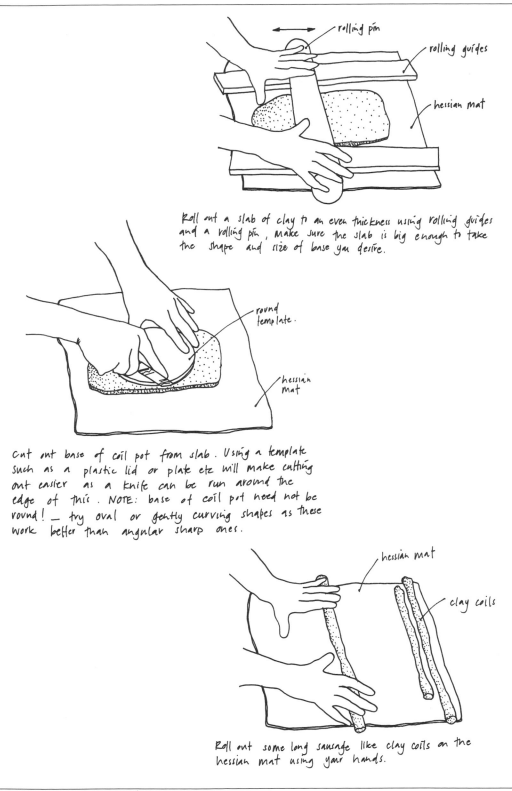

Roll out a slab of clay to an even thickness using rolling guides and a rolling pin, make sure the slab is big enough to take the shape and size of base you desire.

Cut out base of coil pot from slab. Using a template such as a plastic lid or plate etc will make cutting out easier as a knife can be run around the edge of this. NOTE: base of coil pot need not be round! — try oval or gently curving shapes as these work better than angular sharp ones.

Roll out some long sausage like clay coils on the hessian mat using your hands.

Figure 12.12 Making a coil pot

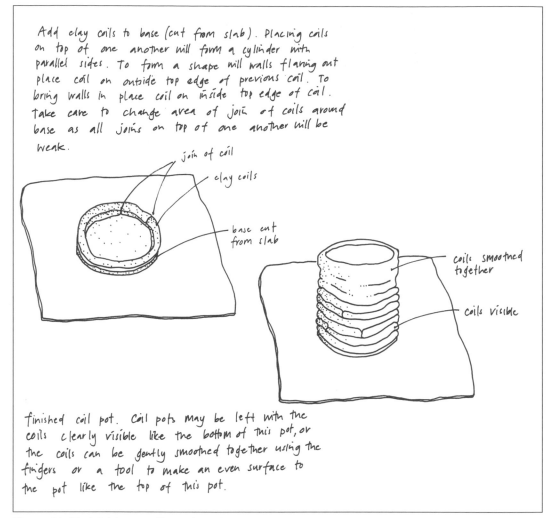

Add clay coils to base (cut from slab). Placing coils on top of one another will form a cylinder with parallel sides. To form a shape will walls flaring out place coil on outside top edge of previous coil. To bring walls in place coil on inside top edge of coil. Take care to change area of join of coils around base as all joins on top of one another will be weak.

join of coil

clay coils

base cut from slab

coils smoothed together

coils visible

finished coil pot. Coil pots may be left with the coils clearly visible like the bottom of this pot, or the coils can be gently smoothed together using the fingers or a tool to make an even surface to the pot like the top of this pot.

Figure 12.12 Making a coil pot (cont.)

Figure 12.13 *Torso*, glazed coil pot by a student. Size: 30 cm high

Figure 12.14 *Bowl*, glazed coil pot by a student. Size: 35 cm diameter

Figure 12.15 *Sunflower Tiles*. Biscuit fired tiles by seven year olds. Size: 15 × 9 cm

Figure 12.16 *Vessel*. Glazed slab pot by a student. Size: 45 cm high

Slab pots and tiles

Pleasing examples of slab pots and tiles are shown in Figures 12.15 and 12.16. The sunflower tiles were based on observation of sunflowers the children had grown themselves. A wide range of processes, including incising, pulling out and applying cut shapes to the surface, contribute to the final effect. For the slab pot, five slabs were used to form the basic 'box' shape, and a circular pattern was applied to the surface as coils and pressed into the slab when soft.

The first stage of the process is identical to that for making a coil pot (see Figure 12.4a). Then the clay is trimmed to the required shapes for the base and the separate sides, or into a continuous piece to make a cylindrical pot. Each component is scored, dampened and put in place to make the overall form, which is embellished or smoothed as required. Slabs can also be used as tiles, to decorate with relief. Adding smaller pieces of clay makes a raised pattern or image. If the clay is thick enough, the surface can be modelled with tools and fingers to create interesting effects.

Cut out a series of shapes to make a box or vessel. Put them together to check that it will work, then join the edges carefully as described to make the form you want as in Figure 12.17. Further possibilities would be to:

- Cut different shapes and join together to make a building, using small slabs for tiles, windows, doors etc. Join each piece carefully.
- Place a cylindrical shape such as a tin on the clay base covering the shape with paper so the clay does not stick. Gently press the clay into shape around it. Join the edges to the base and to each other as described.
- Look closely at a natural object, e.g. a pine cone, seed head, fruit or a flower. Observe its structure, form and surface texture. Roll out a thick clay slab and cut the shape you want. Use the information gathered as a starting point for your own claywork.
- Look at a photograph or sketch you have made of a view or landscape. Roll out a very think slab of clay, and try to represent some aspects of the landscape in the clay. A view through a window can be a good starting point, because it has a ready-made frame within which to focus. Use textural and mark-making tools. Remember to join each piece carefully as described.

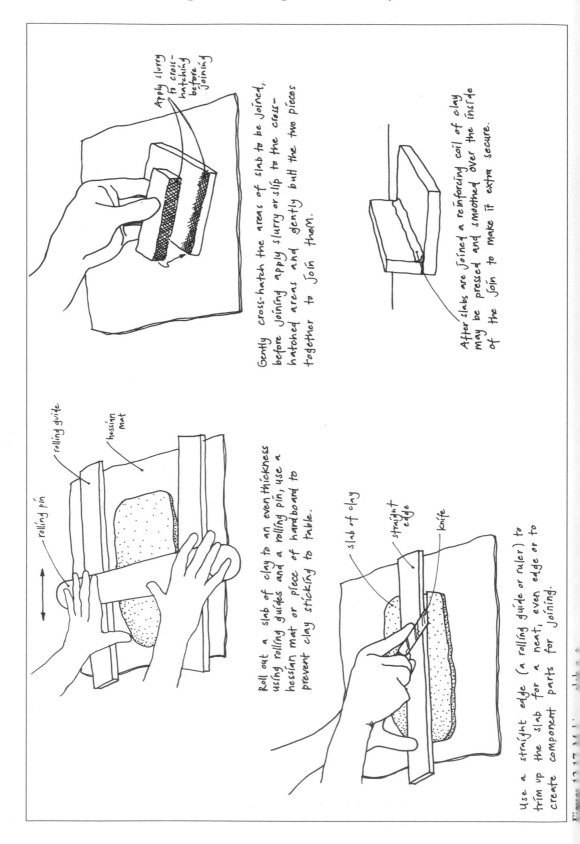

Apply slurry to cross-hatching before joining

Gently cross-hatch the areas of slab to be joined, before joining apply slurry or slip to the cross-hatched areas and gently butt the two pieces together to join them.

After slabs are joined a reinforcing coil of clay may be pressed and smoothed over the inside of the join to make it extra secure.

rolling pin

rolling guide

hessian mat

Roll out a slab of clay to an even thickness using rolling guides and a rolling pin, use a hessian mat or piece of hardboard to prevent clay sticking to table.

slab of clay

straight edge

knife

Use a straight edge (a rolling guide or ruler) to trim up the slab for a neat, even edge or to create component parts for joining.

Moulding

Rolled out clay can be moulded over an existing form such as a dish, a plate or a specially made mould. Avoid using surfaces the clay will stick to. As it dries, the clay will pull in several directions, and may break, so be sure it will come out of the mould, or the mould out of the clay. If not, you may have to cut the clay to remove it, like a plaster cast from a broken limb. Clay shrinks slightly in the drying process, so it is not advisable to leave it to dry around the perimeter of a cylinder. Carefully remove the mould before it dries. A layer of newspaper, or clingfilm, wrapped around and attached tautly with masking tape, allows work to slide off more easily. Once leather hard, clay can be carved or built up or burnished with the back of a spoon to make the surface shiny. The procedure can be summarised as follows:

- Roll out a large piece of clay. Pick it up carefully and lay it on the mould. Gently press it into the mould. Trim off any excess. Make sure the clay is touching the mould at all points, so it dries to the exact shape you require.
- Leave it to dry out a little, and remove from the mould when it is firm enough to take its own weight.
- Add surface texture to the inside before leaving it to dry completely.

KILNS AND FIRING

Claywork is fragile when dry and will soon begin to crumble if not fired in a kiln. The process of firing, or heating clay to a high temperature in a kiln, transforms it chemically. Firing is expensive and time-consuming, so should not be taken for granted. Good claywork can be achieved without a kiln, although children should experience seeing their own work go through the various stages of making, drying out and being fired. Fired clay cannot be reconstituted, and will no longer be absorbent in the same way as unfired clay.

Before any firing takes place, the clay should be thoroughly air dried, so there is no moisture left. Bear in mind the need for safe storage of claywork during drying, when it is so brittle, away from exploring hands! Hollow out solid lumps of clay beforehand, and pierce with a hole. If the shape is effectively completely closed when sitting on the shelf of a kiln, the air inside will expand and the item will shatter. So, ensure hot air can escape during firing.

- The first kiln firing is called biscuit firing, at about 1000 degrees centigrade. This makes the clay particles fuse together and become permanent, although still porous. Biscuit firing takes about 11 hours to complete, and then it has to cool down to a temperature at which the kiln can be safely opened.
- After biscuit firing, glazes may be applied. Then, the item needs to be fired again: for stoneware, at 1200–1270 degrees centigrade; for earthenware, at 1120–1200 degrees centigrade.

Electric kilns

Electric kilns are available in many primary schools, or arrangements can be made with secondary or adult education institutes. Kilns vary in size, capacity and ease of operation.

Consult the handbook for the particular model before use, particularly with regard to health and safety, as well as more technical publications than this purports to be.

Sawdust kilns

A sawdust kiln, often made in a dustbin, is a good use of appropriate technology, and an experience from which all children will benefit, even if there is a functioning electric kiln on site. The following instructions can also be adapted to make a kiln from bricks; further information can be sought from other publications. This type of kiln fires at biscuit stage only. During the firing process in a sawdust kiln, the clay fuses with carbon affecting the colour. Sawdust-fired claywork is usually black, grey or dark brown. The method is:

- Use a metal dustbin with several small holes punched through the sides near the bottom. Collect enough sawdust to fill the bin and some wood shavings, which can be obtained from a carpenter or a woodyard. Place the dustbin in the position where it is to be fired, outdoors (see below). As it will be rather heavy once loaded, packing it in situ is a good idea. If this is impractical, ensure there is help to move it before firing.
- Store claywork to be fired until completely dried out. Sort according to size.
- Put a 5 cm layer of sawdust on the bottom of the bin and then put in some of the heavier claywork. Pack the larger, heavier pieces towards the bottom and the smaller, lighter ones on top, because as the kiln burns through, the top pieces will fall onto the ones below. Fill cavities inside pots or models with sawdust. Leave enough room around each to pack with more sawdust.
- Spread another good layer of sawdust and some wood shavings over the claywork. Press down lightly. Add another layer of clay pieces. Continue to build up layers of claywork and sawdust/woodshavings until near the top of the bin.
- Add another final layer of sawdust, generous wood shavings and some screwed-up newspaper. Light the newspaper. Place the lid on the bin, resting so that it is not completely closed. In this way a draught circulates and sustains the combustion process.
- Leave the sawdust kiln to burn through slowly, a period of some hours. When cool, remove the lid and claywork. A full bin will have been transformed into a pile of claywork and ashes at the bottom.

Health and safety considerations

- Dust is produced from the sawdust while the kiln is being packed. Provide dustmasks. Keep anyone with breathing problems at a safe distance.
- Firing the kiln must take place out of doors in a secure area. The sawdust smoulders only, but the dustbin does get extremely hot. A weekend firing in an internal playground, is ideal. Light it after school and leave to burn all night.
- Carry out firing only with permission of the headteacher and goodwill of the caretaker. No nuisance is caused other than a small amount of woodsmoke.

GLAZES AND VARNISHES

The subject of glazes is very technical. Advice is best obtained from the local adviser about what type to use and where to get supplies for the primary school. There are chemicals involved, and the dry powder which is mixed to make glaze is very fine, so health and safety considerations about its use must be strictly adhered to.

Glazed items need to be fired before the effect is seen. The very high temperature melts the glaze and causes it to fuse into the pot. Wonderful effects can be achieved with very basic glazes, and if you have a kiln available, it is well worth finding out about the potential use of glazes and other decorative finishes.

Most dry clay which has been biscuit fired can be painted with a mixture of powder paint and pva glue, which gives it a sheen but does not make it watertight. 'Newclay' can be varnished with the special product made to go with the clay, which is mixed with a medium and applied with a brush.

Slip, watered down clay, can be coloured with certain pigments and used as a decorative finish by painting it on to the wet item before it is left to dry and biscuit-fired. On the whole, this technique is best left until children are older, as there are so many other things to explore about clay in the primary school.

CHAPTER 13

Fabrics and Thread

Figure 13.1 *Feathers*. Collage sewn from observatin by a seven year old. Size: 8 × 14 cm

Traditionally, textile arts and textile crafts are distinct but closely allied. The clothes we wear and use in our homes are functional but, on the whole, commercially produced. Textile artists produce weavings, collages and embroidery, for decorative, functional and non-functional use. Studying and making textiles and fabrics offers an opportunity to introduce interrelationships between form and function, which also apply to architecture and the built environment.

The surface qualities of a fabric depend both on its inherent structure and the materials used to make it. On the one hand, there is the process of making the fabric, through weaving, felt-making etc. In weaving, the basic loom, warp, weft relationship, once learned, can be developed and manipulated to achieve any number of effects. The scale may vary from very tiny, weaving a wishbone for example, to enormous, depending on the available resources and the preference of the weaver. Materials can include paper, wool, other natural or artificial fibres such as nylon, sisal and linen, and natural materials such as branches and plants.

On the other hand, there is the surface decoration of cloth such as batik, silk dyeing and printing, where the application of pigments or other substances change the surface of a finished piece of cloth. Appliqué, collage and patchwork techniques use the surfaces of fabrics and materials in combination to achieve different effects.

Looking at textiles, children appreciate how particular art/craft forms are influenced by the natural resources available, such as cotton in India, wool in Wales, and the colours by the pigments to hand, as well as the needs and values of the people in the cultural setting in which the artifacts have been made or manufactured.

In some cultures the distinction between craft and art is almost impossible to make. The beauty and aesthetic extravagance of the textiles of parts of South America exemplify how the combination of traditional techniques such as weaving, tasselling and braiding, and an amalgamation of colour and texture, act together to create a visual and tactile impact. The craft becomes an artform in its own right.

Examining old textiles helps children understand relationships between design and manufacture, and the development of associated technology. Access to current work demonstrates how modern textile artists use traditional craft processes in untraditional and unusual ways, softening the boundaries between art and craft.

Appropriate display material is usually easily found at the backs of most wardrobes. Examples of interesting woven, printed or dyed fabrics, shawls, garments, tablecloths and curtains often come to light, and can be assembled, grouped and displayed to look at, handle and sketch.

Knitted items, old and new, show children how different types of wool are used for different purposes, knitted, coloured and shaped in many ways. Kaffe Fassett has elevated the status of knitting into an exciting and free form of making garments, with bold designs, and, quite importantly, provides a role model for boys and men in what has traditionally been regarded as a women's craft.

The National Curriculum requires children to have experience of working in groups. There is certainly a tradition of groups of people working at different stages of the process when making a carpet or wall hanging. Some batik work, paste resist, rag rug making, fabric collage and large embroidery can be carried out by groups of children, individually or in pairs.

It is important for teachers to have recent first hand experience of the techniques and skills they teach children, and to ensure that other adults working with the children also have an opportunity to try out processes before the teaching session.

THE CROSS-CURRICULAR POTENTIAL OF WORK IN FABRICS AND THREAD

Fabrics and thread work offers many opportunities to introduce or consolidate aspects of other areas of the curriculum. While the focus should be on the art, craft and design elements during the process, introductory sessions can highlight cross-curricular links. There is hardly a topic, project or theme in the primary classroom which cannot be enhanced by the inclusion of work related to fabrics, clothes and fabric crafts. Here are some thoughts about potential links, where previous learning can be consolidated through practical application or study in this area.

English

- Using appropriate vocabulary.
- Joint decision-making and collaboration in groups.
- Storying, narrating tales associated with particular items.
- Explaining processes and techniques to each other.
- Use of reference material in the design process.
- Reading about designers and fabric artists.
- In drama, thinking about posture when wearing different fabrics and styles.

Figure 13.2 *Sunflower*. Appliqué sewn from imagination by a seven year old. Size: 22 × 22 cm

Mathematics

- Tessellation, measuring and symmetry in printing on fabrics.
- Exploration of patterns in arranging threads and colours.
- Weaving alternately under/over: odd/even relationships.
- Relationship of perimeter to radius in circular weaving.
- Pattern repeats in already printed fabrics.
- Examining weave patterns such as herringbone, checks and tartans, ribbed, plain and purl patterns in knitting.
- The creation of shaped designs for tie-dye.

Science

- Comparing and testing fabrics.
- Examining textiles, threads and fibres with a microscope and magnifying lens.
- Study of plants used in the production of fibres, e.g. cotton, linen.
- Study of animals whose fur or wool we use, e.g. sheep, goats, camels.
- Comparing different pigments and dyes, their properties and suitability for use in different applications for dyeing or colouring cloth.
- Study of the permeability and other properties of fabrics.
- Study of the principles of dye bath and resist processes.

Information and Communications Technology

- Use of the computer to design symbols for print.
- Using the 'copy' and 'paste' controls to effect different repeat designs.
- Using controls to try out various different colour combinations.
- Working out patterns and compositions on screen to apply in weaving.

Design and Technology

- Experimenting with different simple looms.
- Following through a simple design and make process.

- Working out how fabrics hang together.
- Experimenting with different materials for different purposes.
- Exploring the potential for different threads and fibres as warps and wefts.
- Using fabrics in puppets and other construction work.
- Learning how to join fabrics with glue or thread.

Geography

- Looking at woven fabrics from different cultures.
- Finding out about the production of different materials such as wool, cotton and linen.
- Tracing where fabrics come from, and the effect of the industry or craft on the home economy.
- Identifying appropriate types of dress and fabric use for living in different environments.
- Comparing traditional techniques of weaving and fabric printing throughout the world.
- Looking at the use of symbols in fabric print designs, e.g. Paisley, Alari designs.

History

- Looking at textiles in old prints or paintings.
- Study of design at different periods; recognising where fashion changes and where particular styles endure, e.g. kimonos, kaftans and kilts.
- Study of the work of designers of a particular period, e.g. Morris, Quant, Westwood.
- Comparing textiles of different ages.

Art and design

- Exploring colour combinations in weaving.
- Looking at the way artists/sculptors portray textiles.
- Experimenting with some of these methods.
- Looking at textile artists' work in sculpture, hangings, fashion etc.
- Looking at traditional and innovative uses of colour, pattern and design in weaving, quilting, etc.
- Exploring the issues of women designers, artists and craftspersons in fabrics and thread.

THE BASIC ELEMENTS OF ART IN FABRICS AND THREAD WORK

Pattern and texture

Decoration on cloth in the form of pattern and texture is something children know about. They are familiar with the texture on corduroy and knitted garments, and the patterns on their clothing and furnishing fabrics at home. They may also have made friendship bracelets or painted a design on a tee-shirt or seen hair being plaited. What may be less clear is the relationship between these surfaces, the processes that produced them, and their intended function. Close scrutiny of a range of fabrics can help develop this understanding, e.g.:

- comparing samples of velvet, hessian, tweed, chiffon, knitting, crochet etc.;
- looking through magnifying glasses and microscopes;
- unpicking examples to examine the structure.

Children learn best by actually using the processes that produce these sorts of patterns and textures. Experimental spinning, weaving, painting and printing on cloth also teaches about how artists manipulate materials to produce particular textural and decorative effects, e.g.:

- twisting and spinning different types of thread together;
- weaving on different looms and combining various warp and weft materials;
- using resist techniques such as paste resist or batik;
- creating print blocks to use on cloth.

Colour

Children can select and combine colour when working with fabric or thread to achieve desired effects, in the same way that they mix powder paints or layer pastels. They learn to manipulate different fabric and thread materials, and to exploit their particular characteristics in relation to colour, e.g. the transparency of dyes, the reflective qualities of silken thread or natural fleece colours. Time to experiment is as essential here, as in the use of any other art medium, so children build up a vocabulary of colour combinations and understand how to achieve them. They need to learn about how the colour of threads, fabric paints and dyes combine and interact, in order to use them effectively.

Line

The word 'linen' has the same derivation as the word 'line'. Children use line in much of their fabric and thread work. When practical difficulties are overcome that sometimes hinder fluency, such as threading needles, sewing and embroidery become effective forms of drawing. Even cutting around fabric is a way of making a defining line that becomes the edge. When children dribble wax or squeeze a paste line on cloth, they are in fact drawing. Using these materials involves different manipulative skills from those used with conventional drawing tools, but children are nevertheless making a similar variety of lines and marks in creating their patterns and designs.

Shape, form and space

Fabrics, essentially 2D in structure, are transformed into 3D forms at stages of manufacture. Flat cloth effectively becomes an enclosure for parts of our bodies when it is made into clothing. Using non-traditional looms, where a warp is attached to several adjacent surfaces such as around the legs of a table or around several trees in the field, children can create 3D weavings. Adapting the traditional technique of weaving around nails on the top of a cotton reel (sadly no longer possible with the advent of plastic cotton spools), or using basic knitting techniques very freely, can produce very exciting 3D forms.

CRAFTSPERSONS AND ARTISTS WHO USE FABRICS AND THREAD

Woven techniques are used in sculptural forms and children can also draw on the work of sculptors for their inspiration. Goldsworthy, an environmental sculptor, weaves or twists together leaves, sticks, feathers, and a range of other natural materials in the construction of his sculptures. Hepworth used stretched wires and threads across the interiors of some of her abstract sculptural forms. Soft sculpture, depictions of unlikely things like furniture, apple cores and hamburgers, in soft materials sewn or glued together by artist Oldenburg, challenged the traditional world of sculpture.

Artists who work with fabric and thread are sometimes difficult to locate. Contacts can be made through Crafts Guilds or Associations, and via the Internet. Exploit skills and interests within the school community. Find out which parents or colleagues knit, crochet, sew, embroider or make patchwork, and invite them to share their skills, especially the men. If fabric artists or craftspersons can visit the school, or children can visit them, they might:

Figure 13.3 *Coburg Holly.*
Quilt by Mary Kear.
Size: 2 m × 1.5 m

- observe them at work, in the studio or workshop or in school;
- listen to them talking about their work and how they approach different stages of the process;
- question them about aspects of their work;
- look at examples of their work, scrutinising, drawing and painting to gather information.

Children might be able to work collaboratively with the artist or craftsperson on a piece of work, which will involve combining ideas, understanding the relationship between the expert and the novice or apprentice, developing appropriate expertise and evaluating as work progresses. Children might also work on their own pieces alongside the artist or craftsperson, who then acts as teacher or adviser where necessary.

Embroidery and stitchwork are important elements of fabrics and thread work, from the genteel embroideries of Victorian women with delicate botanical motifs, to the complex stitchery now possible with sophisticated sewing machines and threads (see Figure 13.5). Victorian samplers are fascinating for children, especially the work of girls of the same age.

In the USA and Europe, quiltmaking has attained previously unheard of respect and acclaim as an art form (see Figure 13.3). Wall hangings of Northern Europe and South America are now shown in galleries and afforded new status. Through textiles, children can examine the role of women as

Figure 13.4 *Zenana*. Pleated, printed linen by Caroline Bartlett. Size: 122 × 120 cm

Figure 13.5 *And the Fish Grew Wings (1995)*. Mixed media and machine embroidery on fabric by Sara Dudman. Size: 120 × 120 cm

artists and technicians, and how they have influenced developments such as making and operating looms, sewing machines and knitting machines, as well as dyes and printing techniques.

Quiltmaking in particular, but also weaving, embroidery and knitting, demonstrate how a basic necessity for warmth, linked with a need for embellished and decorative finishes in our homes and our clothes, combined to offer opportunity for women to express ideas and create works of art within often constrained domestic circumstances. Choosing fabrics for a quilt was a skilled process of selecting contrasting or complementary textures and colours from what was available. Reusing materials brought associations that, once incorporated into the quilt, imbued it with further significance.

> I liked assorting those little figured bits of cotton cloth, for they were scraps of gowns I had seen worn and they reminded me of the persons who wore them . . . One fragment in particular, was like a picture to me. It was a delicate pink and brown sea-moss pattern on a white ground, a piece of a dress belonging to my married sister, who was to me bride and angel in one.   (Lucy Larcom, Lowell mill-worker, 1824–1893, *A New England Childhood*)

Early quiltmakers were influenced by the shapes and forms in their environment, using them in the patterns they cut and pieced to make their quilts. As the delight in the process and the popularity of the products grew, the aesthetic preferences and judgements of individual quilters contributed to the development of these designs into a range of highly intricate and complex patterns. The technical knowledge and expertise of the quilter, her appreciation of the characteristics of the materials, combined with skilful aesthetic judgements and enthusiasm for the process, transformed some of the quilts they made into objects of beauty and artistic merit.

Similar processes can be identified in the history of other textile crafts. Recent reassessments of the aesthetic quality of fabric arts have elevated them in status. Exhibitions of textiles are now shown in galleries previously reserved for the work of painters and sculptors. Fine art work using fabrics and threads (see Figures 13.4 and 13.5) is not to be confused with the application of traditional crafts techniques. Many artists, mainly female, use traditional and new techniques to create one-off, individual works as wall hangings, screens etc., to express ideas and record responses, in the same way as we more traditionally view paintings and painters.

RESOURCING FABRICS ACTIVITIES IN SCHOOLS

Second-hand bookshops prove happy hunting grounds for books about craft applications of these traditional skills, sometimes lavishly illustrated. Oxfam and similar calendar pictures offer a wide range of different settings featuring the many different types and uses of cloth around the world. Discussing such illustrations and making links between them highlights common elements which span many cultures, and can introduce the notion of appropriate technology, e.g. why some people wear apparently heavy clothes in very hot climates. Collect or borrow from a variety of sources, garments and samples of fabrics demonstrating different techniques, processes and cultural traditions to stimulate close observation and discussion.

TEACHING ABOUT TEXTILES, FABRICS AND THREAD

The rest of this chapter is divided into sections, to cope with the wide variety of work encompassed in fabrics and thread; first, making fabric, which encompasses all the techniques of spinning and weaving; then, decorating and colouring fabric in different ways, developing previous work in drawing and painting; finally, using fabrics as a starting point for cross-curricular work.

Making fabrics and textiles

Knitting and crochet: with older children who have the necessary manipulative skills, teach basic skills and then encourage them to experiment and create interesting texture rather than to produce articles.

Plaiting, macrame, basketry: these crafts help children explore the potential of materials and textures, through links with hair plaiting and beading, plaited bracelets etc.

Spinning and weaving: encourage children to explore the nature and potential of the process, from fleece or raw cotton to woven or knitted cloth.

Vocabulary

Fabric: any sort of woven cloth or knitted material.

Textile: a woven or machine knitted fabric.

Weave: to make fabric by passing weft under and over warp.

Loom: the apparatus or frame on which weaving takes place; looms to support weaving can be made from cardboard boxes, vegetable trays, circular or rectangular pieces of card, chair legs, twigs or branches, bricks etc.

Warp: the lengthwise threads on a loom, made from any strong thread, e.g. string, twine, raffia.

Weft: the crosswise threads on a loom, made from any of a wide range of different found or commercially produced materials including wool, raw fleece, cotton, any threads, torn or cut strips of fabric, strips of paper or card, leaves, straw, raffia, string, twigs, wire etc.

Spinning: the process of twisting fibres together to make longer stronger thread: raw wool or fleece, cotton fibre etc.

Spindle: a weighted rod for twisting and winding fibres into thread. Spindles can be made from any rod that will act as a downshaft, e.g. pencils, narrow sticks such as dowels. The weight can be made from a lump of plasticine, clay or dough, or a potato pushed onto the bottom of the rod. A small notch near the top of the rod facilitates attachment of the spun thread to the stick.

Spinning

Wool is a hair-like growth, but it differs from hair in that it has tiny scales in rings, like a fir-cone. The roughness of these scales means that the fibres hold firmly together when twisted.

It is sometimes possible to get hold of a whole sheep's fleece, which is a most exciting resource to use with children. It can be rolled for storage and carrying into a large bag, and unravelled before their eyes on a large sheet. The space it takes up is seemingly out of all proportion to the size of an average sheep. It may be possible to get hold of a video of sheep-shearing, so children can see just how the fleece is removed by a skilful shearer, in one piece. Discussion will undoubtedly include questions about why it is so big. This may be explored further by opening out garments to see how much room trousers, gloves and other clothes take up if laid out flat.

Raw wool is full of lanolin, which makes it rather tacky to touch, but which is probably quite good for the fingers. If possible, give each child a small piece of fleece to play with, to roll about in the hand, and then to see what happens during the spinning process. (You may need to check for allergy.)

- Try to pull all the fibres in one direction by holding the ends between fingers and thumbs and gently pulling outward. The fibres will gradually come to lie together in one direction. Then the wool can be twisted, to make a long thin thread where before it was a seemingly tangled mass. The process is shown in Figure 13.6.
- Once they have tried with their hands, the use of carders can be introduced. These are quite sharp, so be sure supervision is adequate. The wool is placed between the beds of the carders, and the spikes comb the fleece fibres so they all lie in one direction. The relationship between this and the painful process of combing tangled or wet hair is obvious.
- Once the fibres have been carded, they are gently removed to make a rolag, which can be spun on a spindle. The fibres should be lengthwise, so the rolag can be gently pulled and retain its length.

To spin wool, a simple spindle can be made with a length of dowel with a weight at the end. A lump of plasticine will suffice. There should be a notch near the top to hold the wool in place close to the spindle (see Figure 13.7).

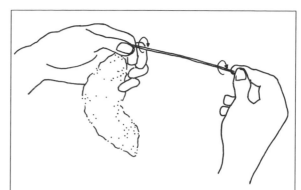

Figure 13.6 Hand spinning without spindle – twist and pull gently between thumb and forefinger

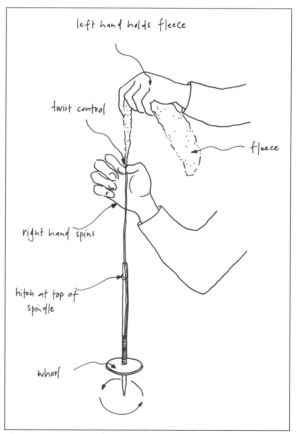

Figure 13.7 Hand spinning using a spindle

- Have some wool already around the bottom of the spindle; commercially produced wool will serve this purpose. Take the end of the wool, and loop it around the notch, leaving an end of about 5 cm.
- Attach the rolag to this (it can be knotted, although it is better to wind it around the end of the wool on the spindle to make a continuous piece). Hold most of the rolag loosely

in one hand with about 10 cm of the fibres, attached to the wool, exposed.

- Let the spindle hang from the wool and set it spinning. It is best to do this standing up, especially for smaller people, because it will have more room to spin. Draw the fibres out of the closed hand with the other hand, while controlling the spin. Try not to let the spindle stop or reverse.
- When you have spun a length of yarn, wrap it around the spindle in a figure of eight, and then around the notch as before.
- When you have finished your handful of wool, pick up another and continue to feed into the twisting thread. You may manage to do this without a knot.

It does take time to achieve expertise in spinning, but it is worth the effort, and sometimes quite young children become very proficient very quickly. Even if they manage only a very small length of spun wool, this can be combined with other resources to make a weaving. Following through this process gives insight into commercial processes, and a range of different wools can be provided for children to sort in different ways.

Spinning wheels are mechanical adaptations of the basic hand-held spindle. They have a fascinating history, and have remained virtually unchanged in design over many years. They can be seen at local craft museums and in working studios, and are sometimes available for loan from local authority school resource collections.

Weaving

This creative craft is truly cross-curricular, since the weaving of fabrics for decorative and practical uses such as clothes and bedding is common to almost every culture, past and present, in one form or another. In some cultures, weaving is traditionally a women's craft, and as such has been under-recognised as an art form, although in Nordic countries, notably Scandinavia and Finland, and in parts of Africa, it is recognised and valued for its true worth as a medium of artistic expression as well as for its utilitarian applications.

It has been remarked that weaving in the primary school is too expensive. It is, if there is an insistence on high grade looms, and only good quality, fine prepared threads and fibres such as wool and raffia. A freer and more imaginative approach is both possible and very beneficial, as well as being cost-effective and satisfying. Teach children that the basic physical technique of weaving involves:

- the *warp*, strong threads, which are attached to
- the *loom*, or frame, to bear
- the *weft*, perhaps less sturdy threads or materials,

to achieve a structure which has literally endless potential for diversity and excitement. Most important to remember, is that you can weave with anything, almost. It is helpful in class to arrange materials according to function: warp threads, weft materials, looms.

Baskets are readily available as resources in all shapes, sizes, patterns and of varying complexity of weave. Drawing a section of a basket or a piece of loosely woven fabric using a magnifying glass encourages close observation and appreciation of the way the piece has been made.

INVESTIGATING WEAVING

- Encourage children to thread small squares of hessian, so they can look closely, preferably through a magnifying glass, to see how the material has been made, and to create their own patterns in the pieces by removing threads at regular or irregular intervals.
- Placing fabrics, especially different loose weaves such as hessian, or decorative weaves such as lace, on the overhead projector enables children to see at great magnification how the threads are put together. If they have made a pattern by pulling threads from hessian, this shows particularly well on the projector, and a whole class can easily see individual pieces. Children can compare and contrast their own with other people's. Baskets show up well too.

Making a paper weaving

Equipment and materials needed are:

- a rectangle of paper of any size, plain or patterned; newspaper or pictures from magazines make interesting textures;
- separate cut strips of paper, all the same width or of different widths, tapering or regular, single width or folded; experiment with a variety made from a range of papers;
- scissors, paper adhesive and sellotape.

The method is:

- Fold the rectangle of paper in half. Make a number of cuts across the fold about 2 to 3 cm apart and up the length of the paper to about 4 cm from the top edge. Do not cut right up to and across the top edge, because the strips need to stay attached.
- Open out the folded paper and you have the warp base on which to weave.
- Use a cut strip as a weft to thread across the warp base under and over alternate strips. Push the strip up to the top of the warp base. Secure the ends of the strip on the back with adhesive or sellotape.
- Take another strip and weave across underneath the first strip. Make sure that you weave in contrast to the first strip, passing it under the warp strip where you went over with the previous one and over where you went under before; this is the essential aspect of weaving that gives it strength. Continue to the bottom of the warp base, securing on the back as you go.

Vary the woven texture, e.g.:

- cut the warp base with strips of varying sizes, tapered or shaped edges;
- weave over and under groups of warps strips instead of only one;
- pull up loops of weft strips to make a more three dimensional effect; (you will need to cut longer weft strips for this);

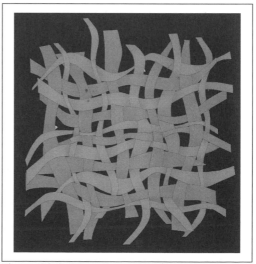

Figure 13.8 *Wavy Paper*. Card weaving by a student. Size: 30 × 30 cm

- pull up weft strips but fold to make triangular or rectangular shapes;
- use images (pictures of faces, figures, objects) for both the warp base and the weft strips. Weaving the weft strips through the warp base will create a different and often unusual image.

Weaving on looms

Looms can be made from almost anything – twigs or branches, table legs, chair legs, old picture frames etc., as well as the conventional wooden or card looms favoured in schools (see Figure 13.9). If using card looms, try to allow the children to decide the size and shape they want, and at what distances to cut notches to hold the warp threads.

Large, collaborative group weavings on tables and chairs, using a wide range of weft materials, inspire exchange of ideas, rapid results and the fun of testing out what works and what does not, e.g.:

- grasses, trailing plants and other natural materials;
- stripped plastic bags or bubble plastic wrapping;
- strips of balloon fabric;
- straws;
- rolls of gummed paper (often found in the backs of school cupboards);
- small thin strips of card and paper from the papercutter.

This list demonstrates how very cheap the process can be, and how easy it is to improvise resources in the classroom, because apart from the educational and social learning, weaving activities are fun. Children who begin by working collaboratively on a large scale are soon able to adapt the skills they have learned for individual work on a smaller scale.

Finishing off the work is sometimes problematic. If a loom is used with ready-made warp, e.g. a fridge shelf, railing or bicycle wheel, it will not be able to be removed at all. The loom, warp and weft all stay together.

For other types of loom, the work can be removed if the warp is appropriately applied. If warp is wound round and round a frame, the threads can be cut across the wrong side to leave a long fringe, which might stay to be part of the finished piece, or trimmed.

If the warp is looped around notches or nails on only one side of the loom, it will need to be snipped to remove the weaving. In some cases, the loom can be bent so the weaving slips off, as with card looms.

It is vital that children should not feel pressured into always producing a neat, even, professional finish to their weaving at this stage, rather that they understand the principles and feel free to experiment, be adventurous and try out different materials to achieve interesting, satisfying and expressive work.

The work of modern weavers, who break traditional rules, proves how adaptable and exciting the process can be, as long as the basic principles of the structure are understood and the piece holds together as required. After all, if a professional piece of work is required, it is best to go to the fabric shop. In primary schools, we perhaps have different aims, which may lead to fine, detailed, accurate and straight-edged work at a later stage. We aim to inspire the use of basic weaving techniques in a creative and exploratory way. They offer all age and ability groups opportunities for:

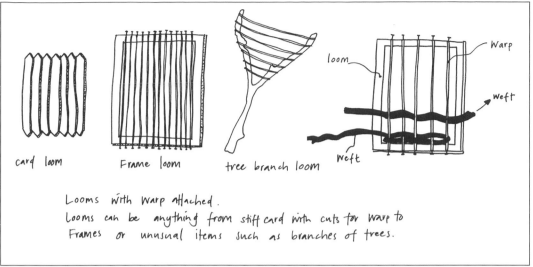

Figure 13.9 Simple looms

- hands-on practical experiences;
- developing manipulative skills and dexterity;
- encouraging extended concentration and focus;
- problem-solving;
- exploring the interaction between process and product;
- making links with traditional and multi-cultural crafts;
- work using the minimum of equipment and materials;
- working individually or in groups;
- comparisons of familiar, everyday articles with historical counterparts;
- promoting a feeling of achievement and self-esteem.

TEACHING THE BASIC ELEMENTS OF ART THROUGH WEAVING

Colour

- Choose one, two or three colours, select warp and weft threads and materials in shades and tones of these colours and weave.
- Make a weaving that represents a season, weather, the elements of water, earth or sky, or a mood such as tranquillity or turbulence.
- Look at a landscape and use the colours you see, or have recorded in your sketchbook, as a basis for weaving.

Texture

- Find contrasting fabrics and weave them to highlight the different textures and finishes: shiny, dull, smooth, rough, sparkly, matt, or natural and synthetic.
- Look at the textures you and your friends are wearing and try to match them in a weaving.

- Use a textured item or artifact, a piece of bark or wallpaper, as inspiration for weaving with different textured materials.
- Make a shiny, smooth weaving or a rough matt one.

Composition

- Make a weaving based on a seascape or landscape you know, using a photograph or sketch as a starting point.
- Make a weaving using geometric shapes: circles, squares or triangles.
- Look through a viewfinder at an area of your room, sketch the arrangement of colours and forms within the rectangle, and use this as a basis for a weaving.

Line

- Use warp and weft lines to make a geometrically based pattern to emphasise vertical and horizontal lines of the weave.
- Make a line weaving, based on two or three colours alternating, varying the width of the line, perhaps starting with very thin lines and building up the width in each colour as the weaving grows.
- Make a circular weaving showing how the line can spiral from the centre to the outside of the piece.
- Make a weaving which uses the warp threads as a feature in terms of colour or texture, emphasising vertical as well as the horizontal lines.

'OURSELVES' WEAVING PROJECT

As part of an 'ourselves' project, children were asked to bring in pieces, preferably strips, of fabric that had some meaning attached. A letter home ensured that parents knew that the pieces would be used as weft for a large weaving. The warp of strong string was attached to nails on the inside of a door, as a makeshift loom. It could equally well have been put on the legs of an upturned table. The fabric pieces were woven into the warp as they arrived, sometimes with the help of parents who brought the children to the classroom in the morning. Each wrote a short piece about his or her piece of fabric, and a scrap was put with the story in a book. (Rumours that one child cut the bottom from her mother's wedding dress without permission remain unconfirmed.) Children learned about:

- *English:* the storytelling, writing and reading of the book, the discussions the work promoted and the active use of descriptive vocabulary in talking about the fabrics;
- *Mathematics:* the longer the strip, the more area it covered;
- *Design and Technology:* making the piece itself and looking at how the structure of the ever-growing fabric worked;
- *Geography:* samples came from all over the world and represented different cultures in being from sari, headcloth, lace, or summer holiday and special occasion materials;
- *History:* the stories of the fabrics and the significance within the family or the earlier life of the child.

DECORATING AND COLOURING FABRICS AND TEXTILES

Of the wide range of dyes and fabric colorants on the market, many are suitable for use in school. Use cotton, from which the processing finishes have been washed out, such as old tee-shirts, sheets or pillow cases. Natural, home-made dyes can also be tested out in class. There are four basic ways of colouring fabric:

- Applying fabric paint or dye to the surface of the material with a brush is rather like painting on paper; paste or wax resist can be applied first, for special effects (see below). Recent development of fluorescent and metallic fabric paints offers an exciting addition to the range available. Some of these are quite expensive, and should be used with care, with especially close attention to the manufacturer's instructions.
- Fabric crayons are available to draw a design directly on to the fabric, or on to a piece of paper which is then carefully ironed on to the fabric. While these are fun for special occasions, they have limited application in the general work of the primary classroom, and are usually too expensive to have generally available.
- Commercially available cold water dyes, including Brusho and Dylon types, are easy to use, relatively inexpensive if diluted according to instructions, and can be made permanent in some cases. Material is dipped or immersed into a dye bath where it soaks up the dye. Home made dyes can be made using vegetables and other plant matter, such as coffee, tea, onions, beetroot, grass and almost any substance that inconveniently stains in other circumstances. It is usually necessary to steep the fabric in a hot solution with water, or even to boil it. Experiment to see which method is most effective.
- Printing with blocks is described in the chapter on printmaking.

Resist methods of colouring cloth

The principle of resist is most commonly known through batik, where wax is applied as a hot liquid, left to dry and colour dyes or paints applied to the cloth. The wax is ironed off to absorbent paper, leaving the original fabric colour showing where the wax was. The colour has been resisted by the wax coating. The process of applying hot wax is clearly potentially hazardous, and should only be used in the most favourable circumstances. The same principle applies if wax crayons or candles are used to draw on paper and painted over: the crayon or candle wax resists the water-based paint. A flour paste can be used as a resist agent, or tie-dye, where tight folds prevent the dye from working on the cloth.

Tie-dye

The tie and dye process is an immediate and satisfying application of a resist process without wax, paste or other substances being applied to the cloth. String, elastic bands or fine thread are tied very tightly around a piece of fabric, which prevents the dye from working in the very tiny folds that are created. So a white pattern is left on the fabric, usually fairly irregular, which has its own unique appeal.

Once the dye has dried, and the string is untied, the cloth can then be re-dipped to make the white area another colour, and to build up layers of colour if the process is repeated several times. The familiar circle of tie-dyed material is only one of the patterns that can be made. Pleating the fabric at different intervals and clipping with paperclips, or even sewing with fine thread, will give different effects.

Preliminary activities for tie-dye are most successful using a range of absorbent papers, such as kitchen roll, blotting papers or paper serviettes. These can be folded, pleated or screwed up, secured with paperclips or clothespegs, and dipped into small containers of Brusho. Once dry and unfolded, children see what happens. They can use their accumulated skill on a more precious piece of cotton later.

Flour paste resist

Figure 13.10 Paste resist

Flour and water paste applied from a squeezy bottle to fabric and allowed to dry forms a thick coating which resists the dyes or paints applied to the cloth. So, when the colour is dry, the dried paste can be removed, leaving white lines where it was. This method is very suitable for primary children (see Figure 13.10). It is similar to many techniques used around the world, in particular the application of cassava in parts of Africa. Where indigo dyes are used, the resultant vibrant range of blues and purples is set off by the white cloth which shows through where the paste was applied beforehand.

The squeezy bottle containing the mixture allows a continuous flow, or individual drops, of paste to be applied. Basic mark-making techniques are used, with increasing sophistication and subtlety depending on the consistency of the paste, the nozzle on the container and the skill of the user.

Before making a cloth paste resist, children need to practice drawing with this strange liquid, and learn how to hold the container in the right way, how to control the drips and the blobs when they start and finish a mark, and how to judge arm and hand movements to obtain the desired effect. Encourage them to use different arm movements as they experiment: sweeping circles, zig-zags and spirals. They can also try to create a series of patterns, using lines, dots, blobs and squiggles.

These preliminary exercises are great fun, very cheap, and help children learn how to control and use the paste to best effect. They teach both the limitations and potential of the stuff. Unless very fine flour is used, the lines are quite heavy, so it is not appropriate to try to produce fine work from what is a rather blunt piece of equipment.

Preliminary work is best done on old paper and then discarded. The paste resist only works well on textiles: the paste has to be picked or rubbed off when dry, and paper is not flexible enough. However, unplanned blobs, dots or lines may well enhance the finished design: an element of the unexpected plays an important part in the making of art.

The materials are:

- a large piece of cotton or individual small pieces: white is preferable but any light colour will do; wash new fabric first to remove the finishing agents;
- empty plastic containers: washing up liquid containers or similar squeezy bottles with nozzles; small ones are easier for younger children to grasp;
- one kilo white plain flour makes enough paste to apply to a large cloth;

- water, mixing bowl, whisk and wooden spoon;
- fabric paints and brushes: these are usually supplied in pots of individual colour with a separate container of mixing medium; check directions supplied for proportions and for procedure for making colour permanent.

For younger children, mix small quantities of colour with the medium ready for them to use; most colours can then be mixed with water, as with other water based paints like readymix and powder paint, to make application to the cloth easy. Some dyes will be opaque, some translucent, some will be quite thick, others thin; first attempts might be best on small scraps of cloth using a fine brush.

Use separate brushes for each colour and wash immediately after use. Provide a range of brushes so that children can use decision-making and mark-making skills familiar through painting and drawing.

Palettes, plates or small tins are useful to mix the paints in, as with powder paints, to achieve the required colour before applying to the cloth; children will need help in working out how much to mix to cover a particular area, and to experiment a little with how the colour looks when applied.

Method

- Mix the flour with sufficient water to give a thick pouring consistency similar to pancake batter, about one litre of water to one kilo of flour. Add the water gradually at first with a wooden spoon and then whisk thoroughly to ensure that all lumps of flour are dispersed or they will clog the opening of the plastic dispensers. A wire coat hanger, bent double, makes a really good whisk. Pour the mixture into several bottles and leave to stand, overnight if possible.
- Spread the cloth out on a suitable large flat space that has been protected with newspaper or polythene, where children have all-round access, and where it can be left to dry overnight.
- On an adjacent area put the bottles of flour paste and some pieces of newspaper where children can experiment with pouring the paste from the dispensers. It does require some practice to get the hang of this and achieve a steady stream with which to draw. Then work on the cloth.
- Transfer the design lightly with pencil onto the cloth. Draw over the pattern with the flour paste, children taking turns. Leave the cloth on table to dry and then fold up or hang until needed. The flour paste will dry to resemble a biscuit crust and will protect the cloth underneath from any paint applied.
- Paint the cloth and leave it to dry. Pick off the dry flour paste to reveal the design in the original fabric colour. Fix according to the fabric paint manufacturer's instructions, usually by ironing.

Batik

Batik is a resist dying process in which hot wax is applied to cloth to stop the colour from penetrating the fibre. It is possible to buy samples of batik fabric, although hand-painted cloth is being replaced by machine-printed fabric where patterns characteristic of the batik process are imitated. These can be examined and perhaps sketched by the children, and used as an inspiration for their own work.

The wax needs to be kept at a high enough temperature to keep it molten so that it can be dribbled and drawn with, and to penetrate right through the fabric. This causes problems for its use with children. Use an electric hot-plate to heat the wax in a double saucepan to avoid burning or scalding. Tape the flex carefully to the floor. The work area should be in a relatively sheltered part of the room to avoid accidents, close, but not too close, to the heater. Wax from the pan needs to be decanted by an adult into a suitable small container, and placed adjacent to where the child will work. No child should be moving around with hot wax.

Before working on the fabric, children should practice on paper, to learn how to use the tools, how long it takes to dry, and the effects the mark-making tools can achieve. It is advisable to have a test run with any adults involved before working with batik, so any potential problems can be dealt with before the children begin. Follow these steps:

- Place fabric on a thick pad of newspaper, with a sheet of white kitchen paper on the top so newsprint does not dirty the cloth.
- A design is applied to the surface of cloth, usually white cotton, with the melted wax. The wax soaks through the fabric and dries to form a hard protective covering. Traditional implements called cantings, that combine a metal reservoir with a spout on the end of a bamboo handle, can be bought. Otherwise use old brushes or spoons. The wax dries very quickly, so work needs to be bold and brave, or the supervising adult needs to have the patience to return again and again to get more wax.
- Make sure the wax is completely dry. Check by holding up to the light, to make sure the wax is really going to resist the dye, or the whole process is invalid. This is where personal experience of adults counts, in teaching the danger signs of too thin a coating.
- The cloth is then immersed in a dye bath. Cold water dyes are used for this technique as immersion in heated water will melt the wax. The cracking of the wax, as the cloth is crumpled to go into to the dye, results in characteristic thin thread-like lines where the dye seeps through. Again, leave to dry completely, on white paper to keep clean.
- The fabric can be dipped several times in different dyes to build up a variety of colours on the surface. In this case wax can be removed from some areas or more wax applied to others to retain some of the original area of colour. The cloth is rinsed dried between dippings.
- If a succession of dippings is required, dip in light dye colours first, progressing to the strong dark colours later, e.g. yellow, red, green, blue, and finally black.
- To remove the wax, place the cloth in a sandwich of white paper, with several layers of newspaper on either side, and a further layer of white paper to protect both the ironing board and the iron from the newspaper. Iron carefully, to melt the wax, which is absorbed by the paper. Replace the top layer of white paper immediately there is any sign of wax, so it does not get on the iron. Once the wax has all been absorbed from the cloth, the piece is ready.
- More wax can be applied in different areas, and the cloth can be put though the same process, to build up different layers of colour and to effect lines of various hues within the design. This is quite a long process, and scarce resources and time rarely permit this extension in primary school.

HEALTH AND SAFETY

- Always read the packet and leaflets of any product you use, e.g. cold water dyes or fabric paints. Instructions from the manufacturer will inform about any necessary precautions, and about any agents needed, e.g. to make ready-mixed paint into a dye suitable for cloth. Always store the packaging with the product if it contains any such information.

- Check if any children have sensitive skin which may be affected even by non-toxic dye-stuffs. Provide adequate protective clothing where necessary and plastic gloves where appropriate. Use old-fashioned laundry tongs to handle wet fabrics.

- To make dyes wash-proof, there are various methods, and it is important to use the right one. Some products should only be used with rubber gloves. Most substances you use will be non-toxic, safe and easy to use. But do check carefully in case there has been an error in storing, or a product has passed its sell-by date, when it may not work or may even be unsafe.

- Particular requirements come into play when children are working with hot wax for batik or using dye baths. The same applies to using hot irons in class. Tape any loose flex firmly to the floor, and ensure adequate supervision and space.

- All helpers, parents and visiting artists or craftspersons must be aware of the requirements for young children to work safely. It is the teacher's responsibility to see that everyone working with children is aware of, and implements, the necessary health and safety codes of practice. Provide a safe area for work. Good principles of basic class-room organisation apply to practical fabrics work of any sort. Work cleanly, tidy up regularly and keep materials well sorted and well arranged for maximum fun with minimum fuss.

USING EXAMPLES OF FABRICS AND TEXTILES

Sewing

Using the tradition of embroidery to create texture on fabric, or as a form of drawing with thread, and to join pieces of fabric to make a garment, 'soft sculpture' or artifact.

Patchwork or fabric collage

Using fabric remnants and haberdashery items, sewn or stuck on to a background, as described in the chapter on collage (see Figure 13.11).

Examining fabrics

'Visability' is a Bristol-based organisation which works with children and adults in a variety of ways to promote expressive activities inspired by global arts and crafts. This idea is based on their work. Children examine the clothes they are wearing: the labels, washing instructions and countries of origin described on the labels. They work in pairs, look at their own and their partner's clothes, and respond to questions.

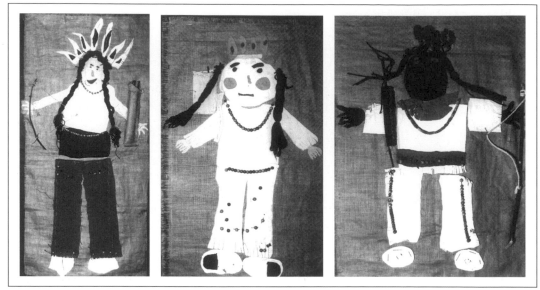

Figure 13.11a–c *Amerindians*. Collage sewn on to hessian, collaborative work by seven and eight year olds. Size: 14 × 27 cm

- What type of fibre is used?
- What is the country of origin?
- Is the fabric woven, knitted, felted etc.?
- How are the pieces joined together?
- How does the garment fasten, e.g. with buttons, a zip, press-studs, or does it simply pull on?
- If so, does it stretch and then go into shape once on?
- What is the surface of the fabric like?
- Is it textured as part of the manufacturing process?
- Is a surface design applied through printing techniques?
- What range of colour is used in the garment, eg. different colours of wool in knitting, or different colours of threads woven together?

Think about taking care of the garment.

- What does the label say about washing it?
- Has anyone got a label that says 'dry clean only'?
- If so, what does it mean? What is dry cleaning? Why is it called that?
- What symbols can you find on the labels and what do they mean? (Packets of different types of soap powders, liquids or bars with the codes explained would be useful: children can read the packets and decide which are suitable for which clothes.)
- How will it get dry after washing?

Think about the people who designed and made the clothes.

- What skills would be needed to make up such a garment?
- If you 'opened out' the garment, what types of shapes would there be?
- How do they know what size to make the different pieces?

For further exploration:

- Children may be asked to record what they find out in different ways, listing for older children while younger or less able children could find their own ways of recording the information they have found out.
- An old garment may be cut open at the seams shows what the pieces look like. Compare this with a paper pattern: sleeves at first seem to bear no resemblance to the shape of the arm it will cover. Trousers too are deceptive in pattern form, as the legs look very large until they are put together. Gloves take up a lot of space when opened out.
- If children have experience of weaving, they might work out if particular bits are cut on the cross, so fabric stretches in a particular way. They might consider why particular fabrics are chosen for particular items, e.g. wool for jumpers and cotton for shirts. Why not the other way around? This also introduces costume and fashion design; some pictures of models on the catwalk will always create excitement and, sometimes, disbelief.
- Much scientific method is applied in the study of clothes. Give the children a set of fabric samples to look at, if possible through a magnifying glass, and encourage them to discuss, compare and contrast the individual pieces.

Before asking specific questions, consider getting the children to sort their samples according to their own criteria. This will get them to look closely, and also inform you as the teacher of how much they are aware of the different properties of different fabrics. It also gives a more open-ended introduction to the subject, and almost always inspires reminiscence and storying about the bit of fabric that 'looks just like the material my mum had in her dress' etc. Some specific questions to focus discussion might be:

- Which fabric is the stretchiest?
- Which do you think would be most waterproof?
- Which would keep you warmest?
- Which might make you sweat?
- Does any of the samples come from an animal?
- Is any of the fabric made from a plant?
- What fabric would make the best trousers for you?
- Which would you choose to make a cushion cover?
- Have you got any clothes made of similar fabrics?
- Does the fabric look the same on both sides? Why?

Such questions will also open up discussions about the wearing of animal products, and the differences between e.g. Nordic people's use of 'local' animal skins for warmth and Western society's use of 'glamour' furs etc. as a status symbol. Also, there is some controversy about the quality of life offered to industrial silk worms.

Sketchbooks can be used to record the ideas, and children might experiment with different drawing media or paint, to try to match textures and colours in favourite fabric samples.

CHAPTER 14

Developing a Context for Learning

Display is an important factor . . . including the display of children's work as a resource for each other. The way in which work and other material is displayed and arranged in a school is more than a matter of convenience: it is a reflection of the atmosphere and attitudes which prevail there. (Calouste Gulbenkian Foundation 1982)

Along with meticulous planning and positive professional relationships, the primary classroom is itself a vital element of successful teaching and learning. Its ethos, its physical arrangement and the quality of work on show contribute to the development of independent learning and critical awareness. It communicates the teacher's priorities, the current class interests and, most importantly, the standard of work achieved, and the value attached to it. Three major considerations for organising the classroom are:

- the creation of a visually stimulating, sensitive work environment;
- access and availability;
- care and maintenance.

The room serves different, often conflicting, purposes, e.g. class and group work, on large and small scales, quiet individual study and more bustling collaborative pursuits. It is also a social setting where children and teachers spend up to 25 hours a week. It is used by assistants, parents, visitors, even pets, and houses equipment, books, materials, coats and bags, lunchboxes, computers etc.

Space itself is a resource, as are all the people who use it. It needs to be in turn relaxing, welcoming, stimulating, and to combine shopfront, workshop, study, library, resource bank and studio. In an ideal world, power points and sinks would be just where we want them, doors would open the right way and furniture would fit. But classrooms reflect the history and educational philosophies of past and current users, and contain immovable, awkward objects. + bank accounts

The function of each area should be clear, so children can access books, tools, equipment etc. without fuss. Organisation should facilitate ease of movement into, out of and around the classroom. Try to keep your room flexible in arrangement, try out different plans and see how they work. Track movement around the room, and see if you can ease bottle-necks and facilitate access to resources. Take your time, work with a colleague, and sketch out your plan on paper before you begin to move furniture, relocate equipment or stick things up. List your priorities, e.g.:

- How often do children need to see the board at the same time?
- Will they have to twist their heads to copy?
- How much whole-class time is spent in the carpet area?
- What uses are made of this space at other times?
- Do children have easy access to reference material?
- Is there enough space to line up for playtime etc.?

'Aesthetically pleasing surroundings influence both learning and social behaviour. They show to a wider audience what children have achieved while reaffirming the value of their work'

(Lancaster 1990).

Art is not messy if carefully planned and organised. Teaching children basic workshop rules is vital, for a safe and happy working environment. To encourage children to become independent, the teacher needs to ensure they can access and replace materials, tools and equipment easily; teachers need to teach, not wait at table. Too much time spent fetching and carrying is a cue for rethinking organisation and planning. Encourage children to organise for their personal needs within the workspace, with everything to hand so they do not have to lean across others for access.

- Ensure that there is adequate flat working space, if possible close to a sink.
- Make appropriate, accessible and safe storage available for both flat and 3D items, during the making and display of finished work.
- Store materials and equipment in general and regular use where it is easily accessible in the room.
- Store separately, but with ready access, materials and equipment for specific art activities, e.g. printmaking equipment or claywork tools.
- Ensure all materials are clearly labelled and well maintained: care and maintenance should be seen as a joint responsibility between children and teacher.
- Make sure that everything is clean, tidy and sorted before storing it, e.g. that paint containers are topped up, brushes replaced in the right containers, printing ink tubes wiped clean and sorted etc.

Materials should invite exploration, and be appropriately housed and look appetising. The teacher is responsible for the basic organisation of the classroom, and needs to ensure that:

- pencils are always sharp and stored attractively (see Figure 14.1);
- there are enough for children to make informed choices;
- wax crayons are clean with a selection of sizes and types;
- pastels' colours are clearly visible;
- pastels, crayons and oil pastels are distinguishable;

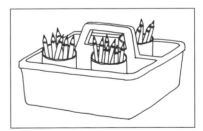

Figure 14.1 Storing pencils

- felt pens can be selected according to colour, size and type;
- only water-based felt pens are available;
- paper is available in different weights, sizes and colours;
- draft paper is that – not scrap;
- paintbrushes are clean, sorted and not used for glue;
- paint is stored in small, separate containers;
- modelling materials are attractively sorted and stored;
- a range of non-toxic glues and spatulas is available;
- sharp scissors are readily available.

HOW TO PROMOTE GOOD WORKSHOP PRACTICE

1. Before the lesson:
- cover tables with thick, even layers of paper to mop up spills: single layers crumple up and float away on the breeze;
- use newspaper table mats for glues, paints etc.;
- tape carrier bags to tables to collect ongoing waste; they can be jettisoned at the end of the session (see Figure 14.2);
- make a plan of how you will organise the room, which often throws up ideas and potential problems of access, storage etc.;
- consider before you start what you will do with the products: too much unfinished work may mean there are too many pieces of work on the go.

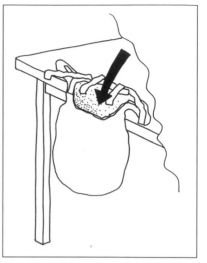

Figure 14.2 Dealing with rubbish. Place rubbish directly into carrier bags taped to the edge of tables.

2. During the lesson:
- remind children to keep work surfaces clear, e.g. to replace pencils into containers if not actually in use;
- pace yourself and the children: stop every 20 minutes or so to share work to date, and to remind them about maintaining their working space in good order;
- do an interim clear-up before break, so children return to an orderly and inviting space, not chaos;
- always give due notice of finishing time.

3. At the end of the lesson:
- allow plenty of time to review work and to clear;
- ensure children take collective responsibility for clearing up;
- allocate jobs so everyone knows what to do;
- ask children to tidy their own tables while class monitors stack, clean and put away: the unpleasant jobs might otherwise always be somebody else's!
- remember, it is not the cleaner's job to scrape paint off the walls: it should not be there.

RESOURCES

> A variety of resources, including natural and manmade objects and artifacts, should play their part as everyday necessities in children's education. Nothing can take the place of first-hand study and experience, both in and outside the school. The steady build-up of knowledge and understanding about the nature and qualities of things cannot be gained in any other way, and this forms a sound basis for all aspects of learning. (Morgan 1989)

The content of the National Curriculum and current practice in primary education require the provision of a range of resources to support art teaching, including collections of natural objects and examples of the work of artists and materials for children to use.

Museums sometimes operate loan systems where a range of items can be borrowed for school-based study. The following may operate in your area:

- schools art services can offer a variety of artifacts, prints, paintings, specialist books and slides for schools to borrow;
- schools library services can supply sets of books, charts, film strips on a topic;
- local museums, art galleries, art centres may have departments or personnel that offer facilities for schools to visit, or personnel who work in schools.

Accumulate a range of resources and items to support classroom work and display:

- with pupils, collect natural materials such as groups of feathers, bones, seedheads, rocks, fossils, pebbles, shells, bark, plants and bulbs etc., artifacts, examples of fabric, metal objects etc.;
- encourage children to bring in items to support topic work;
- seek out charts, visual reference material, from a range of sources;
- mount pictures from old calendars, cheap art books from second-hand shops etc., to add to the collection of 2D art work in reproduction.

Beg, borrow, or:

- collect consumables and ask parents for donations;
- ask parents for paper: this can often generate items from family members working in computing or printing;
- contact woodyards or small joinery businesses for wood shavings, off-cuts or sawdust;
- ask local packaging businesses for spare off-cuts of card;
- check if there is a local Scrapstore that collects throwouts from industry; for an annual subscription educational organisations can visit and select card, paper, fabric, collage and construction material;
- save picture resources from newspapers, magazines and postcards, prints, greeting cards.

Resources for colour work

Paint sample cards from manufacturers have many uses, apart from being useful additions to the collage box. Here are some ideas:

- on the weather chart, stick colours that match the sky at different times of day;
- in the sketchbook, use the samples to stick on sketches as an aide-memoire for later painting work;
- make a collection of colour samples which match those on display, for instance in preparation for a still life painting;
- find a range of colours which match your many skin tones, then try the same with your hair, your clothes and your shoes;
- look at a reproduction of a painting, and try to match all the colours that are used.

Resource for texture work

Samples of textured materials can be stuck on to small cards, for children to sort into texture groups, using Venn diagrams (mathematical links); classify materials according to other criteria (science links); describe to each other, noting words in a word bank (language links).

They can also be used to introduce rubbing as a technique. Use masking tape to secure them to the worktop, and provide different fairly firm but thin papers (e.g. kitchen, tracing, greaseproof, photocopy) and a range of wax crayons. Tape the paper lightly over that card, and experiment by rubbing the side of the crayon gently over the paper to achieve a range of texture impressions.

Resultant rubbings can be sorted with the cards, and discussion may ensue as to what variations in effects were achieved and how. Rubbings are useful for collage work etc. The surface that produces the most satisfactory rubbing will often prove the best material for making a print block.

How to make a set of cards

Cut cards of approximately 10 cm square. Use impact adhesive to affix textured materials onto the cards (i.e. coat both surfaces thinly with a suitable adhesive, wait until it goes transparent, then press the two surfaces together).

Examples of materials which might be on the blocks:

- wallpapers, various qualities and weights: woodchip, embossed;
- sandpapers and glasspapers of various grades;
- foam rubber, polystyrene, bubble wrap, other packaging;
- woven fabrics, felt, knitted and crocheted fabrics, fake fur;
- cotton, threads, strings, wools etc. of different qualities;
- card: various weights: strawboard, thin laminated, corrugated;
- balsa wood;
- wood shavings (eg. from pencil sharpeners);
- sawdust, (house dust?);
- mosaic pieces;
- pasta;
- leaves, bark and other natural items;
- sugar or other granular foods like coffee, tea, herbs;
- rubber (eg. a deflated balloon).

Visual resources

Teachers need a bountiful supply of visual resources to inspire and inform. Some may come from reference texts associated with the topic or project. Illustrators of children's stories also undertake a vast amount of research, and fiction books may also provide information. A rich supply of other images is to be found in magazines, postcards, calendar illustrations etc. It is useful to make sets of these, mounted on a neutral colour card, for display, to promote imaginative storytelling and to support the design and making of artifacts.

A4 cards, pre-cut, can be used to mount and easily stored in commercially available files. They can be put in plastic wallets in a ring binder, used for classroom display and for research purposes. The following process is one that older children can handle, once they have been carefully taught how to use the equipment.

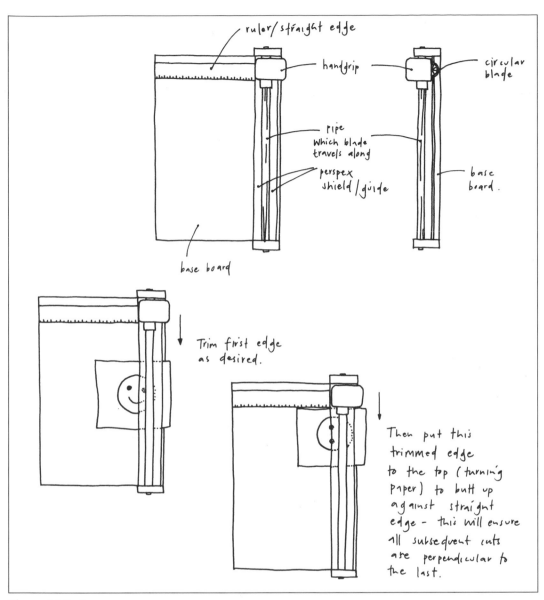

Figure 14.3 Paper cutter

- Get the pile of magazines, a good paper-trimmer (see Figure 14.3), a good supply of pre-cut card, a glue-stick, a small pad of newspaper slightly larger than the pictures, and a clean rag or tissue.
- Go through the magazines, and tear out the whole page containing any illustration which might be of interest. Look in the first instance for any interesting or thought-provoking illustrations. Discard the rest of the magazine, or leave for others to find what they want.
- Mark on the paper cutter the measurements for 3 cm less than A4 to give a margin of 1.5 cm all the way round: 26.5 cm × 18 cm. Crop the pages torn from the magazine to these dimensions.

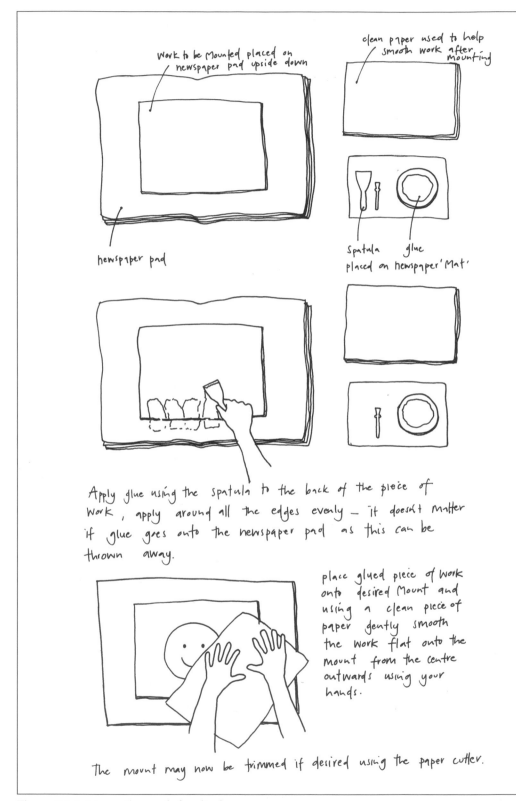

work to be Mounted placed on newspaper pad upside down

clean paper used to help smooth work after mounting

newspaper pad

Spatula   glue
placed on newspaper 'Mat'

Apply glue using the spatula to the back of the piece of work, apply around all the edges evenly — it doesn't matter if glue goes onto the newspaper pad as this can be thrown away.

place glued piece of work onto desired Mount and using a clean piece of paper gently smooth the work flat onto the mount from the centre outwards using your hands.

The mount may now be trimmed if desired using the paper cutter.

Figure 14.4 Mounting work for display

- Illustrations can then be speedily mounted centrally on the cards, gluing all around the edges; a dab at each corner is generally a false economy. A pile of old newspaper can be placed under the picture as it is glued (see Figure 14.4). The top piece is discarded each time, to avoid glue getting onto the work surface or onto the front of the next illustration. Place the picture carefully in the centre of the mounting card and rub it into position with a clean rag or tissue. Always note the source, artist, date, and scale of the original.

Postcards (see Figure 14.5) can be mounted two-up on an A4 card. Calendar pictures may require larger mounting boards. Similar resources can be made by photocopying from books, e.g. large format art books from the local library. Smaller illustrations can be blown up with modern photocopiers. Check copyright for anything you use in this way. A mask-making project might be inspired by the display of a range of illustrations of masks alongside classic portraits in reproduction. A body adornment project may be resourced through illustrations from the Oxfam calendars, photocopies from books, magazine illustrations of fashions in face-paint and cosmetics, or placing items of jewellery directly on the photocopier to enlarge.

Figure 14.5 Mounting postcards

Even for 3D work, the work of artists and painters in 2D can be most helpful, in that paintings of buildings, portraits of people in different costumes, animals etc. can be used as source material. There are, for instance, excellent animal and plant paintings by Victorian artists of weird and wonderful species of flora and fauna. These artists generally worked from life, and wherever possible, the source material used in the classroom should be backed up with first-hand experience, direct observational work of their own, and moving images through video.

Topic-based displays do not always need to contain children's, and only children's work. Mounting a display of resources and information, using artifacts, reproductions, the cards mentioned above, blow-ups of texts from information books, story books and poems relating to the topic can provide excellent starting points, and invite the exploration of accompanying books and magazines. Such a display can be the teacher's most useful resource. Children can browse, sketch and make notes.

Small images can be used in class in many ways, e.g. as visual stimulus to creative writing, for sorting and researching, as well as starting points for the study of art and visual imagery. Photocopies of favourite poems, or extracts from books might be added. Useful collections might include:

- reproductions of works of art on postcards, greetings cards etc.;

- examples of contemporary media, such as computer-generated images, photographs and advertising images;
- pictures of urban and rural dwellings, bridges, religious observance buildings, from different places and times;
- examples of landscapes, seascapes and skyscapes;
- transport images;
- images of people, old and young, to represent a wide cross-section of people on special occasions, at work, at home, at play, in different cultural settings;
- unusual images, often found in style magazines, such as a woman carrying a house on her back, a railway running through a house etc.

Positive images of women, black people, the disabled and the elderly are not always easy to come by; these should be in the collection in their own right, filed under 'people at work', 'people and their hobbies', 'musicians', etc., rather than being isolated as disabled or elderly, which only endorses the fringe label, and further pigeon-holes people according to their minority status. Look through and check if:

- women are all in submissive, servile, domestic or glamorous roles;
- men are all in dominant, non-domestic, business or workman roles;
- elderly people are all dependent, weak or fragile;
- black people are all exotic, sporty, poverty-stricken or musical;
- disabled people are passive, dependent and sad.

Some topics or themes occur regularly. For these, mounting a series of images on A1 size card can save time and effort. They can be arranged on display boards to inform, inspire and introduce the work. Such boards may be about art per se, e.g. about line, colour or a particular medium such as clay or paint or drawings. Or, they may have illustrations of art from a particular period, e.g. Victorians or Tudors, or a theme such as the sea.

Keep an even border around the boards, and avoid elaborate mounts. A wide border will allow for trimming in future if edges get tatty. Two or more boards can be hinged together to make a 'big book', for whole class discussion. Itinerant teachers might find it useful to fit a handle for easy carrying.

DISPLAY

Displays themselves can be either a short-term celebratory experience or something which is kept in the classroom or school to be used and developed. This involves skills such as labelling, notetaking, creative or descriptive writing, painting, modelling and the skill of adding appropriate reference books.

(Jackson 1993)

Most schools have guidelines on type and size of lettering, mounting policy, colours of backgrounds etc. which should be adhered to. Display is usually the responsibility of the class teacher, although helpers may play a large part in this work. It is important to discuss and negotiate the task, since it is, after all, a major teaching resource as well as being a decorative feature in the classroom. Display is a vital aspect of the school environment, in the classroom or other areas of the school, to:

- communicate information to parents, visitors, other pupils and staff, about activities that are carried out in school;
- raise the self-esteem of pupils by displaying their work;
- develop and stimulate visual awareness;
- create an interesting and attractive environment;
- provide a model and teaching aid for other classes.

Different school or classroom areas may be for permanent displays of framed prints, selected children's work and notice boards, for regularly changed displays of children's 2D and 3D work featuring all areas of the curriculum, for collections of artifacts/natural objects, and for stimulus displays to encourage engagement with ideas, concepts and matters of current relevance.

A central display to introduce a new topic or theme is a very valuable resource. Typically, it contains pictures, artifacts, books, poems and other stimulus material, e.g. grown-ups' picture books about artists, or architecture, or maps. Questions may promote discussion and interaction, and accompanying lesson plans may address aspects of speaking and listening as well as other curricular areas represented.

Displays reflect priorities as much by omission as inclusion, e.g. evidence of information technology in use, or offering a fair reflection of the richness of our multi-cultural society. Where classrooms lack evidence of the personalities, interests and heritages represented both by the children and in the wider world, the matter needs to be positively addressed through appropriate resource provision.

There is a school of thought which insists that every child's work should be displayed on every occasion, although this will clearly be impractical sometimes. If so, children should be informed about why you chose particular work, and they might even contribute to the selection process, according to agreed criteria. One compromise is to display a selection on boards, and to put further examples in a large plastic folder which can be leafed through. Artists often do this at exhibitions, so gallery visitors can see further examples of work for which there is no room on the walls. In principle, all work should be named, although there may be good reasons to make exceptions.

Fancy angular display often makes children's work unreadable, whether it is a graphic image, written or number work. It can be useful to mount different sized work on similar sized paper, to give a feeling of unity and regularity to the display (see Figure 14.6). The eye should always be attracted to the work itself, not to the background. Practical suggestions:

- check the school policy for mounting, display etc.;
- make clear if the work is finished or ongoing;
- allow sufficient space and time for preparation;
- work with a colleague to make the process more enjoyable and speedy;
- if possible, encourage children to help and learn about mounting and display for themselves;

Figure 14.6 Mounting difficult sized work on similar sized paper. Choose a size of paper or card large enough to take the largest image and mount all work on a similar size no matter how big or small it is.

- make sure all your equipment is in good working order;
- make sure staples fit the stapler; the best way to ruin a stapler is by inserting the wrong size or type of staples;
- cut work carefully on the papercutter; line guides and rules ensure straight edges and accurate right-angles;
- use neutral colours for backing papers and boards; bright colour overpowers the children's work;
- use good adhesive, and make sure all edges are firmly attached to the backing;
- use a wad of large newspaper to place work on when you apply the glue; work to the edge, and discard the top layer;
- mount small work in sets on large sheets, then arrange on the wall;
- work out the arrangement before you start, with a sketch, or lay it out on the floor in front to gauge the overall effect before you begin;
- keep sides and top parallel to the display board;
- remember children's eye level: always bear in mind the visibility of the work; if in doubt, check with them;
- pin work in position with drawing pins, so you can adjust it easily before using staples or pins for the final fixing: avoid brass drawing pins on the final display;
- consider using a spirit level to check that work is straight;
- avoid work on windows: it cuts the light and the glue never comes off;
- consider keeping a note of measurements of boards, to make estimates about how much work will fit.

Children's artwork should (almost) never be cut around. The composition is destroyed and if it is then mounted on a dark or bright background, it is difficult to focus on the work. Grubby or frayed edges can be trimmed, but always keep to the basic shape in which the child made the work.

Lettering for display

Headings, titles, labels and longer pieces of text can inform the observer about the origins of and stimulus for the work. They can also encourage closer scrutiny, and spark off the interest and curiosity of the children. Decide on a title, text and lettering that reflects the school's handwriting style and policy, to serve as an exemplar for the children.

Consistent lettering styles on displays give a more professional look. Lettering need not be enormous to be legible, though sometimes a big, bold headline for a display is eye-catching and effective.

Lettering can be hand-written (calligraphy pens are a pleasure to use), stencilled, computer printed or cut out from paper or card. When planning display lettering, consider:

- its purpose and function within the display;
- the age of the children in the school;
- clarity and legibility;
- where to place lettering on the display;
- position of the display and of the observer in relation to it: how much space in front there is to move back to view it;

- the relationship between the height of the lettering and the width of the strokes that make up individual letters: letters that are too thin or too thick look unsatisfactory.

Many writing and drawing implements can be used effectively to produce good display lettering, e.g. chisel-tipped brushes, pen and ink, felt pens. The latter are quickest and easiest to use. Ranges of specially produced lettering felt pens can be bought in a variety of widths and colours, and with a little practice, quite professional lettering can be achieved.

Take time and trouble to rule lines as a guide for letters, parallel to the sides of the paper on which the letters are positioned. Alternatively have black, ruled guide lines underneath, as for a writing pad. Large maths paper with faintly printed squares can be helpful. Capital letters are the same height as ascenders: half as big again as lower case letters. Descenders should be the same depth as the ascenders' height.

There is now a range of excellent fonts available on computer that can be produced in a variety of sizes. Choose for clarity and legibility: some of the more elaborate fonts are rather difficult to read.

Hand cut letters can be simply achieved, of any size, based on a 3:4 ratio rectangle. A third of the width of the rectangle is the width for all the horizontal and most of the vertical strokes of the letters. Diagonal strokes are slightly less than this width.

To save time when cutting letters:

- cut over a waste-paper basket;
- count how many letters you need and cut that number of rectangles to begin with;
- cut several letters at the same time;
- fold rectangles when cutting symmetrical letters;
- try to work with the minimum of prior drawing;
- keep a store of cut letters.

USING EXHIBITIONS WITH CHILDREN

Trips and outings can be an invaluable addition to school and classroom experiences, to inform, entertain, stimulate and excite curiosity while consolidating, reinforcing or challenging previous experience. They can act as an introduction to the topic, timed mid-way to sustain interest, or as a grand finale.

When planning to visit an exhibition, consider the age group, although never underestimate the ability of children to respond to a range of different work, nor how well it might address aspects of the National Curriculum.

Some children may never have visited an exhibition before; some may be quite familiar with the experience. Prepare the children for the visit so they know what to expect, what to do and how to behave. Consider how to structure the visit, how long to spend, how to focus children's attention on particular aspects of the work, whether worksheets are appropriate, what handouts or drawing materials the children might need. Contact the site, visit if you can, pick up any literature or worksheets supplied for children

Before detailed planning, check school and local authority policy and procedures for off-site visits, particularly regarding charges for transport and entrance fees, required adult/child ratios, and guidelines for safety procedures. Discuss your proposal with the headteacher and involved colleagues and research costs and possible dates well ahead of your proposed visit. Ask the school secretary about insurance and transport; the school may use a particular company. Then:

- estimate costs, check with head;
- confirm bookings and transport;
- prepare information for parents; the school may have a proforma with a reply strip for guardians to sign; you may want to add notes about the educational aims, and read through with the children;
- co-opt any extra adult help that you need;
- prepare supplementary resources, e.g. worksheets or questionnaires;
- organise equipment, e.g. clipboards, pencils, crayons, magnifying glasses, first aid;
- order packed lunches where necessary well in advance;
- identify children with health problems, e.g. travel sickness, asthma, allergies, and arrange appropriate medication;
- brief children; give information about times of departure and arrival back, lunches, spending money, suitable clothing, appropriate behaviour and safety procedures.

Brief accompanying adults thoroughly. Explain the aims for the trip, and your expectations for children's work. Find out if any of them are familiar with the work you are going to see, and use catalogues or leaflets to inform others. Establish points of focus to help other adults in their discussions with groups. Afterwards, make time to find out what other conversations and interests emerged during the day which you can capitalise on in follow-up work. Enjoy the experience!

> Visual understanding is vital in an image-oriented society . . . An understanding of the visual arts develops aesthetic sensibilities through making, which lead to the skill of visual discrimination and a greater understanding of one's surroundings and the world
>
> (SCAA/Department of National Heritage 1997)

Artists and their Work

All the artists listed below are practising professionals, whose work is regularly exhibited. Some of the work reproduced in this book can be seen in full colour via web sites on the internet. Addresses are given below.

CAROLINE BARTLETT: *ZENANA* (PLEATED, PRINTED LINEN)

Caroline's work is based on imagery related to specific sites or places, and draws on architectural references, myths, legends, history and culture. *Zenana*, a Persian word, refers to women's apartments in Indian royal palaces (and elsewhere in the middle east), where women lived in purdah, with a view of the world through jali (net work) screens.

SARA DUDMAN: *AND THE FISH GREW WINGS* ... (MIXED MEDIA AND MACHINE EMBROIDERY)

This work celebrates regeneration, with birds and fish representing stages of evolution and 'breaking free'. Influenced by Indian textile work, Sara challenges the boundaries between art and craft, allowing colours, patterns and textures within the materials to influence the work. The sewing machine is used as a drawing tool, along with traditional techniques such as appliqué, embroidery and felt-making to create pieces of artwork to be hung on the wall.

LEE EDWARDS: *APOTHECARY* (COMPUTER PRINT: POWERMAC 8600/250; PHOTOSHOP; WACOM GRAPHICS TABLET)

Lee uses both conventional and computer printmaking in his work, scanning in hand-made prints which often already contain digitally produced material and photographs. He sees his current images as having a 'song-like' quality.

ANITA FORD: *HARPYIA* (OPEN BITE ETCHING AND AQUATINT)

This is the Harpyia, the snatcher, the personification of the storm wind, a bird of authority and power, not always alluring or polite, who embraces the winds of change. She has teeth. She also has vulnerability and sensitivity: synonyms so long ascribed as weaknesses, are in essence her strength.

ELEANOR GLOVER: *COLLAGE ON BARK PAPER* **(MIXED MEDIA, FOUND OBJECTS);** *WOODEN FIGURE WITH LETTER FORMS* **(PINE AND ACRYLICS)**

Eleanor's work is largely autobiographical. Her training in bookmaking, typography and illustration can be seen in her affection for letter forms, and her toymaking experience also shows in her work, which represents and celebrates the beauty and the diversity of human beings.

STEPHEN HOSKINS: *GOLDEN SECTION. L.A.* **(SCREENPRINT WITH GOLD FOIL)**

Stephen's work is based on the Golden section proportion and simple Euclidean geometry, with colours influenced by his interests in Renaissance Art (Piero de la Francesca, Botticelli and Albertini), and a fascination with Renaissance frescoes. When painted surfaces disintegrate to reveal the support below, there remain small patches of order amongst a background of random chaos.

ALFRED HUCKETT: *WINDOWS* **(MIXED MEDIA DRAWING)**

Alfred works principally in watercolour, finding the medium offers strength and direction, despite its fragility and elusiveness. Pen and wash and drawing ink allow him to express his love of working on paper, preferring its finer textures to that of canvas. His work is seemingly figurative but has strong abstract undertones, and ranges in size from a few inches to several feet.

MARY KEAR: *SKETCHES TOWARDS A QUILT* **(MIXED MEDIA);** *COBOURG HOLLY* **(QUILT)**

Mary works her intricate patterns in line and colour before beginning to cut and stitch, although designs may be modified during the making process. The quilt reflects the colours of the holly tree outside Mary's then workroom: its pale green new leaves changing as the year passes, through appley-green to very dark, sometimes almost yellow in the sun; its white flowers, and its berries growing from green to orange to scarlet and finally crimson-red. Mary sees quilting as 'painting with material: it can look quite flat, but when someone snuggles down under it, the patterns, colours and shapes look completely different'.

LALIT KUMAR: *THE DANCE OF THE COCKEREL* **(OIL CRAYONS)**

Lalit grew up on a farm in Africa, and always enjoyed seeing the extravagant mating dances of the birds. Now, in England, he occasionally finds himself constructing nostalgia, and describes this picture as being 'the juice of all those dances'.

ABIGAIL LEACH: *SKETCHES* **(CHALK PASTEL, CHARCOAL);** *CLOCK* **PIECE (EARTHENWARE WITH COLOURED SLIP)**

Abigail uses clay to create forms, in this case inspired by sculptors Moore and Hepworth, conceived of as being sited in a landscape. Some of her work is functional, but in this case she was trying to move towards a more non-functional approach. Abigail uses sketches to work on ideas.

BARBARA MUNNS: *GOLDEN SHELL* **(COLLOGRAPH PRINT WITH GILDING METAL)**

Damaged frescoes, and how their edges reveal all the workings and films of pigment that have been laid down, have influenced Barbara's own images, like this print, one of a series concerned with ideas about fossils and shells. Barbara uses quite complex processes, including this special type of collograph when a mixture of acrylic paste, fine carborundum grit and acrylic medium have been applied to a metal plate, into which an impression of a shell is made.

YANI NICHOLS: *UNTITLED* **(CLAY BOWLS, MOULDED AND GLAZED)**

These pieces were designed to be placed in the garden, where rainfall and dew would accumulate in the crevices and the clay's texture would be changed by the growth of small mosses etc. on the pots. In fact, they have been enjoyed so far in an interior setting, and still await an outdoor home.

ANDY PINNER: *UNTITLED* **(LITHOGRAPH)**

The hand-drawn image was photographed on to a light sensitive lithography plate, of which 60 'miniprints' prints were made. The image is intended as a testament to the wanton destruction of an industry and the communities it supported.

ELZA SCOBLE: *BILLY'S BALLOONS*; *PORTRAIT OF CARLA* **(OIL PAINT ON CANVAS);** *MONICA* **(PAPIER MACHE WITH PLASTER OF PARIS)**

Elza works on both personal and imaginative themes, often in domestic settings, sometimes using photographic references. The paintings were inspired by her son, Billy 'flying' around the room holding balloons, with his father, and by Carla's joie de vivre. The reclining figure is imaginary, but the pattern and colours (reds, oranges and yellows) were inspired by a book of Coptic art.

JULIAN SCOTT: *MIR – VERSION 2* (SYNTHETIC RESINS ON PANEL)

Julian uses film, video, various kinds of photography and satellite images alongside more traditional sources to explore some of the possibilities for landscape painting at the end of the millennium.

LUCKY THOMAS: *WHISTLE FOR IT!* (CARNIVAL COSTUME: MULTIMEDIA), PHOTO-GRAPHED BY NICK STRANGELOVE

Designed, and made with Carla's help, by Lucky, for her to wear at the Notting Hill Carnival in 1995, as part of the theme 'Play Ball, Play Mas', with the Perpetual Beauty Carnival Club from Hackney. (Reprinted with courtesy of the Independent from the 28.8.95 edition.)

KAMINA WALTON: *KEEP OUT OF REACH* (COLOUR PHOTOGRAPH)

In this work, Kamina used a transparency in a liquid filled glass jar to achieve this powerful image. In it, she sets out to challenge preconceptions about mental anguish, by articulating individual experience ranging from anxiety and stress to phobic behaviour and depression. She believes that a non-technical approach to photography facilitates its use as a means of individual expression. Kamina works extensively with children and adults in education and community contexts.

Bibliography

Ashcroft, K. and Palacio, D. (1997) *Implementing the Primary Curriculum: A Teacher's Guide*. London: Falmer.

Barnes, R. (1989) *Art, Design and Topic Work 8-13*. London: Routledge.

Barrett, M. (1990) 'Guidelines for Evaluation and Assessment in Art and Design Education', in *Journal of Art and Design Education*, **9**, 3. Corsham: NSEAD.

Bearne, E. (ed.) (1996) *Differentiation and Diversity*. London: Routledge.

de Bono (1972) *Children solve Problems*. Harmondsworth: Penguin Education.

Calouste-Gulbenkian Foundation (1982) *The Arts in Schools, Principles, Practice and Provision*. London, CGF.

Chambers, M. (1989) *An Introduction to Computer Graphics in Art and Design Education*. Corsham: NSEAD.

Clement, R. and Page, S. (1992a) *Principles and Practice in Art*. Harlow: Oliver and Boyd.

Clement, R. and Page, S. (1992b) *Knowledge and Understanding in Art*. Harlow: Oliver and Boyd.

Clement, R. and Page, S. (1992c) *Investigating and Making in Art*. Harlow: Oliver and Boyd.

Cox, M. (1997) *Drawings of People by the Under-5s*. London: Falmer.

DFE (1995) *A Guide to Safe Practice in Art and Design*. London: HMSO.

DES/HMI (1978) *Primary Education in England*. London: HMSO.

Gardner, H. (1990) *Art Education and Human Development*. Jill Norman: London.

Gentle, K. (1993) *Teaching Painting in the Primary School*. London: Cassell.

Green, L. and Mitchell, R. (1997) *Art 7–11 Developing Primary Skills*. London: Routledge.

Hampshire County Council (1992) *Further Guidelines for Art Education Key Stage 1-5*. Hampshire County Council.

Hole, D. (ed.) (1997) *Primary Arts Education: Contemporary Issues*. London: Falmer.

Jackson, M. (1993) *Creative Display and the Environment*. London: Hodder and Stoughton.

Jayhem, J. and Walton, K. (1987) *As Easy as ABC. An Introduction to Photography and Language Work in the Primary Classroom*. London: Arts Council of Great Britain.

Johnsey, R. (1998) *Exploring Primary Design and Technology*. London: Cassell.

Kear, M. and Callaway, G. (1999) *Looking Afresh at the Arts in Primary Schools*. London: Falmer.

Lancaster, J. (1990) *Art in the Primary School*. London: Routledge.

Meager, N. (1993) *Teaching Art at Key Stage 1*. Corsham: NSEAD.

Mathieson, K. (1993) *Children's Art and the Computer* London: Hodder and Stoughton.

Micklethwaite, L. (1991) *I Spy: An Alphabet in Art*. London: Collins.

Micklethwaite, L. (1991) *I Spy: Numbers in Art*. London: Collins.

Morgan, M. (1989) *Art 4-11: Art in the Early years of Schooling*. Oxford: Blackwell.

Morgan, M. (1993) *Art in Practice*. Oxford: Nash Pollock.

Moyles, J. (ed.) (1995) *Beginning Teaching: Beginning Learning*. Buckingham: Open University Press.

The National Curriculum Council Arts in Schools project team (1989) *The Arts 5-16, A Curriculum Framework*. London: Oliver and Boyd.

The National Curriculum Council Arts in Schools project team (1989) *The Arts 5-16, Practice and Innovation*. London: Oliver and Boyd.

Newlands, M. and Rubens, M. (1983) *Learning on Location*. London: Calouste-Gulbenkian Foundation.

Newlands, M. and Rubens, M. (1989) *A Tool for Learning*. Calouste-Gulbenkian Foundation.

Nicholls, D. (1997) *Pooling Ideas on Art and Imaging*. Stoke-on-Trent: Trentham Books.

North, M. (1989) *Bristol Print '89* International Mini-Print Exhibition Catalogue.

OFSTED (1998) *The Arts Inspected*. Oxford: Heinemann.

Peter, M. (1996) *Art for All: I The Framework*. London: David Fulton.

Peter, M. (1996) *Art for All: II The Practice*. London: David Fulton.

Phillips, T. (1997) *Aspects of Art - A Painter's Alphabet*. London: Bellew.

Piotrowski, J. (ed.) (1996) *Expressive Arts in the Primary School*. London: Cassell.

Powell, J. (1996) *The History of Britain Through Art*. Hove: Wayland.

Richardson, J. (1997) *Looking at Pictures*. London: A. & C. Black and National Gallery Publications.

Ritchie, R. (1995) *Primary Design and Technology*. London: David Fulton.

Roalf, P. (1992) *Looking at Pictures: Families*. London: Belitha Press.

Roalf, P. (1992) *Looking at Pictures: Children*. London: Belitha Press.

Roalf, P. (1992) *Looking at Pictures: Self-portraits*. London: Belitha Press.

Robinson, G. (1993) *Sketch-books: Explore and Store*. London: Hodder and Stoughton.

SCAA/The Department of National Heritage (1997) *The Arts in the Curriculum*. SCAA.

Sedgwick, F. (1993) *The Expressive Arts*. London: David Fulton.

Sedgwick, D. and Sedgwick, F. (1993) *Drawing to Learn*. London: Hodder and Stoughton.

Sedgwick, D. and Sedgwick, F. (1996) *Art across the Curriculum*. London: Hodder and Stoughton.

Sharp, C. and Dust, K. *Artists in Schools*. London: Bedford Square Press.

Taylor, R. (1992) *Visual Arts in Education*. London: Falmer.

Taylor, R. and Andrews, G. (1993) *The Arts in the Primary School*. London: Falmer.

Tickle, L. (1996) *Understanding Art in Primary Schools*. London: Routledge.

Tickle, L. (1996) *Understanding Design and Technology in Primary Schools*. London: Routledge.

Thistlewood, D. (1989) *Critical Studies in Art and Design Education*. London: Longman.

Treacher, V. (1989) *Classroom issues in Assessment and Evaluation in the arts*. Reading: Berkshire LEA.

Walton, K. (1995) *Picture my World*. London: The Arts Council of England.

Wenham, M (1995) Not by Bread Alone: Developing Thinking and Skills in the Arts. In J. Moyles (ed.) *Beginning Teaching, Beginning Learning*. Buckingham: Open University Press, 129–143.

Winser, K. (1996) in Peter, M. *Art for All: II The Practice: Developing Art in the Curriculum for pupils with Special Educational Needs*. London: David Fulton.

Withey, D., Graze, E. and Fulton, M. (1996) *A Primary Teacher's Handbook – Art*. Dunstable: Folens.

Woolf, G. (1997) *Childen's Art*. London: Bellew.

Woolf, G. (1997) *Activity Book*. London: Bellew.

(1994) *The Art Book*. London: Phaidon.

WWW SITES OF ARTISTS WHOSE WORK APPEARS IN THIS BOOK

Edwards, Lee (computer artist)   http://www.yellowmoon.demon.co.uk
Anita Ford (printmaker)   http://www.toba.demon.uk
Caroline Bartlett (fabric artist) http://www.users:globalnet.co.uk/~abanks/

Index

Aalto, Alvar 118
abstract 10, 38, 40, 116, 142
adhesives 125
Africa, African 117, 118, 146, 147, 156, 184, 190
aims 4, 12, 13, 48, 66, 67, 69, 116, 120, 129
Alari 49, 177
alphabets 60
American Indian 49, 147
animals 7, 14, 51, 84, 86, 110, 116, 128, 132, 142, 146, 152, 163, 176, 203
animation 86, 94, 134
appliqué 109, 175
apprenticeship 9, 40
appropriate technology 181
Arabic 60
architects, architecture 8, 14, 34, 38, 116, 117, 118, 135, 155, 174
Arnolfini Marriage, The 112
Art Deco 14, 109
Art Nouveau 133
art therapy 111
artists in schools 14
Asia 133
assessment 3, 6, 12, 13, 49, 121, 130, 151
Attainment Targets 3, 4, 12, 78, 83
Australian Aboriginal 15, 17, 38, 40, 49, 117

baskets 182, 184, 185
batik 174, 175, 189, 191–192
Beatles, the 109
Beaton, Cecil 89
Blake, Peter 90
body adornment 116, 132, 155, 203
bookmaking 96–104
books 4, 6, 12, 14, 19, 24, 34, 51, 53, 57, 60, 75, 81, 86, 89, 90–121, 128, 130, 135, 145, 149, 157, 181, 200, 205
box modelling 106, 110, 115–130
bridges 116, 119, 128, 132, 204
brushes 42–43, 47
Brusho 42, 53, 189
building up 61, 127, 157, 162, 163

calligraphy 21, 27, 38, 96, 99, 206
camera 76, 83–95

Canaletto, Antonio 38
carnival 116, 117, 129, 144, 145, 146, 147
carving 61, 116, 127, 159, 161, 162, 163
CD roms 47, 37, 61, 119, 146, 155
Celts 132
Cézanne, Paul 38, 50
China, Chinese 27, 61, 147, 148
clay 7, 8, 10, 16, 22, 27, 37, 58, 62, 69, 72, 115, 127, 131, 153–173,
clay, types of 158
collaboration 2, 53, 97, 108, 119, 180, 186
collage 4, 22, 52, 56, 72, 80–84, 95, 98, 106–117, 134, 174, 175, 193
collograph 56, 59, 62, 72
colour 4, 7, 14–17, 22, 26, 32, 36–54, 62, 67, 76, 79, 81, 82, 88, 94, 108–111, 156, 178, 187
colour mixing 46
colour wheel 46
composition 5, 17, 29, 38, 40, 50, 51, 62, 67, 84, 85,
computer 6, 7, 15, 20, 22, 37, 61, 61, 63, 74–82, 85–89, 98, 107, 109, 130, 155, 176, 204
Constable, John 49
continuity 12, 55
coordinators 15
copies, copying 40, 51
costume 116, 117, 129, 135, 203
creativity 1, 110, 116, 129
crochet 179, 182
cross-curricular work 3, 6, 9, 11, 19–22, 37–38, 60–61, 77–78, 97, 107, 116, 121, 129, 145, 154, 175, 181, 184
crowns 116, 132

da Vinci, Leonardo 24
dance 8, 113, 144, 145, 146, 151
découpage 107, 109, 133
Degas, Edgar 142
design and technology 7, 37, 61, 78, 87, 98, 107, 115, 132, 142, 146, 155, 176, 188
differentiation 10
Disney, Walt 90
display 3, 4, 12, 13, 30, 35, 37, 46–53, 75, 85, 96, 113, 119, 127–149, 155, 196–208
Divali 145, 147

dolls houses 116, 117
drama 8, 84, 95, 111, 113, 144, 151, 176
drawing 2, 10, 14, 17, 18–35, 75–77, 81, 88,
    91, 92, 97, 106, 128, 178, 191
drawing development 22–24
drawing media 26–31, 32, 82
Durer, Albrecht 24, 62, 66
Dutch school 49
dyes 178, 189–195

Egypt, Egyptians 98, 113, 118, 132, 133, 148,
    156
elements of art 3, 10, 15–17, 22, 36, 38, 61,
    78–80, 88, 99, 107, 133, 156, 177, 187
elements of learning 13
Elizabethans 132
embroidery 109, 174, 175, 179, 180
English 4, 6, 37, 60, 78, 87, 97, 107, 119, 121,
    145, 154, 176, 188
etching 58, 62
evaluation 3, 12, 13, 47, 49, 61, 67–70, 86, 94,
    95, 107, 112, 121, 130, 142, 151
exhibitions 35, 48, 85, 130, 205, 207–208

fabrics 7, 16, 17, 22, 27, 32, 33, 37, 38, 56, 62,
    67, 80, 106–109, 122, 174–195
Fassett, Kaffe 175
Fawkes, Guy 147
Finland 184
firing – see kilns
form, forms 9, 10, 17, 21, 37, 50, 51, 116, 134,
    157
Frink, Dame Elisabeth 14, 142

galleries 3, 15, 48, 80, 199, 205
Gaudi, Antonio 109, 118
genre 6, 8, 84, 90, 111
geography 4, 7, 61, 87, 98, 11, 116, 132, 154–
    157, 177, 188
Giacometti, Alberto 142
glaze 153–156, 172–173
glues 125
Goldsworthy, Andy 89, 94, 179
Gormley, Antony 142
Goya, Francisco 24
Greece, Greeks 16, 60, 61, 98, 113, 156
groups 3, 11, 53, 122, 145, 150, 166, 175, 176,
    186
gummed paper strips 151

Hamilton, Richard 90
handwriting 16
hats 116, 119, 150
Hausman, Raoul 90
health and safety 7, 45, 53, 69, 86, 119, 121,
    125, 130, 150, 160, 172, 193

Hebrew 60
Hepworth, Dame Barbara 142, 179
Heron, Patrick 48
Hirst, Damien 99
history 4, 8, 52, 61, 87, 98–99, 111, 116, 132,
    135, 154–157, 177, 181, 188
Hockney, David 6, 24, 63, 89, 93
Hokusai, Katsushika 4
humanities 37, 78, 146

imagination 9, 36, 51, 52
impact adhesive 126, 200
Impressionists 14, 49
India, Indian 17, 38, 49, 175
Indonesia 148
Information and Communications Technology
    7, 37, 61, 78, 87, 98, 107, 146, 155, 176
intaglio 57, 59
internet 15, 129, 179
Inuit 147
Islam, Islamic 8, 17, 38, 49

Japanese sketchbook 104
jewels, jewellery 117, 132, 133, 153, 203

kilns 153, 171–172
kites 116, 121
knitting 175, 178, 180, 182

landscape 7, 21, 38, 40, 52, 117, 169, 187,
    188, 204
language 6, 15, 19, 61, 115, 154, 200
lettering 71, 80, 204, 206
Lichtenstein, Roy 80
line 8, 16, 20, 22, 24, 27, 31, 32, 62, 78, 82,
    156, 178, 188
lino 59
lithography 59, 62
Long, Richard 89, 94
loom 174, 176, 180, 184–188

Mackintosh, Charles Rennie 133
macrame 182
magnifying glasses 21, 31, 48, 53, 54, 178, 195,
    208
maps 16, 34, 53, 116
marbling 57, 110
masks 99, 116, 119, 128, 130, 135, 144–152,
    203
match 10
mathematics 7, 9, 37, 60, 78, 98, 107, 115,
    116, 142, 146, 154, 155, 176, 188, 200
Matisse, Henri 38, 62, 109, 147
microscopes 178
Mills and Boon 96
Miro, Joan 24

modelling 131–143, 161
modroc 131–143, 151–152
Mondrian, Piet 48
Monet, Claude 40
monochrome 17, 62, 64
monoprinting 56, 57, 72–73
Monroe, Marilyn 80, 90
Moore, Henry 24, 142
Morris, William 14, 62, 177
mosaic 106–110, 134, 155
moulding 115, 140, 171
mounting 204
movement 8, 51, 87, 88, 113, 129, 145, 146
Munch, Edvard 8
museums 15, 80, 96, 117, 157, 184, 199
music 2, 8, 38, 146
musical instruments 8, 116, 132
myths and legends 6, 36

National Curriculum 3, 4, 6, 10–12, 19, 36, 77, 78, 83, 84, 175, 198
National Geographic 132, 146
newspaper 32, 43, 65, 70, 71, 85, 93, 101, 131–143, 159, 160
Nightwatch, The 33
Noh Theatre 146
North American Indians 117
numeracy 9
numerals 80

O'Keeffe, Georgia 40, 49
observational work 20, 22, 32, 33, 49–51, 116, 129, 184, 203
Oldenburg, Claes 179
Oxfam 181, 203

paint 10, 15, 16, 27, 40–42, 75, 108
painting 2, 8, 11, 14, 17, 31, 36–54, 76, 81, 82, 88, 91, 92, 97, 10–6, 113, 117, 139, 178, 191
painting equipment 40–44
Paisley 17
Paolozzi, Edward 117, 147
paper 7, 8, 28, 37, 42, 47, 53, 64, 73, 76, 80, 96–104, 106, 108
papier mâché 10, 16, 129, 131–143
paste resist 190–191
patchwork 60, 107, 109, 175, 179, 193
pattern 7, 8, 16, 17, 20–22, 32, 38, 49–51, 54–56, 60, 62, 67, 76–80, 88, 107, 108, 116, 117, 134
perspective 33
photocopier 3, 5, 40, 83, 85, 88, 157, 203
photographs 4, 7, 12, 34, 49, 51, 54, 97, 110–112, 121, 127–132, 142, 169, 188, 204
photography 53, 83–95, 109

physical education 8, 61, 84, 88
Picasso, Pablo 8, 24, 117, 147
pigments 7, 36–41, 79, 175, 176
Pink Panther 86
planning 3–4, 11, 15, 33, 45, 81, 86, 68, 116, 119, 121, 129, 131, 145, 146
plants 7, 37, 51, 84, 142, 174, 176
plaster 5 8, 62, 154, 159
plasticine 3, 7, 56, 69, 72, 131–143, 154, 183
play dough 37, 131–143, 154
poems, poetry 8, 12, 19, 24, 37, 52, 53, 119, 121, 203, 205
policies 4, 12, 119, 205, 207
polystyrene 56, 58, 62, 70, 72, 108, 124
pop-up cards 116
portrait 4, 14, 21, 89, 92–93, 111, 129, 203
potato 58, 69, 70, 72
pots 164–171
printmaking 14–15, 27, 31, 44, 55–76, 79, 82, 85, 89, 91, 104, 110, 178
printmaking equipment 63–65
printmaking techniques 56–60
problem-solving 6, 12, 18, 76, 115
progression 3, 12, 55
projectors 53, 85, 92, 113, 148, 185
Punch and Judy 147
puppets, puppetry 8, 10, 84, 99, 116, 117, 135, 144–152

Quant, Mary 133, 177
quiltmaking 109, 177, 180, 181

rag rugs 175
Rama and Sita 8, 147
reading 4, 9, 14
relief 55, 56, 115, 134, 139, 157
Religious Education 8, 88, 111
Rembrandt (Harmensz van Rijn) 15, 33, 49, 112
Renaissance 14, 49
researching 10, 21, 51–53, 98, 107, 110, 112, 119, 122, 145, 154, 200
resist 175–178, 189
resources 34, 24, 47, 198–204
Riley, Bridget 38, 48, 49, 80
Rococo 135
Rodin, Auguste 142
Rogers, Richard 118
Romans 16
Rousseau, Henri 51
rubbings 56, 71, 110, 200

salt dough 131–143, 154
Santa Fe 118
Scandinavia 184
Scarfe, Gerald 89

Schwitters, Kurt 90
science 7, 37, 61, 87, 115, 121, 142, 146, 154, 155, 176, 200
Scrapstore 122, 199
screenprinting 60
scribbling 18, 23, 24, 28, 77
sculptors, sculpture 10, 11, 14, 15, 17, 31, 98, 106, 109, 110, 115–131, 135, 142, 158, 162, 164, 177, 179, 193
sea 4, 8, 53, 110, 111, 188, 204
Sergeant Pepper 109
sewing 31, 193
shade 16, 24, 92
shape 8, 10, 17, 22, 32, 37, 51, 79, 81, 82, 108, 134, 157, 178
shields 116
Shoga, Folake 142
sketchbooks 12, 19, 20, 24, 32, 34, 35, 39, 50, 51, 53, 54, 85, 89, 99, 116, 132, 142, 187, 195, 199
sketches, sketching 7, 8, 18, 19, 34–35, 112, 127, 132, 169, 188, 203
skills 13
sound 35
South America 175, 180
speaking and listening 4, 9, 78, 205
special needs 11
spectrum 7, 37
spinning 178, 181–184
stained glass 106, 109
Steadman, Ralph 89
stencils 56–59
still life 32, 49
stories 12, 19, 24, 52, 53, 84, 87, 97, 11, 119, 121, 132, 145, 149, 176, 188, 195, 203
storyboard 53, 86, 95
Surrealists 14, 51, 93, 109
symbols symbolism 8, 23, 38, 60, 132

talk 4, 6, 13
tape recorder 146
television 112, 118, 149

templates 113, 145
textiles 174, 175
texture 4, 7, 10, 14, 17, 20, 22, 26–30, 32, 34, 37–40, 49, 50, 54–56, 61, 89, 94, 106, 107, 117, 156, 187, 199
Thomas, Dylan 119
tie-dye 189
tiles 134, 138, 153, 155, 157, 159, 169
tone 16, 20, 26, 29, 31, 32, 76, 84, 88, 89, 92
topics, projects 3, 4, 12–14, 19, 97, 110, 116, 175, 203, 204
trails 118
Tudors 204
Turkey 148
Turner, Joseph Mallord William 4, 38, 49
typefaces 6, 80

values 13
Van Eyck, Jan 112
Van Gogh, Vincent 24, 39, 49
Vasarely, Victor 80
Victorians 8, 98, 113, 147, 180, 203, 204
video 4, 8, 15, 51, 83, 86, 89, 94, 95, 116, 119, 130, 134, 142, 149, 150
viewfinder 21, 31, 33–35, 48–54, 91, 188
Vikings 3, 132
Visability 193

Wales 175
Wallace and Grommit 134
Warhol, Andy 80, 90
water 30, 53, 88
weather 13, 38, 89, 145, 187, 199
weaving 7, 174–188
website 80
Westwood, Vivienne 133, 177
wire 28, 128–131
wood 127–8, 131, 132
writing 4, 9, 16, 87

zig-zag books 35, 97